PURSUING THE SPIRITUAL ROOTS OF PROTEST

Pursuing the
Spiritual Roots of Protest

Merton, Berrigan, Yoder, and Muste
at the Gethsemani Abbey Peacemakers Retreat

GORDON OYER

To Cindy -
Thanks for your
wisdom & support
over many years,
Best

FOREWORD BY
Jim Forest

AFTERWORD BY
John Dear, SJ

CASCADE *Books* · Eugene, Oregon

PURSUING THE SPIRITUAL ROOTS OF PROTEST
Merton, Berrigan, Yoder, and Muste at the Gethsemani Abbey Peacemakers Retreat

Cascade Books
An Imprint of Wipf and Stock Publishers
199 W. 8th Ave., Suite 3
Eugene, OR 97401
www.wipfandstock.com

ISBN 13: 978-1-62032-377-9

Cataloging-in-Publication data:

Oyer, Gordon.

Pursuing the spiritual roots of protest : Merton, Berrigan, Yoder, and Muste at the Gethsemani Abbey Peacemakers Retreat / Gordon Oyer.

xxii + 276 p.; 23 cm—Includes bibliographical references and index.

ISBN 978-1-62032-377-9

1. Protest movements. 2. Peace—Religious aspects. 3. Merton, Thomas, 1915–1968. 4. Berrigan, Daniel. 5. Yoder, John Howard. 6. Muste, Abraham John, 1885–1967. I. Title.

JZ5560 O95 2014

Manufactured in the USA.

Papers of John Howard Yoder used with permission of the estate of John Howard Yoder and the Thomas Merton Center at Bellarmine University.
Unpublished letters, handwritten outline, and audio recordings of Thomas Merton used with permission of The Merton Legacy Trust and the Thomas Merton Center at Bellarmine University.
Thomas Merton's reading notebook material used with permission of The Merton Legacy Trust and Syracuse University Library.
Papers of A. J. Muste used with permission of the Swarthmore College Peace Collection.
Fellowship of Reconciliation Records and unpublished letters of John C. Heidbrink used with permission of the Fellowship of Reconciliation.
Reprinted by permission of Farrar, Straus and Giroux, LLC: Excerpts from *The Hidden Ground of Love: The Letters of Thomas Merton on Religious Experience and Social Concerns* by Thomas Merton, edited by William H. Shannon. Copyright © 1985 by The Merton Legacy Trust. From "Retreat, November, 1964: Spiritual Roots of Protest" from *The Nonviolent Alternative* by Thomas Merton. U.S. and Canada copyright © 1980 by The Merton Legacy Trust.
Reprinted by Curtis Brown, Ltd.: From "Retreat, November, 1964: Spiritual Roots of Protest" from *The Nonviolent Alternative* by Thomas Merton. U.K. and British Commonwealth copyright © 1980 by The Merton Legacy Trust.
Reprinted by permission of HarperCollins Publishers: Excerpts from pp. 96, 98, 133, 142, 159–61, 166–8, 260 from *Dancing in the Water of Life: The Journals of Thomas Merton, Volume Five, 1963–1965* by Thomas Merton and edited by Robert E. Daggy. Copyright © 1997 by The Merton Legacy Trust.
Reprinted by permission of University of Notre Dame Press: Excerpts from *Testimonies and Reflections: Essays of Louis Massignon*, edited by Herbert Mason. Copyright © 1989 by Herbert Mason.

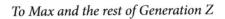

To Max and the rest of Generation Z

Table of Contents

Illustrations

Foreword

Since Christian monasticism began to flower in the deserts of Egypt, Sinai, and Palestine in the fourth century AD, millions of people have gone on monastic retreats, and it still goes on. It's not hard to find those who would welcome a few days of tranquility in a place where the core activity of one's quiet hosts is worship and prayer.

Many people who seek monastic hospitality say they are there to experience peace. What is truly unusual is for someone, still less a group of people, to seek the shelter of a monastery in hopes of becoming better equipped to be peacemakers, but this is exactly what fourteen people did for three days in November 1964 at the Abbey of Our Lady of Gethsemani in Kentucky. We used our time together both to explore what we were up against and how best to respond.

Our host was Thomas Merton, one of the most respected Christian authors of the twentieth century. At the time he had been a monk at Gethsemani for almost twenty-three years and was serving the community as Master of Novices. What had made him well known to the outside world was his autobiography, *The Seven Storey Mountain*, a hard-to-put-down account of what led him to Christian faith, the Catholic Church, and a monastic vocation. Published in 1948, it had become an international bestseller and finally a modern classic. It is often compared to Augustine's *Confessions*.

Merton had been thinking about war from an early age. His birth in France (his mother was from America, his father from New Zealand) coincided with the initial months of World War I, a catastrophe his antiwar father managed not to take part in. By the time World War II had begun, Merton's recent conversion to Christianity had led him to pacifist convictions—it was obvious to him that killing was incompatible with the teaching of Jesus. While others were putting on military uniforms, Merton put on a monastic robe. By the time of the 1964 retreat, he was the best known and most widely read Christian monk in the world.

In 1961, writing for *The Catholic Worker*, Merton had argued that "the duty of the Christian in this [present] crisis is to strive with all his power and intelligence, with his faith, his hope in Christ, and love for God and man, to do the one task which God has imposed upon us in the world today. That task is to work for the total abolition of war." Many essays along similar lines followed as well as a book, *Peace in the Post-Christian Era*, but its publication had been stopped by the head of the Trappist order in Rome, Dom Gabriel Sortais, who felt that it was inappropriate for a monk to write on such controversial topics.

By the time of the retreat, Merton had become one of the founders of the newly launched Catholic Peace Fellowship, which just a few weeks later would open a national office in Manhattan. Besides Merton, four others taking part in the retreat were CPF cofounders: Tom Cornell, Daniel and Philip Berrigan, and myself.

One of the striking aspects of the retreat was that not all those taking part were Catholic, a fact that is unremarkable today but was rare and controversial in 1964. The most senior retreat participant was seventy-nine-year-old A. J. Muste, a Quaker who had once been a minister of the Dutch Reformed Church; by the time of our gathering he was perhaps the most distinguished leader of the U.S. peace movement—former executive secretary of the Fellowship of Reconciliation and now chairman of the Committee for Nonviolent Action. There was John Howard Yoder, the distinguished Mennonite scholar; eight years later he would publish *The Politics of Jesus*, a book still widely read. W. H. Ferry, vice president of the Center for the Study of Democratic Institutions, was a Unitarian at the time who, later in life, described himself simply as a Christian. Elbert Jean was a Methodist minister from Arkansas who had been deeply immersed in the civil rights movement. Last but not least was Presbyterian John Oliver Nelson, a Yale professor who was a leader of the Fellowship of Reconciliation and founder of Kirkridge, a conference and retreat center in Pennsylvania.

My memories of the retreat begin with place and weather. Rural, rolling Kentucky was wrapped around the abbey on every side. The monastery in those days was mainly made up of weathered, ramshackle buildings, with the oldest dating back more than a hundred years. The weather was damp and chilly, the sky mainly overcast, with occasional light rain. It was due to the weather that we met mainly in a small conference room in the gatehouse that normally was used by family and guests visiting monks. There were only two sessions at Merton's hermitage, a simple flat-roofed, one-story structure about a mile from the monastery. It was made of gray cinder blocks. Heat was provided by a fireplace. Whether in gatehouse or hermitage, it was a squeeze fitting all fourteen of us into the available space.

Merton, wearing his black-and-white Trappist robes, served as the retreat's central but never dominant figure. At each session, by prearrangement, one of the participants made a presentation, at the end of which there was freewheeling discussion.

What did we talk about in those intense three days?

While many issues were aired, three major themes survived in my unaided memory: conscientious objection to war, the challenge of technology, and a provocative question Merton raised: "By what right do we protest?"

Conscientious objection: Before the Vietnam War, conscientious objection had been mainly linked with several small "peace churches"—Quakers, Mennonites, and the Church of the Brethren—while the Catholic and large Protestant churches produced relatively few conscientious objectors. But the times were about to change with Vietnam, a country few Americans could find on the map, providing the catalyst. Several months earlier Congress had approved the Gulf of Tonkin Resolution, granting President Lyndon Johnson unilateral power to launch a full-scale war in Southeast Asia if and when he deemed it necessary. As far more soldiers would be needed than voluntary recruitment could hope to provide, drafting hundreds of thousands of young men would prove essential.

One element of our discussion was to consider the case of Franz Jägerstätter, an Austrian Catholic layman who had been executed in Berlin in 1943 for refusing to fight in what he judged to be an unjust war. What if his story and stories like it were to become better known? What if significant numbers of young American Christians were to follow Jägerstätter's example and say no to war? (In the years that followed the retreat, the Catholic Peace Fellowship did much to promote awareness of the Jägerstätter story, its New Testament basis, and its implications in our time. The CPF's draft counseling and educational work help explain the astonishing fact that the Catholic Church in the U.S. produced the largest contingent of conscientious objectors during the Vietnam War.)

Technology: Thanks especially to W. H. Ferry, technology was a major topic for us. "Ping," as he was known to friends, brought home to us the implications of the technological credo, "If it can be done, it must be done." Every possibility, once envisioned and no matter how dangerous, toxic, or ultimately self-destructive, tends to become a reality, nuclear weapons being only one of countless examples. The technology of destruction as it advanced war-by-war had become truly apocalyptic. The threat was fresh in all our minds—two years before the retreat, during the Cuban Missile Crisis, the world had been poised on the brink of nuclear war. But it wasn't only a question of weapons of mass destruction. Increasingly our lives were being shaped and dominated by technology.

Protest: For me, Merton's question—"By what right do we protest?"—was something of a Zen *koan*—an arrow in the back that one's hands cannot reach to dislodge. Coming from a left-wing family background, it seemed so obvious to me that, when you see something wrong, you protest, period. Protest is part of being human. Merton and others at the retreat made me more aware that acts of protest are not ends in themselves but ultimately must be regarded as efforts to bring about a transformation of heart of one's adversaries and even one's self. The civil rights movement was a case in point; in recent years it had already brought about significant positive change in America. Thanks to its largely nonviolent character, it was an example of how to protest in ways that help change the outlook of those who are threatened by change. Merton put great stress on protest that had contemplative roots, protest motivated not only by outrage but by compassion for those who, driven by fear or a warped patriotism, experience themselves as objects of protest.

In the years that followed, I never forgot these three elements in our exchange, but there was a great deal more that slowly faded from memory. How often I wished I had brought along a tape recorder in order to listen in once again, or at least had kept better and more legible notes. Now decades later I've found the next best thing: the curiosity and relentless digging of Gordon Oyer. Drawing on notes made by myself and others, plus letters and other writings of those who took part, as well as interviews with the few of us still alive, Gordon has done an amazing job of reconstructing our conversations—as you are about to find out.

Jim Forest

February 7, 2013

Preface

If there's a book you really want to read, but it hasn't been
written, then you must write it. —Toni Morrison

Toni Morrison's words aptly anticipate how this book came to be.
Having embraced the peace tradition of my Mennonite upbringing, I
naturally appreciated John Howard Yoder's contributions to Christian
peace literature. My reading on the topic also led me to the peace writings of Thomas Merton, which in turn provided a segue into his material
on contemplation and social criticism. Little surprise, therefore, that the
passing reference in a Merton biography to Yoder's presence with Merton
at a gathering of peace activists piqued my curiosity. This event occurred
November 18–20, 1964 at Merton's Gethsemani Abbey. It was organized
as an informal retreat that had been given a theme of "The Spiritual Roots
of Protest" to guide discussion. On such an occasion, what would conversations between the Mennonite ethicist and the monastic contemplative
have entailed?

In response to my probing, Yoder scholar Mark Thiessen Nation
shared a reference where Yoder had noted his deposit of related material
with Bellarmine University's Thomas Merton Center archives. Soon after
learning of this collection, a Catholic Worker friend announced he and his
community would launch their newly established Catholic Worker school
with a workshop on Merton, and they would include discussion of Merton's
views on nonviolence. On a whim I contacted the Center archives to see
if they could provide any material on the Gethsemani retreat that I might
share in workshop discussion. They graciously responded with a copy of
Yoder's own notes taken at the event.

From there, the project began to assume a life of its own. A handful of brief published accounts, pieced together from secondary sources,

served only to expand my questions rather than resolve them. The Yoder notes—cryptic in many ways, as such records tend to be—further stoked my curiosity about what else his files and the Merton Center archives might divulge. And so a few weeks later, I found myself gliding down I-65 toward Louisville and the Merton archives.

Yoder's papers revealed that, at the prodding of his University of Notre Dame department head, he had assembled an array of background information, along with some relevant correspondence, that would provide any researcher a helpful leg up on documenting the retreat. At that point, what started as a recreational adventure to satisfy my curiosity began morphing into aspirations to write an article about the event, and perhaps even prepare a longer narrative that might be deposited at the Center for others to reference. Only through periodic hints and nudges by Dr. Paul Pearson, Director of the Thomas Merton Center, did the awareness materialize that I might actually publish a book on the topic. It was a book I wished to read. It had not been written. I should write it.

During the coming months, while negotiating workplace demands and relying on accumulated vacation time, I embarked on several more research adventures. These involved the delightful and edifying privilege of meeting and interviewing the five surviving retreat participants and visiting with the family of a sixth, conversing with three monks who resided at Gethsemani in the sixties, and visiting additional archives at Swarthmore College, Cornell University, Boston College, Columbia University, Syracuse University, and Dartmouth College, along with other trips to the Thomas Merton Center. Gradually, a manuscript unfolded. Still skeptical, however, that a publisher would view this material worthy of publication in today's challenging market, I began to submit proposals with minimal expectations of reward. Thankfully, Cascade Books opted to negate my pessimism.

The experience of reconstructing this story cannot help but affect its writer. One cannot enter into such a world of deep and sincere reflection on the place of protest without being confronted by hard questions about one's own responses to social ills. Much that surrounds us starkly contradicts the insights fostered by biblical narratives and spiritual truths as I have grown to understand them. The process of compiling this narrative often elicited an unsettling cognitive dissonance that challenged and prodded for more consistent effort to better illuminate and challenge those contradictions.

The story that resulted from vicariously entering into that discussion at Gethsemani Abbey, however, does not explore specific acts of protest per se. The event fell during a lull in peace activism between cold war antinuclear protests and anti-Vietnam War activity. It therefore fails to capture the era's energy and passion that permeated the literal movement of protesters through America's streets, campuses, draft boards, and institutions of power. Such stories naturally carry great force and meaning. Actions taken and events played out in real time offer powerful instruction, guidance, and inspiration. Fortunately, biographies exist or are in progress for nine of the fourteen (the Berrigans, Ferry, Forest, Merton, Muste, Nelson, Walsh, and Yoder) to provide such narratives. The lives and contributions of the remaining five (Cornell, Cunnane, Grady, Jean, and Ring) prove equally inspiring and instructive, as their brief biographical outlines in chapters 1 and 6 would suggest. Hopefully their full life stories will also become accessible.

Rather than recount such historic *acts* of protest, however, this book mostly addresses *ideas* about and *motives* for protest. These matters are important as well, for actions of protest can seem superficial and lack integrity when we do not understand what we act against or fail to reckon with our motives for doing so. And acting with depth and integrity mattered greatly to the fourteen who gathered to discuss "the spiritual roots of protest."

This story seeks to accomplish two main objectives. The first is simply to establish a clearer picture of a particular historical event: where the idea for a retreat came from, how it came to be realized, and what happened when it occurred. The second goal, however, is to capture the array of ideas and motives that emerged from the synergy of fourteen peacemakers who gathered to probe the foundations of their practice. In doing so, they raised essential, timeless questions we would do well to also ask ourselves fifty years later. They also helped model the mutual support required for people of faith to embark on and sustain active, resistant, nonviolent protest against the cultures of domination that human civilization seems destined to evoke.

Aside from sating historical curiosity, then, this is a story that can speak to us today. Those forces of domination pondered and protested a half century ago have not been tamed. They have only grown more sophisticated, tightened their grasp on global experience, and entrenched themselves more deeply within our human psyche. We need strong actions of resistance and protest now more than ever, especially actions nourished by deep roots of spiritual integrity. The quest of these activists therefore can surely nurture our own need for such roots, whether we expressively protest those forces in the streets or more quietly resist them in daily routines. Hopefully what follows illuminates that quest and, through it, supplies some degree of nourishment to each reader.

Acknowledgments

THE PILGRIMAGE OF COMPILING this story has relied on the support, encouragement, and wisdom of many, some at particular points in the effort and others throughout it. Attempting to sort through this material and create a meaningful narrative within the margins of an otherwise full and busy life becomes discouraging at times. I have been blessed by infusions of energy at various junctures through the interest, appreciation, and interaction others have offered.

I am particularly grateful for the generosity of the five surviving retreat participants—Daniel Berrigan, Tom Cornell, Bob Cunnane, Jim Forest, and Elbert Jean—who shared their time and memories during interviews, fielded many subsequent inquiries, and reviewed portions of the text for accuracy. This opportunity to tap into living memory of the event and its times nearly fifty years later has inspired, adding color and nuance to the story. Thanks also to Monica Cornell, Anne Walsh, and Joy Jean for their roles in making time and space for my visits with their spouses. I also benefited by visiting with the wife of John Peter Grady, Theresa Grady, and their daughters Mary Ann Grady Flores, Claire Grady, and Ellen Grady, who shared memories of him and provided a helpful sense of his colorful personality.

A substantial debt of gratitude is also due Dr. Paul Pearson, Director and Archivist at the Thomas Merton Center, foremost for encouraging my pursuit of this work. He and Assistant Director Mark Meade are also due considerable thanks for generous assistance with many aspects my research. This includes helping navigate the rich resources of the Merton archival collection at Bellarmine University, track obscure references to Thomas Merton's life and works, and decipher his sometimes cryptic handwriting, as well as offering timely responses to a range of related questions. Dr. Pearson provided helpful counsel in navigating the publication process, in addition.

I also greatly appreciate the perspective added to this material by Jim Forest in his foreword and Fr. John Dear in his afterword. Elizabeth McAlister, Ched Myers, Jake Olzen, and George Packard supplied indispensable insights on contemporary faith-based protest for use in developing the epilogue.

In addition to these, several others provided helpful assistance along the way. Jim Forest, Ched Myers, Paul Pearson, and Anke Voss read various iterations or major sections of the manuscript and offered invaluable feedback. Brother Patrick Hart, Fr. James Conner, and Br. Frank Gorzinski shared helpful memories of the Gethsemani Abbey layout and routine in 1964; Br. Hart and Fr. Conner also proved indispensable in reviewing photographs of the retreat to identify settings. Dr. Herbert Mason generously shared his insight and personal experiences of Louis Massignon and Thomas Merton, which helped me gain a better understanding of their work and their relationship to each other. Bill Wylie-Kellerman likewise shared of his relationship with Daniel Berrigan and his research on William Stringfellow and Jacques Ellul. Andy Alexis-Baker graciously pointed me toward helpful material about Jacques Ellul. Martha Yoder Maust offered comments regarding the career of her father, John Howard Yoder. Conversations or email exchanges with Eric Anglada, Paul Dekar, Gerry Twomey, Mark Nation Thiessen, and Tom Yoder Neufeld all facilitated this work as well. Thanks also to Gray Matthews and David Belcastro, coeditors of the 2012 *Merton Annual*, for publishing a significant portion of this material before Wipf and Stock accepted this book proposal, and also for granting permission to include it here.

Crucial logistical support was offered by Kate Hennessy, whose transcribing skill proved invaluable for turning audio recordings of interviews into manageable text. Likewise, Dr. Hollie Markland Harder provided timely and effective translations of four otherwise inaccessible Louis Massignon essays, and Virginie Realie provided a fifth. I also thank Christian Amondson, Dr. Christopher Spinks, and Justin Haskell of the Wipf and Stock editorial staff for their ongoing assistance in processing this manuscript.

The writing of history rests on archival foundations, and the value of institutions that collect and preserve such material cannot be understated. Several collections beyond the holdings at Bellarmine University contributed to this work. I am indebted to these institutions and their staffs for preserving and making available this material: the Daniel and Philip Berrigan Collection at Cornell University, the Thomas Merton Collection at Syracuse University, the James Forest Thomas Merton Collection at Boston College, the W. H. Ferry Collection at Dartmouth College. Special thanks are due to Dr. Wendy Chmielewski, the George R. Cooley Curator of the Swarthmore College Peace Collection, for assistance with material in its A. J. Muste, Fellowship of Reconciliation, and Church Peace Mission collections, as well as to its archivist Anne Yoder. My research was also greatly facilitated through access to the University of Illinois Library with its substantial research collection and academic services, and to the Champaign County Historical Archives for its public access to needed technological resources.

On a personal level, my thanks go out to Eric Anglada, with whom I share a mutual appreciation of Thomas Merton's writings and thought, and whose well-read awareness of Merton's work has expanded my own appreciation for Merton. I also offer personal gratitude to Ched Myers, whose writing and speaking has deepened and enriched my understanding of the biblical narrative and its political-social implications. Ched also offered timely encouragement of my efforts to complete this project and affirmation of its value to the faith community. Special thanks as well to Anke and Max for the moral support they have provided over this project's five years. Anke's impressions and feedback have made this a better book.

Abbreviations

CNVA	Committee for Nonviolent Action
CORE	Congress of Racial Equality
CPC	Christian Peace Conference
CPF	Catholic Peace Fellowship
CPM	Church Peace Mission
CT	*Courage for Truth*
CUL	Cornell University Library, Ithaca, New York
DWL	*Dancing in the Water of Life*
FOR	Fellowship of Reconciliation
HGL	*The Hidden Ground of Love*
NCC	National Council of Churches
RJ	*Road to Joy*
SANE	Committee for a Sane Nuclear Policy
SCPC	Swarthmore College Peace Collection, Swarthmore, Pennsylvania
SDS	Students for a Democractic Society
SUL	Special Collections Research Center, Syracuse University Library, Syracuse, New York
TMC	Archives of the Thomas Merton Center, Bellarmine University, Louisville, Kentucky
TTW	*Turning Toward the World*
WF	*Witness to Freedom*

1

The Antiwar "Movement Aborning"

REMNANTS OF THE MORNING'S rain still glistened as a dozen scattered walkers emerged from the monastery retreat house and trod along a pathway through the adjoining garden. Exiting the opposite side through a gap in the monastic enclosure's gray block walls, they ambled past the abbey reservoir and strode along a dusty lane for several yards, then disappeared into the trees of a wooded hillside. Fallen leaves, slippery wet beneath their feet, slowed their pace as they made their way up the dark and muddy footpath, sheltered from sunlight by the arched canopy of thinning branches that stretched over their heads. About a mile north of the abbey they emerged from their gentle climb into a clearing. Reentering the sunlight they turned toward a small cinder block building perched at the edge of the grassy field, barely visible through a stand of trees on their left. In the middle of the opening, next to a barbed wire fence that bisected the clearing, they noted their host, a robust middle-aged monk in a white Trappist robe and black scapular. He slowly paced across the grass, face downward, glasses donned, intently peering into an open notebook cradled in his extended hands. Deep in thought, his demeanor conveyed a serious focus as he studied the jottings on the pages before him. Upon noticing that his guests had arrived, he waved a friendly greeting and strode toward them. As he joined them, they continued toward the cottage, crossed a sheltered cement porch that extended the full width of the structure, and entered its front door. Once inside they settled into the seating available within its austere walls, and the monk began to share with them his carefully chosen words.[1]

---

1. Chapter opening based on details in Cornell, "Merton on Peace," 23; photographs taken by Jim Forest held in the James Forest—Thomas Merton Collection, John J. Burns Library, Boston College; and general knowledge of monastery grounds.

The individuals assembled at this bucolic Kentucky site had arrived intent on probing religious motives and rationales for challenging some of their nation's more oppressive habits, particularly that of making war. The pastoral setting, when coupled with the monastic ambience offered by the Abbey of Our Lady of Gethsemani, provided an ideal venue to conduct this retreat from the daily bustle of modern urban life. That morning back at the monastery they had begun their conversation by reviewing an outline headed "The Spiritual Roots of Protest." The monk in question—Gethsemani's (and America's) most renowned monastic figure Thomas Merton—had sketched the outline to guide their three-day discussion. Now, this afternoon at his hermitage, Merton would launch the first of four in-depth dialogues by elaborating on his views about "The Monastic Protest."

Although the idea for this gathering had taken more than two years to coalesce from inception to fruition, its timing proved ideal. The summer of 1964 had elicited both explicit demands for equal access to civil rights and stirrings to challenge expanding U.S. military support of South Vietnam's anticommunist regime. In calling for this event, one of the retreat's initiators, John C. Heidbrink of the Fellowship of Reconciliation, had observed that, "We are faced here and abroad with a super-structure of protest and non-conformity building up daily in nearly every country which can loosely be called a movement for peace." Lest this activity remain grounded only in secular hopes and materialistic priorities, he had sought a venue for confessing men of peace to examine "the subject of spiritual roots of the US peace movement as well as the international movement aborning."[2] And here, amid the hills, trees, and monastic solitude, they intended to accomplish exactly that.

The Movement at Hand[3]

The emerging U.S. antiwar movement of the mid-1960s reflected one of several ebbs and flows of American peace activism, and understanding the goals of those gathered at Gethsemani and the conversations they shared first requires a glimpse of activity that came before. Its most recent flow had built upon and superseded what one historian dubbed a "small band of isolated of pacifists" who sustained their convictions during the worst

2. Heidbrink to Merton, 17 Sept. 1964, TMC.

3. This peace movement summary largely relies on DeBenedetti and Chatfield, *An American Ordeal*, especially 9–102. Other works consulted include Chalmers, *Crooked Places*; Chatfield, *American Peace*; Farrell, *Spirit of the Sixties*; McNeal, *Harder than War*; Peace, *Just and Lasting Peace*; Wittner, *Rebels Against War*.

years of the McCarthy era's anticommunist obsession.[4] This revival in peace advocacy responded to mushrooming nuclear arsenals and the atomic testing needed to further develop them. Some of these activists dreamed of dismantling nuclear arms altogether, but most peace advocates of the later fifties and early sixties invested in the more modest goal of eliminating—or at least reducing—nuclear weapons testing. In attempting to describe what motivated them and framed their objectives, historians Charles DeBenedetti and Charles Chatfield have suggested that most of them focused their work primarily through one of two lenses.

The first lens consisted of "liberal internationalism" and generally aligned with what some refer to as "nuclear pacifists."[5] These advocates were often heavily vested in the institutions of liberal democratic society, seeing in them the vehicles through which humanity would advance toward peace and prosperity. They sought collaborative structures to police conflict and regulate atomic energy and research, and their vision focused pragmatically on reformation of political and social institutions to accommodate such oversight. The leading outlet for liberal pacifist impulses was the Committee for a Sane Nuclear Policy, or SANE.[6] Though championing liberal agenda, SANE often included radical pacifists as well, while serving as the core of nuclear test ban activism. It shepherded a scattered array of local groups comprised of widely diverse members that promoted various petition drives, community meetings, advertisements in major newspapers, and public demonstrations that called for limits to nuclear testing. By 1960 SANE was mobilizing events with participation in the tens of thousands.[7]

The second lens that focused the work of peace advocates concerned itself less with broad political reform than with expression of personal moral convictions that rejected violence and required active engagement. Drawing on currents that ranged from historic peace church perspectives to secular conscientious objection to Gandhian nonviolent resistance, those viewing peace through this lens promoted focused actions to directly confront and challenge rather than simply reform existing institutions.[8] In contrast to

4. Wittner, *Rebels Against War*, 228.

5. Wittner distinguishes between "nuclear pacifists," who opposed arms proliferation because of the consequences of nuclear engagement, and "radical pacifists," who opposed all forms of violence on principle.

6. DeBenedetti and Chatfield, *American Ordeal*, 13–19.

7. Ibid., 104, 107.

8. The "historic peace churches"—Mennonite/Amish, Quaker, Church of the Brethren, and historically related groups—originated in Europe and held nonviolence as an integral aspect of Christian faith. Of these, Quakers historically were more politically and socially engaged, whereas the others were more withdrawn well into the twentieth

seeking venues for global governance, this "radical pacifist" lens set its sights more intensely toward justice, decentralized power, self-determination for developing countries abroad, and freedom of personal conscience at home. They sought to reconstruct values and elevate human consciousness rather than improve legislation, and they above all embraced an engaged, absolute rejection of violence. For inspiration they often looked to iconic figures such as Abraham J. Muste and Dorothy Day and to like-minded networks such as the religiously based Fellowship of Reconciliation (FOR), Day's Catholic Worker Movement, the War Resister League, and the American Friends Service Committee.[9] The journal *Liberation*, founded in the mid-fifties, provided a significant voice for their ideas. In particular, radical pacifists channeled their nuclear opposition through the Committee for Non-Violent Action (CNVA),[10] which sought venues to confront directly the systems that supported atomic testing by organizing protests and other direct actions at testing sights, Atomic Energy Commission offices (which oversaw the tests), military installations, and elsewhere.[11]

The views these two lenses promoted would often overlap. Their distinctions were not clear and their boundaries were quite fluid. Some who opposed U.S. militarism simply did not fit well within either. Those loyal to the Old Left opposed atomic testing mainly within a framework of rigid Marxist/socialist ideology. Most in the "nonresistant" peace churches such as Amish and Mennonites absolutely embraced pacifism but rejected direct action and political lobbying. Certain nuclear pacifists no doubt cared little for the grand global vision of internationalism. Other historians would add the nuance of a "progressive" lens that focused beliefs and actions against what such activists considered "imperialist" U.S. intervention.[12] But the DeBenedetti and Chatfield "internationalist"/"radical" lenses form something of a fault line that can help unravel the complex web of personalities, organizations, and activity that together formed a peace movement at mid-century. It can also help to better frame the ideas that formed the worldviews of

---

century. Most other groups identified themselves as "nonresistant" to reflect their absolute rejection of violence (in contrast to "nuclear pacifists") and their reluctance to directly confront power structures (in contrast to "radical pacifists"). All historic peace churches articulated Christian theologies of nonviolence since their origins, dating to the Protestant Reformation.

9. DeBenedetti and Chatfield, *American Ordeal*, 19–22.

10. This organization was originally named "Non-Violent Action Against Nuclear Weapons," and reorganized as the CNVA in late 1958. Wittner, *Rebels Against War*, 246–47.

11. Chatfield, *American Peace*, 104.

12. Peace, *Just and Lasting Peace*, 29.

those who gathered at Gethsemani in 1964, just as the unfolding political developments of the early sixties helps better explain the agenda that retreat planners pursued.

In particular, the August 5, 1963 signing of a Partial Test Ban Treaty and its ratification that September deflated and dissolved the primary objective that had focused and unified the energy of peace advocates.[13] This treaty served to reinforce a growing political consensus that the most prudent course the United States should pursue rested with efforts toward verifiable arms control rather than disarmament. Although a handful pressed on to eliminate nuclear weaponry, many others rested comfortably on an arms control platform, and the peace movement as a whole atrophied.[14] In response, many former test ban supporters soon refocused their energy on civil rights activism rather than issues of war and peace.

The pursuit of equal African American rights within U.S. society had traditionally held a special relationship with peace advocates, especially with radical pacifists who opposed war on moral principles and were predisposed to challenge other failures in social morality, such as rampant racism. The tight intertwining of these movements—or perhaps these two emphases of a larger social agenda—makes it difficult to tease apart their relationship. Radical pacifists naturally welcomed the civil rights movement's embrace of nonviolence, and they had in fact supported and nurtured nonviolent opposition to racism since the Second World War. For example, the Congress of Racial Equality (CORE), a catalyst for nonviolently pursuing racial justice, originated with support from FOR staff during World War II, and it matured through the input of leaders who worked either for or closely with FOR.[15] An even greater source of reciprocal peace/civil rights movement influence emerged in 1960 when students and others "sat in" to integrate Southern lunch counters, giving birth to the Student Non-Violent Coordinating Committee (SNCC).[16] Its success and aftermath played a large role in confirming the potential to foster social change nonviolently and placed direct action squarely into America's public awareness as a legitimate tactic of political and social engagement. Such inroads toward raising America's consciousness and realizing social change during the early sixties therefore

---

13. Its formal title was: "Treaty Banning Nuclear Weapons Tests in the Atmosphere, in Outer Space, and Under Water" (*Encyclopedia Britannica Online*, s.v. "Nuclear Test Ban Treaty." Online: http://www.britannica.com/EBchecked/topic/421810/Nuclear-Test-Ban-Treaty).

14. Chatfield, *American Peace*, 113.

15. Wittner, *Rebels Against War*, 233–35.

16. Ibid., 269.

served to affirm, train, and motivate many who would mobilize to protest war only a few short years later.[17]

At the turn of the decade, however, the American civil rights movement dwarfed U.S. nuclear disarmament activism. The Southern Christian Leadership Conference budget stood at five times that of SANE and its staffing exceeded SANE's by a factor of eight.[18] More to the point, although peace and antiwar advocates consistently supported civil rights causes, the opposite proved less reliable, especially as the roiling national debate over Vietnam accelerated. Many civil rights workers looked to nonviolence primarily as a political tactic, not a moral absolute. They saw nonviolent persuasion of one's immediate neighbor as more credible than seeking nonviolent resolutions to international tensions abroad. As the fifties bled into the sixties, other social transitions also affected peace work. The liberal embrace of internationalist solutions such as verifiable arms control would gradually morph into a new platform of "pragmatic realism" that called for more assertive U.S. leadership in shaping global developments. This waning liberal commitment to peace advocacy and the departure of liberals from peace activism paved the way for radical pacifist priorities to gain greater traction within peace movement agenda. Meanwhile, as this transition gained momentum, a "New Left" identity also began to coalesce and adopt a worldview that resonated with many radical pacifist concerns. This element drew heavily from the ranks of college students and other young people, becoming most evident in formation of the Students for a Democratic Society (SDS). The New Left encompassed a wide diversity of concerns and issues, however, and what mostly provided it coherence was a common desire to remake society through employing Marxist-style critique.[19]

The convergence of disarmament, civil rights, New Left, counterculture, and other impulses during the early sixties reflected a shifting social paradigm within the United States. Disparate as they were, they all relied on a sense of group consciousness rather than traditional organizational principles for the glue that connected them, and they lifted up the power of consciousness-raising rather than institutional stability as the most effective vehicle through which to improve society. Though they sought changes on a national level, they invested in local, grassroots experience as their primary medium of change. They exuded a spirit of what has been called "political personalism," and their activity reflected confidence that the "personal" was also "political" well before that phrase was coined in the context of

17. DeBenedetti and Chatfield, *American Ordeal*, 41–42, 64–65.

18. Chatfield, *American Peace*, 115.

19. DeBenedetti and Chatfield, *American Ordeal*, 39–40.

late-sixties feminism. This spirit would also characterize the early years of the "aborning" antiwar movement.[20]

The potential to unite these disjointed elements and exert visible and viable antiwar pressure remained latent for some time, however. The Kennedy Administration expansion of military consultants in Vietnam, rising from 3000 to 11,000+ during its first year and a half, had elicited minor ripples of disjointed criticism, but few noticed. Eventually a core of informed critics within the administration began to articulate the risks of U.S. involvement, strengthening the commitment and credibility of those who opposed it. In contrast to domino theory alarmists who asserted that resisting communism in Vietnam served vital American interests, critics countered that U.S. intervention not only supported oppression of the Vietnamese people, it also aggravated Cold War tensions and subverted democratic processes at home. When in 1963 the Diem regime expelled certain U.S. reporters and violently repressed protest by Buddhist monks—some of whom expressed their protest through self-immolation—Americans in general began to take note. More observers began to conclude that prolonged U.S. involvement in this conflict halfway around the world would be immoral, futile, and fail to serve U.S. interests. By the close of 1963, public figures were publishing open letters that challenged the U.S. presence, and the appearance of anti-Vietnam placards in nuclear disarmament protests began to unsettle and further alienate liberal peace advocates.[21]

Activist priorities and public attention in the first half of 1964 remained heavily focused on civil rights issues, however, as a concerted—and for some lethal—Mississippi voter registration drive ensued that summer and the 1964 Civil Rights Act passed in July. Nonetheless, the antiwar voices that also murmured in the background began to amplify as the year progressed. Some in Washington sharpened their rhetoric for avoiding military escalation and seeking a negotiated withdrawal from Vietnam. Old Leftists vocalized their absolute opposition to the war, peace groups organized small protests in early spring, and a small cluster of radical pacifists burned draft cards in May signaling the emergence of conscription as a potent motivator for antiwar involvement by young people. Although these ripples received scant attention and delivered only marginal impact, the gears of antiwar protest had begun to engage, and the engine driving those gears soon received injections of added fuel from actions taken by President Johnson that

20. Chalmers, *Crooked Places*, xvii–xviii; Chatfield, *The American Peace Movement*, 121–22; Farrell, *Spirit of the Sixties*, 6–8.

21. DeBenedetti and Chatfield, *American Ordeal*, 81–91.

summer.[22] In late July, just eight months after President Kennedy's assassination, he added 5,000 troops to Southeast Asia. Then in August a U.S. ship engaged North Vietnamese vessels, which prompted the congressional Gulf of Tonkin Resolution—a virtual carte blanche to escalate military engagement. Some in the press responded skeptically to this turn of events, and radical pacifists held a small antiwar vigil at the Democratic National Convention in late August. Still, disagreement within antiwar ranks regarding immediate versus negotiated withdrawal impaired a sense of unity in their opposition. It did not, however, prevent the start of plans for a national protest in mid-December that would prove to be the first substantial demonstration against the U.S. presence in Vietnam.[23] Also before the year closed, SDS leaders would agree to sponsor a demonstration the following Easter to demand U.S. withdrawal from Vietnam.[24]

Although dissent would gel and accelerate among antiwar camps during the months that followed the November 1964 Gethsemani event, nothing about the nascent movement seemed clear or obvious as the retreat approached. With students, leftists, selected liberal politicians, critical journalists, and traditional radical pacifists all beginning to weigh in against the war, those who grounded their opposition in faith convictions could understandably question where they fit and what might constrain their participation and collaboration. The movement's growing secular priority of fostering a new and greater consciousness sounded a familiar and recognizable chord for those who responded to a religious calling, but it did not embody the same motives or ultimate vision. In a letter to Merton, John Heidbrink shared his view of this incipient movement as something fragmented and "torn loose from cultures." It fed off of "pragmatic bits of political analysis" that often seemed "justifiably anti-church without being anti-religious" in character. It "admits only one attitude to nature, history, and human life: an attitude restricted to elements which are rationally explainable." For churchmen it was urgent, he felt, to "ask the questions that need to be asked regarding the *why* and *what* of protest and political analysis" with spiritual priorities in mind. "That is why we need to come to Gethsemani."[25]

22. Ibid., 92–97.
23. Wittner, *Rebels Against War*, 281.
24. DeBenedetti and Chatfield, *American Ordeal*, 98–101.
25. Heidbrink to Merton, 17 Sept. 1964, TMC.

Those Who Gathered

The circle of men sequestered in Merton's hermitage on that November afternoon mostly fit within a religious niche of radical pacifism, and many had accumulated impressive résumés in the realm of pacifist thought and action. They certainly embraced the sense of the times that translated personal commitment and experience into political relevance and action. This group was necessarily comprised of men, since the monastery retreat house was not prepared to lodge women for an overnight event until its renovation twenty-five years later. We can therefore only speculate on the impact that Dorothy Day or some other female pacifist voice may have provided in its conversations. Though retreat organizer John Heidbrink in the end could not attend, some who did had close ties to the Fellowship of Reconciliation. This body had formed at the onset of World War I and took root in the United States shortly thereafter. It drew on religious tenets to ground its rationale against war, but as a membership organization, it held no direct ties to formal church structures. By the 1960s, the FOR drew mainly on Protestant members configured into a series of denominational peace fellowships.

One of the 1964 retreatants, the venerable Abraham "A. J." Muste[26] (1885–1967), had in 1916 helped found an early U.S. FOR chapter in Boston and chaired the U.S. FOR from 1926–1929.[27] Following an extended flirtation with Trotskyism, Muste recommitted to his earlier pacifism as World War II approached. From 1940 through 1953 he served as the FOR executive director, where he played a role initiating CORE. His journey led to close interaction with the work of Martin Luther King Jr., leadership in CNVA, and service on the War Resister's League national committee. Muste also helped found *Liberation* magazine in 1956 and then served on its editorial board well into the sixties. He joined Dorothy Day and others in 1957 to publically refuse cooperation with New York City civil defense drills, and he participated in a 1961 CNVA San Francisco to Moscow Walk for Peace that advocated for unilateral disarmament. Resting on impeccable peace movement credentials, he was widely respected for his sincerity and intellect, even by those who disagreed with him; he lived and modeled his pacifism with integrity. Muste was easily the most prominent guest at Gethsemani that week.

John Oliver Nelson[28] (1909–1990), a second participant with FOR ties, chaired its National Council from 1950–1955. Nelson's father had begun his

26. Information on Muste generally from, DeBenedetti and Chatfield, *American Ordeal*, 20–21; Robinson, *Abraham Went Out*; Henthoff, *Peace Agitator*.

27. Henthoff, *Abraham Went Out*, 100. For a history of the FOR, see Dekar, *Creating*.

28. Information on Nelson from Yeasted, *JON*.

career in Pittsburgh, serving as secretary to Andrew W. Mellon and eventually rising to become vice president, treasurer, and a board member of Gulf Oil. He accumulated considerable wealth in the process, and as his son, John Nelson gained access to an excellent education. This included study for a year in Edinburgh, Scotland, where he met George MacLeod, who would soon establish an ecumenical community on the Island of Iona, an ancient monastic site. MacLeod deeply inspired him and fostered Nelson's aspirations to create a similar community in the United States. After graduating, Nelson began his career as a Presbyterian pastor, followed by positions with the Presbyterian Board of Christian Education and the Federal Council of Churches Commission on Ministry. He also played a prominent role in the YMCA, serving as its national secretary for a time as well as editor of its Association Press. Given his upper class background, Nelson presented himself with polish, but he interacted congenially and unpretentiously with those he met and was known for his personal benevolence to the poor and underprivileged he encountered.[29] From the start of his theological career, he advocated for peace and justice; during World War II he supported contentious objectors. Nelson also held a great passion for the development of church leaders and for establishing a retreat center modeled on MacLeod's Iona. In 1942 he established Kirkridge Retreat Center near Bangor, Pennsylvania to pursue both. The center's motto expressed his commitment to effecting both social change and spiritual depth: "Picket and Pray."

Nelson's professional career took an academic turn in 1950, when he became Professor of Christian Vocation and Director of Field Work at Yale Divinity School. Then in the summer of 1964 he left Yale to become director of Kirkridge Retreat Center. The Center's longstanding commitment to social issues, including peace, was readily apparent that year. A June retreat addressed "Liturgy and a Radical Apostolate," featuring John Heidbrink, Catholic Archbishop Thomas Roberts of Great Britain, an outspoken supporter of peace and justice concerns, and John Nelson himself.[30] Two months later Kirkridge sponsored "Christian Faith and the 'American Faith,'" led by Paul Peachey of the Church Peace Mission (CPM).[31] At the time of the Gethsemani retreat, in addition to having just launched his new vocation at Kirkridge, Nelson also served as chair of the Church Peace Mission. This organization, sponsored by historic peace church agencies, the FOR, and a handful of mainline Protestant peace committees, first convened in 1950

29. Paul Peachey, conversation with author, 16 June 2012.

30. "Proposed Retreat Schedule. Liturgy and a Radical Apostolate. June 10–14, 1964," A/234, Berrigan Collection, CUL.

31. Lawrence Young to Paul Peachey, 4 Aug. 1964, C/3, CPM Records, SCPC. Paul Peachey to Lawrence Young, 6 May 1964, C/3, CPM Records, SCPC.

as an ad hoc gathering to process how American churches had accommodated World War II. It eventually morphed into an ongoing organization to promote pacifism within Christendom, providing a level of institutional engagement that the FOR lacked. The CPM's core work promoted Christian pacifist/non-pacifist dialogue through ecumenical scholarly discussion among American just war and pacifist theologians and social scientists. By 1963 CPM conferences were also addressing civil rights questions. A. J. Muste had figured prominently in the CPM, as well, serving on staff as its "Missioner" from the early fifties until 1962. In some ways the CPM's agenda mirrored the liberal reformist agenda of institutional dialogue across differences, but it rooted its program in deep moral convictions about peacemaking as an inherent Christian vocation. It also played a role in co-organizing the Gethsemani retreat along with John Heidbrink's FOR.[32]

Two other participants held special relationships to the FOR at the time of the event. Jim Forest[33] (1941–) had joined the New York City Catholic Worker community in 1961 after receiving discharge from the Navy as a conscientious objector. After arriving at the Catholic Worker he quickly immersed himself in the contemporary radical pacifist milieu, participating in antinuclear protest actions at Atomic Energy Commission offices sponsored by the CNVA and others. He was jailed for fifteen days in 1962 following his participation in one such action. Forest's talents earned him managing editorial roles for *The Catholic Worker* and *Liberation* periodicals, and he served briefly on CNVA staff and worked closely with the War Resisters League—both of which provided venues for interaction with A. J. Muste. He also worked for Catholic Relief Services during this era. Building on his editorial activity for *The Catholic Worker*, Forest struck up a friendship with Thomas Merton, initially through correspondence and later during a February 1962 visit to Gethsemani. Forest's relationship with the FOR began in 1961 when John Heidbrink first proposed formation of a Catholic peace group that would affiliate with the FOR. The end product of that effort— PAX—chose not to affiliate, however, and adopted an agenda that focused more on work within the U.S. Catholic community than on ecumenical or activist engagement. In early 1964, again at Heidbrink's urging, Forest once more launched groundwork for a more activist Catholic FOR affiliate. He began to make contacts, gather lists of names, issue mailings, and perform other core organizational work. Forest also spearheaded development of a

32. CPM description from Peachey, *Usable Past*, 107–18; Robinson, *Abraham Went Out*, 150–56; Yoder, "Racial Revolution," 97–124. Yoder described the CPM as "one of the most undersung intellectual forces at work behind the American religious and social scene during the troubled 1960s."

33. Information on Forest from Forest, conversation with author, 29 May 2011.

statement of purpose for the group, and by the time of the retreat a fledgling Catholic Peace Fellowship (CPF) affiliate of the FOR was coalescing, with Forest serving as one of its three cochairs. Six weeks after the Gethsemani retreat, Forest began to work full time for the CPF.

The retreat also included another CPF organizer, Tom Cornell[34] (1934–), who had joined the Catholic Worker movement in the mid-fifties at age nineteen. He likewise embraced the era's antinuclear peace activism, participating in CNVA and related events. Moving in these circles would introduce him to John Oliver Nelson and create close and ongoing ties with mentor A. J. Muste. Cornell's civil disobedience also extended to draft resistance; beginning in 1960 he would burn each of his nine consecutively issued draft cards, often publically. Cornell was deeply committed to the Catholic Worker movement, serving as editor of *The Catholic Worker* from 1962–1964; when Jim Forest arrived in 1961, they began a close friendship that continues to the present day. In mid-1965 Cornell joined Forest as a part-time FOR employee to support the emerging CPF as its educational advisor. For Cornell, the CPF would provide a formal venue to advance Catholic Worker radical pacifist priorities, describing it as "a benign front for the Catholic Worker movement through the institution of the FOR." The CPF would serve as an important network for the journalistically-tagged "Catholic Left," or "Catholic Resistance," that played a significant role in antiwar resistance during the latter half of the decade.

A handful of other Catholics on the initial CPF rolls (or with strong relational ties to it) participated in the retreat, as well. Daniel Berrigan[35] (1921–), a Jesuit priest, provided considerable support to Forest and Cornell in their work to establish the CPF, sharing names to contact, helping raise funds, and ultimately serving on its list of formal sponsors. He also developed close personal bonds with Thomas Merton and John Heidbrink. Berrigan's studies and experiences introduced him to such influences as the writings of Teilhard de Chardin, who emphasized an incarnational God present here and now, and the French "worker priests," who voluntarily accompanied laborers deported to Germany during World War II and worked alongside them in French mines and factories after it ended. A man of letters, Berrigan began to publish poetry early in his career, and in 1957 he was appointed as a professor of New Testament studies at Le Moyne College in Syracuse, New York. His advocacy regarding issues of poverty, open clergy/laity relations, and ecumenical interaction stretched boundaries of

34. Information on Cornell from Cornell, email to author, 13 Apr. 2010; Cornell, conversation with author, 29 May 2011.

35. Information on Daniel Berrigan from Polner and O'Grady, *Disarmed and Dangerous*, 92–106.

the pre-Vatican II Catholic Church and positioned him on its cutting edge. He used his monthly spot on a national Catholic radio show to promote awareness of poverty and other socioeconomic concerns. Not surprisingly, he also interacted with Dorothy Day and the Catholic Worker movement. While at Le Moyne he offended the local bishop by establishing a Catholic Worker-like house in Syracuse and exposing as slumlords various financial supporters of the diocese. In both 1961 and 1963, his attempts to participate in "freedom rides" to support integration in the South were rebuffed by his superiors.

Beginning in 1962, Berrigan and John Heidbrink collaborated to lead retreats for Protestant clergy. That same year Berrigan initiated correspondence with Merton, seeking counsel regarding challenges to his advocacy, and he visited Gethsemani to see Merton and lecture for his novices that June. They soon became close friends and confidants. His outspoken voice on social issues prompted Berrigan's dispatch to France for a half-year "sabbatical" in 1963–1964 to cool the embers that his agitation regularly seemed to stir. In late August he returned to his new assignment in New York City as a writer for *Jesuit Missions* magazine. He had arrived in good time to not only join the November retreat, but to play an important role in executing it.

Another friendship of Daniel Berrigan's that formed through his activist adventures was that of Anthony "Tony" Walsh[36] (1898–1994). Unlike most other participants, this British-born Canadian and World War I veteran does not fit neatly into American peace and civil rights movement categories. As a lay Catholic intuitively drawn to service, he established a noteworthy career among First Nations people in British Columbia and fulfilled his World War II military requirement by establishing healing and morale-building opportunities for soldiers stationed in that province. After a few more years of wandering, he settled in Montreal where he co-founded and operated Benedict Labré House. This house of hospitality followed the Catholic Worker model, and his success prompted visits from many interested parties, including Dorothy Day. It also earned him local and national awards for his devotion to the poor. Walsh also possessed a contemplative nature and would sometimes retreat to a Trappist monastery not far from Montreal for times of rest and renewal. While at Le Moyne College in nearby Syracuse, Daniel Berrigan visited Labré House, and he and Walsh became friends. Berrigan led annual retreats at Labré during the late fifties and early sixties. Walsh accompanied Berrigan to Gethsemani in 1962—also lecturing for Merton's novices—in addition to rejoining him there at the 1964 retreat.

36. Information on Walsh from Buell, *Travelling Light*; Smith, "Portrait of a Teacher."

A third participant in both the 1962 and 1964 Gethsemani visits was Daniel's younger brother, Philip Berrigan[37] (1923–2002). If Daniel Berrigan's gateway into activist circles rested on issues of poverty and ecumenicity, matters of race relations and civil rights characterized Philip's. More brash, outgoing, and athletic than the introspective and scholarly Daniel, Philip nonetheless shared his brother's spiritual sensitivity for those oppressed. His military training in the Deep South during World War II and his observation of racial prejudice and disadvantage within military ranks exposed him to the pervasive presence and debilitating consequences of American racism. Following his military service Philip entered a Josephite seminary, an order dedicated to serving African American Catholics, and he was ordained priest in 1955. From the start of his first assignment among indigent blacks in the nation's capital, Philip challenged local whites to consider their complicity in the trials that African Americans experienced in the United States. Within a year he had alienated many of the city's white Catholics, even as he became popular in African American activist circles. Predictably, he was soon transferred to a New Orleans boy's high school, where he undauntedly pressed onward at integration issues.

The resistance and slow responsiveness of the church and constituents alike only served to heighten his frustration and intensify his efforts. In New Orleans Philip also awakened to concerns over nuclear war when the 1962 Cuban missile confrontation left him ill-prepared to address the crises of faith it prompted in many of his parishioners. Along with his brother, Philip was denied permission to participate in 1961 and 1963 freedom rides that they attempted to join. Shortly after the 1963 denial, Philip was transferred to a parish in the Bronx—where once more his vocal criticism of slow-moving bishops forced his removal in mid-1964, this time upriver to a seminary in Newburgh, New York, a conservative community noted for its racist atmosphere. After his arrival in New York, Philip also joined Jim Forest as one of the CPF's initial co-chairs.[38] By the time he arrived at Gethsemani for his second visit, then, Philip Berrigan had already logged considerable experience confronting power and culture in pursuit of religious/moral objectives.

Two other participants moved closely within the Berrigan brothers' Catholic activist circles. John Peter Grady[39] (1925–2002) was born in

37. Information on Philip Berrigan generally from Polner and O'Grady, *Disarmed and Dangerous*, 92–106.

38. The third initial CPF cochair, along with Phil Berrigan and Jim Forest, was Martin Corbin. CPF letterhead from October 1964 in D/32, FOR Records, SCPC.

39. Information on Grady from Flores, "Obituary"; McGowan, *Peace Warriors*, 21; *Disarmed and Dangerous*, 240–41; Teresa Grady, Mary Anne Grady Flores, and Ellen Grady, conversation with author, 12 June 2012.

the Bronx to Irish immigrants. His World War II service in the Navy was bracketed by attendance at Manhattan College, and he subsequently pursued (but never fully completed) a PhD in sociology at Fordham University, where he was awarded a Fulbright scholarship to Ireland. He met his future wife on a visit home for the wedding of a friend in Chicago. After their marriage, Grady served as business manager of *Jubilee*, a popular Catholic magazine published between 1953 and 1967 that is sometimes credited with helping prepare American Catholics for the changes ushered in by Vatican II. Thomas Merton was a regular *Jubilee* contributor and the godson and classmate of its founder and editor Edward Rice. This particular role of Grady's no doubt deepened his awareness of movement figures and issues. Following this editorship, the Grady's moved to Chicago where he worked in a Catholic family/marriage support program, but then returned to the Bronx to raise their family of five children. Here he participated in local politics and in 1959 and 1960 helped conduct a crosscultural program in Puerto Rico.

Robert Cunnane[40] (1932–) came to know Philip Berrigan through his brother, a classmate of Philip's at Holy Cross College. Cunnane had studied for the priesthood in Rome, and in 1959 he was ordained as a Stigmatine priest, an order dedicated to youth education and clergy formation. His work included developing retreats at the order's Espousal Retreat House near Boston. While serving there, Cunnane was also appointed part-time director of the Packard Manse Ecumenical Center in Stoughton, Massachusetts, near Boston. Here he sought to build bridges between Protestants and Catholics, Christians and Jews, and different economic classes. Philip Berrigan's mentorship proved foundational to his future involvement in the peace movement. After the younger Berrigan returned north, he sometimes visited Cunnane, who in turn would drive from Boston to Newburgh and together with Philip continue into New York City to join company with Daniel Berrigan and others of similar ilk. His pilgrimage into the peace movement was just beginning when he joined the others at Gethsemani.

Charles Ring[41] (1925–1986) served with Bob Cunnane at the Espousal Retreat House at the time of their trip to Gethsemani. He also grew up in the Boston area and went to Rome for biblical studies. His arrival there preceded Cunnane, but their stays in Rome overlapped. When Ring returned to the United States in the mid-fifties he taught in the religious studies department of Catholic University in Washington, D.C. for several years. Declining a

40. Information on Cunnane from Cunnane, email to author, 15 Apr. 2010; Cunnane, conversation with author, 31 May 2011.

41. Information on Ring from Cunnane, 27 Oct. 2012, conversation with author.

post there as department head, he joined Cunnane at the Stigmatine retreat house in 1963 and became acquainted with Philip Berrigan during the Josephite priest's visits.

An eleventh member of the party filled a quite different niche in the pacifist realm. John Howard Yoder[42] (1924–1997) held deep roots—both spiritual and familial—in the Mennonite historic peace church tradition. In addition to Yoder's perpetual exposure to those religious peace teachings as a child, his parents, progressive by the era's Mennonite standards, brought him along when they attended FOR meetings in Wooster, Ohio. In 1949 Yoder joined a postwar relief effort in Europe sponsored by the Mennonite Central Committee. His tasks included offering material aid, administrating a couple of children's homes, and bolstering French Mennonite interrelationships and awareness of their own historic peace tradition. Besides his work with the French Mennonites, Yoder engaged in ongoing ecumenical peace and social dialogues and completed studies for a PhD in theology from the University of Basel, which was ultimately awarded in 1962. In 1955 he administered earthquake relief work in Algeria, where he witnessed violent opposition to French colonial control. Yoder also engaged in the European Study Conference of American Mennonite Students in Europe, also known as the "Concern" group, which challenged certain Mennonite institutional presumptions. The *Concern* pamphlet series injected fresh views on church and society into the postwar American Mennonite milieu.

Following his return to the United States in 1957, Yoder increasingly moved among Mennonite and ecumenical academic and institutional circles, often focusing on topics of peace and nonviolence. By 1964 he was serving as an administrative assistant with the Mennonite Board of Missions, a part-time instructor at Mennonite Biblical Seminary, and in ad hoc capacities with the National Council of Churches and World Council of Churches. Yoder's personal history did not include extensive protest, but by the time he arrived in Gethsemani he had accumulated years of experience sorting through both practical and theoretical nuances of countering the impact of war and other social ills. Further, he had grown well-practiced within diverse ecumenical contexts at articulating a solid biblical/theological rationale for nonviolence and for considering the roles and relationships of church, government, and other social institutions. In other words, he arrived at Gethsemani with a solid foundation for tapping spiritual roots of engagement to seek peace and social change in a post–World War II world.

---

42. Information on Yoder from Nation, *John Howard Yoder*, 13–23; "John H. Yoder, Theologian At Notre Dame, Is Dead at 70." *New York Times*, January 7, 1998. Online: http://www.nytimes.com/1998/01/07/us/john-h-yoder-theologian-at-notre-dame-is-dead-at-70.html; Mennonite Church USA Archives, "Inventory."

Another Protestant participant, Elbert Jean[43] (1921–), represented a unique element of the civil rights movement. Born in rural Arkansas, Jean observed firsthand from early life the impact of Southern rural poverty and racism. After serving in the military during WWII, studying for the ministry at Southern Methodist University, and becoming ordained in the Methodist church, Jean was assigned to various Methodist pastorates in rural Arkansas. His path of assignments eventually led him to St. Luke's Methodist Church in Little Rock. There, he became deeply involved in local efforts of clergy and laity to integrate the city's Central High School. This measure gained national attention when federal troops were deployed in 1957 to implement the 1954 Supreme Court's Brown v. Board of Education school integration ruling. Intense local resistance, backed by the governor's refusal to support the school's integration, polarized the community. During the controversy Jean became acquainted with Will Campbell, an outspoken advocate of integration in the South who participated in aspects of the Little Rock episode. Campbell had assumed leadership of the National Council of Churches (NCC) "Southern Project" in 1956, an effort to provide resources and guidance to smooth conflict in local integration efforts throughout the South. Locals would be more receptive, it was felt, to the persuasion of white Southern men than to imported Northerners.

Following his contentious Little Rock involvement, Jean was relegated to pastor a rural backwater congregation at Mena, Arkansas. Here his previous participation in Little Rock and positions on race relations prompted ostracism by some colleagues, as well as dwindling financial support for his ministry. At Campbell's invitation, Jean left the paid pastorate and moved to Nashville where he served with Campbell as a "minister at large" on the project and filled a part-time pastor role at a black African Methodist Episcopal congregation named Seay-Hubbard in Nashville. The Campbell and Jean families grew close during these years; Will Campbell would later quote Jean as saying he had "left the Church to enter the ministry."[44] In 1963 Campbell resigned from the NCC project to develop his own similar program, formed under the dormant structure of an organization known as the Committee of Southern Churchmen. Campbell would eventually come to know Merton. He visited Gethsemani in 1965, and Merton later contributed to the Southern Churchmen periodical, *Katallagete*. Following Campbell's departure from the NCC, Jean stayed on staff to administer its Southern

43. Information on Jean from Jean, 23 Apr. 2010, email to author; Jean, 18 Apr. 2011, interview with author; Lori Cameron, 12 Feb. 2013, email to author; Findlay, *Church People*, 24, 43. Information on Will Campbell from Hawkins, *Will Campbell*, 40–62.

44. Campbell, *Brother to a Dragonfly*, 261.

Project until it was terminated in 1964. At that point, he rejoined Campbell as staff for the Committee of Southern Churchmen. Jean's experiences with ecclesial authority and the influence of the iconoclastic Campbell fostered a distrust of the institutional church and its ability to respond to unpopular and difficult social and moral issues. Though not a radical pacifist, Jean brought to the Gethsemani gathering broad experience working for justice and reconciliation in situations of tense conflict.

The thirteenth and final guest at Gethsemani, Wilbur H. "Ping" Ferry[45] (1910–1995), represented the greatest anomaly among this particular circle. His lineage included a capitalist father, who climbed the ranks of the Packard auto company from accountant to president to board chair, and an activist grandmother, who had agitated for women's rights and local causes. After graduating from Dartmouth College, Ferry briefly taught at a boys school that placed Joseph and John Kennedy under his care. In 1945 Ferry joined a public relations firm whose clients included the Ford Foundation and its Fund for the Republic, for which Ferry became a pivotal advisor in distributing enormous funds to social causes. In 1954 he joined the Fund's staff and influenced support for progressive and controversial projects that included battling the era's McCarthyist agenda. In 1959 the Fund founded a new think tank—the Center for the Study of Democratic Institutions in Santa Barbara, California. Its purpose, in harmony with liberal internationalist agendas, was to organize conversations among intellectuals to address diverse challenges that humanity faced. Ferry joined its staff as vice president; a longstanding friend with Catholic Worker ties, John Cogley, also served a staff role. Ferry's path to the Gethsemani retreat originated through Thomas Merton. In 1961, Merton's publisher suggested he might do well to become acquainted with Ferry, and Merton wrote to him. Despite Ferry's estrangement from organized religion, an unlikely but close friendship formed between the men. At the time of the retreat he self-identified as a Unitarian.[46] Later in life he considered himself an agnostic, though during his last years he named "Christian" as his religious affiliation.[47] Ferry helped distribute many of Merton's writings in mimeographed form during a period (1962–1964) when Merton's order severely restricted publication of his works on peace. He would come to see the Trappist monk as one of three or four "great men in my life." Ferry's presence could not help but inject a healthy dose of liberal democratic/internationalist perspective into the retreat's mix of discussion.

45. Information on W. H. Ferry from Ward, *Ferrytale*.

46. Tom Cornell, 7 Feb. 2013, email to author.

47. Ward, *Ferrytale*, 18.

Rounding out the list of participants was the host and hub of the event, Thomas Merton[48] (1915–1968). The early life of Father Louis, as he was known to his fellow Trappists, held few hints of his monastic life to come. Born to artist parents, both of whom would die before he reached age sixteen, Merton experienced a transient childhood and bohemian youth. Through the subtle influence of friendships and literary academic pursuits, he was eventually drawn to Catholicism and its mystical tradition. Merton entered the Trappist monastic order just as the United States entered the Second World War, eventually applying his literary talents within his new vocation. Following publication of his 1948 best-selling autobiography, *The Seven Storey Mountain*, Thomas Merton emerged on the national scene as a one of the most respected and widely read religious writers.

In March 1958 Merton experienced an often-referenced epiphany credited with helping to alter his perceived selfhood, his monasticism, and his relationship to the people and world around him. This famed "Fourth and Walnut Experience," which alludes to the location of this experience in downtown Louisville, intensified his awareness of the interconnectedness among all humanity and placed his vocation in a newly understood social context. It marked a pivotal transition toward dialogue with a wide variety of intellectual and mystical colleagues as his quest for greater insight and broader understanding extended beyond the boundaries of Catholicism and Christianity. Merton soon became increasingly engaged in correspondence with writers from Jewish, Sufi, Hindu, and Zen traditions, as well as others of the Christian West.

This transformation also led to more engaged and critical thinking about larger social issues, including the futility and immorality of nuclear war as a threat to human life itself. Expressions of Merton's concern with the issue begin to recur in journal entries logged during late summer in 1961, and by the end of August he had resolved to speak out on the issue.[49] This resolution began to bear considerable fruit that October. His first venture into antinuclear writing was marked by publication of "The Root of War is Fear" in the October 1961 issue of *The Catholic Worker*. The bulk of the essay comprised a chapter in *New Seeds of Contemplation*, which had been approved by church hierarchy for publication. His submission to *The Catholic Worker*, however, contained added paragraphs that focused his critique more sharply on American policy and the dilemmas it created for U.S. Christians. The mad scramble on all sides of the geopolitical divide to

48. Material on Merton from Shannon et al., *Merton Encyclopedia*; Merton, *Passion for Peace*; Forest, *Living with Wisdom*.

49. Merton, *TTW*, 29 Aug. 1961, 157.

build bomb shelters and protect them with machine guns, even in a "nation that claims to be fighting for religious truth," surely signaled our entry into a "post-Christian era," he asserted. Those who advocated for an American "first strike" in nuclear war toward the end that "the glorious Christian West can eliminate atheistic communism for all time and usher in the millennium" had surely fallen prey to "the most diabolical of illusions." Rather, the Christian's duty in such a world, "the one task which God has imposed on us in the world today," was simply "to work for the total abolition of war."[50]

October 1961 also marked the start of a string of correspondence on the topic that would come to be known as his Cold War letters. Late that month he recorded in his journal a conviction to "set everything aside to work for the abolition of war," which meant "getting into contact with the others most concerned," such as a British Catholic peace organization, the Fellowship of Reconciliation, and *The Catholic Worker*.[51] Over the next year, into October of 1962, Merton would pen over one hundred letters related to the topic, circulating many of them to numerous people in mimeograph form.[52] On the same day as the October journal entry that voiced his commitment against war, Merton also launched a proposal to collect an anthology of essays by various writers that would articulate the urgency of the issue.[53] His publisher, James Laughlin, eagerly concurred, and the resulting work titled *Breakthrough to Peace: Twelve Views on the Threat of Thermonuclear Extermination*, reached the reading public in August 1962.[54]

It should come as no surprise that such direct engagement with political issues prompted concern from within Catholicism in general and his Trappist order in particular. It ventured beyond the accepted prerogatives of contemplative monks, whose pursuit of solitude and withdrawal supposedly precluded an informed understanding of real world necessities that would contaminate their vocation. Besides, as the Berrigans and others in this circle had learned, dabbling in topics with political implications could alienate and offend important people. Sensing what was to come, he hurriedly put together his own book manuscript to be titled *Peace in the Post-Christian Era*. Just as he was completing the draft in April 1962, however, the Trappist Abbot General Gabriel Sortais ordered Merton to stop publishing his own antiwar material. The book was therefore shelved, at least for the time

50. Merton, *Passion for Peace*, 11–12. See also Forest, *Living with Wisdom*, 152–54.

51. Merton, *TTW*, 30 Oct. 1961, 175–76.

52. The correspondence would eventually be published in book form as *Cold War Letters*.

53. Merton to James Laughlin, 30 Oct. 1961, in Merton and Laughlin, *Selected Letters*, 183–84.

54. Merton, *TTW*, 27 Aug. 1962, 240.

being.[55] Merton chafed under the restriction, writing to Jim Forest shortly afterward, "Imagine that: the thought that a monk might be deeply enough concerned with the issue of nuclear war to voice a protest against the arms race, is supposed to bring the monastic life into *disrepute*."[56] Though Merton obeyed the terms of the order, with the support of his abbot he sought every opportunity to circumvent its spirit, continuing his dialogue with other pacifists and distributing mimeographed copies of his work through a network of friends and correspondents. Some of these were present at the gathering in November 1964, when it seemed his censorship might be lessening enough to permit publishing comments supportive of peace, provided they did not tackle nuclear weapons or warfare in general.[57] Merton also permitted his name to appear among the list of Catholic Peace Fellowship sponsors. At the time of the retreat, then, more than two decades of contemplative reflection, disengagement from the priorities of cultural conformity, and frustration with institutional authority had melded with a sharpening social awareness to grant Merton unique insight into motives for protest.

A Prescient Event

On many fronts, U.S. society pulsated with change and uncertainty as the latter months of 1964 drew near. Especially since the October 1962 Cuban Missile Crisis two years prior, the religious, domestic, and political worlds that these fourteen men observed and experienced had undergone significant flux. Within Roman Catholic circles, Pope John XXIII had launched an irreversible sea change by convening the first Vatican II council session just three days before U.S. spy planes captured proof of Soviet missiles on Cuban soil. The following spring, two months before his death, John XXIII would lend credibility to Merton's writings on peace by issuing the groundbreaking encyclical *Pacem in Terris*.[58] Each of the next three Septembers his successor, Pope Paul VI, followed his initiative and convened additional Vatican II sessions. The legacy of John XXIII offered great strides toward liberating traditional relationships within the Catholic Church and helped to challenge its acceptance of state military ventures.

55. Segments of it would be included as essays in Merton, *Seeds of Destruction*, and the full work was eventually published as a whole with the same title, *Peace in the Post-Christian Era*.

56. Bochen, "Censorship," 49.

57. Merton to Ferry, 8 June 1964, *HGL*, 218.

58. The encyclical was dated 11 Apr. 1963.

Domestically, the civil rights movement continued to steadily erode white racial privilege during these two years, but only through painful disruption. Five days after Pope John XXIII released *Pacem in Terris*, the moral leader of the U.S. African American church issued his own encyclical in the form of Martin Luther King Jr.'s "Letter from a Birmingham Jail." Two months later—nine days after the Pope's death in June 1963—a defender of the Old South murdered civil rights leader Medgar Evers. Stakes in the campaign for civil rights continued to rise that year with an August 28 "March on Washington for Jobs and Freedom" that climaxed with King's iconic proclamation, "I have a dream," reverberating across the capital's mall. Barely a month later, four young black girls lay dead in the wreckage of a bomb detonated at Birmingham's Sixteenth Street Baptist Church. The following year's Freedom Summer campaign in Mississippi endured the murders of advocates James Cheney, Andrew Goodman, and Michael Schwerner on June 21. But the Civil Rights Act passed eleven days later, and that October, black America's bittersweet nonviolent pilgrimage through brutal racist terrain received international vindication when the Nobel committee awarded Martin Luther King Jr. its Peace Prize. The next month's election of Lyndon Baines Johnson as president capped a political campaign fueled as much by fears of his opponent's agenda abroad as by his own stance on justice at home.

In the realm of international politics, President Kennedy's assassination followed his August 1963 atmospheric test ban treaty triumph by only two months. The treaty failed to slow nuclear proliferation, however—by mid-October of 1964 China had detonated its own atomic bomb to join the club of nuclear super-powers. The Cold War logic that relied on nuclear threat to deter hot war engagement likewise proved false. Troop expansion by Kennedy's successor during the summer of 1964 accelerated policies that would wreak havoc on America's moral standing at home as well as abroad and ignite loose strands of domestic discomfort into widespread antiwar protest.

For the retreatants at Gethsemani, this kaleidoscope of tense change deeply affected their worldview and fostered serious urgency. Events within and without the church seemed to be careening out of control. Even Merton the contemplative could express to his confidant Daniel Berrigan during the summer of 1964 that he felt "sick up to the teeth . . . [with] explanations about where we are all going because where we are all going is . . . over the falls. We are in a new river and we don't know it."[59] Their collective personal experience with the institutional church offered these men scant

59. Merton to Berrigan, 4 Aug. 1964, *HGL*, 83–84.

optimism that they could turn to it for prophetic guidance or leadership, any more than they could turn to governmental institutions to lead its citizens through hard moral choices badly needed at such a time. Instead, to help chart their path as America's military commitment grew, they seized this retreat opportunity and turned to one another and their collective spiritual wisdom for insight. But someone first needed to arrange for them to assemble. Just as national and global events around them had evolved to this juncture, so the idea of gathering at Gethsemani had evolved and adapted during the preceding months.

2

Assembling "A Few Strong People with a Passion for Peace"

WITH SNOW SWIRLING BEYOND his windshield and the Louisville skyline receding in his rearview mirror, Paul Peachey guided his rented car southward into the hilly knobs of Nelson County, Kentucky. After an hour navigating the highway's twists and turns, he approached a sign that marked the way toward "Trappist." Turning left onto a narrow country road, Peachey followed it for a few short miles and then pulled into a tree-lined lane. He parked to the side of the lane beneath one of the trees, exited his car, and strode toward the large door of the long, faux-stone gatehouse that granted access to the Abbey of our Lady of Gethsemani. Peachey announced himself to the gatehouse porter attending to the entry way, and the monk ushered him into a small greeting room within the gatehouse. His colleague William R. Miller, who had arranged his visit and made plans to meet him here, soon joined Peachey. As the porter telephoned the main complex to announce their arrival, Peachey and Miller passed the time together until their host appeared to guide them through the enclosed courtyard and on into the imposing monastic structure that loomed behind it. Upon entering a large meeting room, the two visitors were offered seats before an assemblage of Trappist monks and novices who had gathered to share the next hour or so with them. When all had settled into their places, the novice master, Thomas Merton, rose to speak.[1]

---

1. Chapter opening based on details in Peachey to Irene Leaman et al., 17 May 1995, 2, Yoder Papers, TMC; recording 42.4, 27 Jan. 1963, TMC; Br. Patrick Hart and Fr. James Connor, 3 Nov. 2012, conversations with author.

The Idea Sparks

"This is a very new situation, here," Merton began on this afternoon in late January of 1963.[2] "It hasn't been before in the history of a Trappist monastery, as far as I can see. First of all," he noted, "this particular group—brothers, and choir novices, and choir professed, and priests—this is a cross section of the monastery." Merton further explained that this occasion was also unique because these current and future monks would be addressed by representatives of two Protestant groups: Peachey, Executive Secretary of the Church Peace Mission, was Mennonite, whereas Miller belonged to the United Church of Christ and edited its periodical, the *United Church Herald*. The topic at hand, Merton explained, was nonviolence. "Both of these individuals are very interested in the peace movement, and the peace movement . . . is probably stronger among Protestants than it is among Catholics."

Merton continued to frame the occasion and its topic for his brethren, demonstrating his familiarity with the nuclear disarmament movement that was engaged beyond their enclosure. As he spoke, he groped for words that would intrigue and connect. "What is this idea of nonviolence, anyway?" he posed. "In the present context of nuclear war . . . anybody who proposes the idea of a solution . . . other than that of nuclear war . . . has got to offer a positive solution. These men are interested in the possibilities of solutions that are not violent. Is it possible to arrive at peaceful solutions of international problems? Now this is of course an enormous question." Merton then brought the topic closer to home. "Is this something totally foreign to us?" he asked. "Well it shouldn't be. The Epistle in today's Mass is an Epistle about nonviolence. It goes like this—the last part of the twelfth chapter to the Romans: 'Be not wise in your own conceits, to no man rendering evil for evil.' See this is what nonviolence does, it goes right against the policy of rendering evil for evil." He then continued reading the passage:

> Providing good things not only in the sight of God but also in the sight of men. If it be possible, as much as it is in you, have peace with all men. Revenge not yourselves, my dearly beloved, but place unto wrath, for it is written, vengeance is mine, I will repay, sayeth the Lord. But if thy enemy be hungry, give him to eat; if he thirst, give him to drink. For in doing this thou shalt heap fires of coal upon his head.

Here, alluding to this painful imagery, Merton injected a side comment, "There's a problem of interpretation about that passage," which elicited

---

2. Merton's comments taken from recording 42.4, 27 Jan. 1963, TMC.

considerable laughter. He then closed out the text: "But be not overcome by evil, but overcome evil with good."[3]

Driving home the import of the discussion to follow, Merton summarized that, "I would say that's just about the keynote of the whole idea of nonviolence . . . As Christians, I think there is no denying that we have to think it is possible. If we don't believe it is possible, we put ourselves in a position where we are no longer going to solve this thing as Christians . . . If we solve [it] as non-Christians, if we are non-Christian enough, we lose our soul." Having set the stage and captured their attention, Merton turned the discussion over to Miller, who for the remainder of the session embarked on a rather lengthy discourse that mostly consisted of historical anecdotes about nonviolent responses that produced results. He closed with questions. Peachey had remained silent throughout the joint assembly, but he would get a chance the next morning for a more intimate exchange with Merton, the primary purpose of his visit. Reflecting on these interactions in his journal the following evening, Merton noted how he "was eventually strained and tense from all the talk" the previous day, but that "it was quieter this morning with Peachey alone. We discussed my peace book which is not being published[4] and his translation of Dumoulin's *History of Zen* which has just appeared.[5] It was a fruitful morning."[6] Peachey would garner personal copies of Merton's books before departing,[7] and Merton would later comment that Peachey had struck him as a "fine fellow."[8]

This encounter in the closing days of January 1963 was not the first contact the two visitors had with their venerable host. Miller had previously served as managing editor of the FOR periodical, *Fellowship*, prior to his current United Church of Christ position.[9] In his editorial capacities Miller had interacted with Merton regarding the monk's writings on nonviolence and other matters of peace and the Cold War climate, and he would presently publish his own book on the topic of nonviolence.[10] Those exchanges

3. Rom 12:17–21.

4. *Peace in the Post-Christian Era* was completed in April 1962 but prevented from publication by his order's Abbot General in Rome.

5. DuMoulin, *History of Zen Buddhism*. While on assignment in Japan with Mennonite Central Committee, Peachey met the German Jesuit theologian Heinrich DuMoulin, who taught history and philosophy at Sophia University in Tokyo, Japan. For Peachey's story of his translation, see Peachey, *Usable Past*, 100–102.

6. Merton, *TTW*, 28 Jan. 1963, 294–95.

7. Peachey to Leaman, et al., 17 May 1995, Yoder Papers, TMC.

8. Merton to Tom McDonnell, 8 Feb. 1963, TMC.

9. Thomas Merton Center, "Merton's Correspondence with: Miller," biography para.

10. Miller, *Nonviolence*.

undoubtedly prompted Merton's arranging to expose his community to a sampling of the larger movement and its biblical relevance. No doubt the past spring's censorship pressures still stung. Perhaps on some level Merton may have hoped Miller's words might help vindicate—or at least explain to the Gethsemani community—his passionate desire to write about peace.

Peachey, for his part, had corresponded with Merton regarding his Dumoulin translation during the past year. This visit represented his third attempt to meet Merton for a conversation about his study of Zen history.[11] After the formal release of Peachey's book several days following the Gethsmani visit,[12] Merton wrote Peachey again and inquired about his rendering of a particular phrase.[13] Peachey's response addressed the translation, but then went on to pursue another matter—would it "be feasible for you or your Abbey to host an interfaith retreat on Peace?" In this context, "interfaith" meant the mingling of Catholics and Protestants. Their January visit had apparently touched Peachey's heart regarding the potential such conversations held, for in closing his letter Peachey shared that, "My visit with you meant more they I can tell, for it reassured me at a deep level that there is a fruitful urgency about these dialogues."[14]

Promoting Peace—A Gathering to Support the Nuclear Test Ban Movement

Peachey's proposal to Merton emerged from a conversation with John Heidbrink, then serving as the FOR's Director of Interchurch Activities. Peachey would credit Heidbrink with suggesting the Gethsemani venue for a retreat to discuss matters of peace, but in truth the suggestion had come full circle. Three months before Peachey's Gethsemani visit, John Heidbrink had taken his own pilgrimage to meet the monk while on an extended tour to connect with FOR constituents. As a highly visible contributor to the FOR periodical *Fellowship*, Merton warranted a spot on his itinerary. During Heidbrink's day at Gethsemani, Merton guided him on a four-hour walk through the forests and wooded landscape that surrounded the abbey. As they walked, Merton praised the FOR and its magazine, offering to be "used as often as we can use him" in its pages. He would continue to "write fiercely"

11. Merton to D. Berrigan, 15 June 1962, TMC; Merton, recording 20.3, 29 Aug. 1962, TMC; Merton, *TTW*, 13 Nov. 1962, 264.

12. Merton to McDonnell, 8 Feb. 1963, TMC.

13. Peachey to Merton, 13 Mar. 1963, TMC, mentions Merton's letter to Peachey of 6 Mar. 1963; no longer extant.

14. Ibid.

on matters of peace, but do so anonymously to, in Heidbrink's words, "avoid the hatchets of the censors." Heidbrink relished Merton's open warmth and found him to be a "keen man" whose monastic withdrawal only intensified his view of the world.[15]

Neither man could have known, however, that even as they walked across the Kentucky hillsides, CIA officials 500 miles away busily pored over U2 spy plane photos taken the day before. That evening these analysts would brief the U.S. State Department that they had identified the installation of Soviet missiles in Cuba. One week later, their discovery would explode across global news outlets, publicizing the so-called Cuban Missile Crisis and edging the two superpowers toward the brink of nuclear war as the rest of humanity held its collective breath. It seems no small irony, therefore, that as the CIA scrutinized its evidence that afternoon, Merton casually suggested to his guest that perhaps the FOR might convene a three day peace conference at Gethsemani Abbey some time the following year. Merton hoped for an occasion when U.S. peace leaders might engage in "deep self-analysis and exchange" and named A. J. Muste as one he particularly wished to meet. Merton also noted that Archbishop Thomas Roberts, a vocal supporter of peace issues in his native England, would be visiting the United States the coming year, hinting at his desire that the controversial Catholic leader also participate. Merton added that his superiors had approved such an event and were prepared to accommodate the visitors.[16]

John Heidbrink carried this standing invitation with him to Pittsburgh the following February, when Paul Peachey convened the Church Peace Mission's Committee on Study Program on which Heidbrink served. Peachey had assembled this collection of seminary and other religious leaders to counsel him regarding current trends in theological thought. This inaugural meeting of the committee occurred just thirteen days after Peachey's own visit to Gethsemani, and there Peachey and Heidbrink first connected regarding a dialogue hosted by Merton.

Pursuit of such a gathering fell easily within the bailiwick of both Heidbrink and Peachey. In practice, their paths perpetually crossed, intermingled, and blurred as they fulfilled their roles as institutional peace advocates. FOR was a sponsor of the CPM, and numerous individuals—including A. J. Muste and John Oliver Neslon—played roles in each, sometimes simultaneously. In 1961 Peachey, a sociologist by training, had accepted the assignment as CPM Executive Secretary, and by 1963, he was casting

15. John C. Heidbrink, "Report. John Heidbrink Trip. Oct. 14–Nov. 2, 1962," D/37, FOR Records, SCPC.

16. Heidbrink, "Report. John C. Heidbrink Trip," D/37, FOR Records, SCPC.

beyond the CPM's traditional Protestant core to include Catholic thinkers in its conferences and dialogues.[17] Heidbrink's work with the FOR engaged similar terrain, though perhaps at a more grassroots level. In his role coordinating interfaith activities he worked with a variety of denominational peace groups, each with varied ties to denominational structures. Heidbrink facilitated ecumenical dialogue as well. For example, he helped recruit fifteen or so Presbyterian ministers to the June 1962 retreat co-conducted with Daniel Berrigan. In following years they teamed to facilitate gatherings that included priests as well as ministers. By 1964 Berrigan, Merton, and several other prominent Catholics were on the rolls of the Fellowship of Reconciliation via their roles with the emerging Catholic Peace Fellowship.[18]

In a letter to Heidbrink several days after their committee meeting Peachey urged, "Your suggestion at Pittsburgh of a retreat at Gethsemani with Tom Merton is something we should really take up." He went on to offer suggestions and solicit input in how to move forward with it. Did Heidbrink wish to make first contact with Merton? "Would it be possible to get first a few strong persons, both Catholic and Protestant, who would carry a profound passion for peace, and then bring in some key church leaders who should be gotten off the fence?"[19] Heidbrink followed with a short note sharing that he supported Peachey making the contact with Merton and suggesting that Daniel Berrigan could serve as the medium for gaining Roman Catholic participation. Heidbrink affirmed that a gathering of "strong people (R. C. and Prots) calling upon the rail sitters is a superb approach" and advocated keeping participation within the academic community, including both lay and clerical individuals. "A proposal before hand (your's) is all Merton needs to do the work in [Kentucky]," he advised.[20]

A gathering along these lines fit within the CPM's niche in religious peace advocacy, and Heidbrink's suggestion in the context of a CPM planning meeting is understandable. The Partial Test Ban Treaty had not yet been ratified, nor had U.S. involvement in the Vietnam conflict escalated. The coalition of radical pacifists and liberal internationalists still more or less held together at the time, and the CPM sought to bridge the religious counterparts of that spectrum. Peachey's initial contact with Merton in mid-March reflected this agenda, echoing the tentative thoughts he and

17. Peachey to Merton, 13 Mar. 1963, TMC. Peachey, *Usable Past*, 110–15.

18. D. Berrigan to Merton, 16 May 1962, TMC; D. Berrigan to Merton, 14 June 1963, TMC; D. Berrigan to Merton, 2 June 1964, TMC.

19. Peachey to Heidbrink, 21 Feb. 1963, D/4, CPM Records, SCPC.

20. Paul Peachey, "Report to the CPM National Committee," 26 Mar. 1963, D/6, CPM Records, SCPC. Heidbrink to Peachey, postcard, n.d. [postmark Feb. 1963], D/3, CPM Records, SCPC.

Heidbrink had shared. He suggested equal Catholic/Protestant participation and proposed they include both pacifists and non-pacifists who were "creative 'key' people." Such an event would require a great deal of thought, with a purpose and focus "approached with utmost seriousness." If Merton's venue might work, Peachey offered that he and Heidbrink would develop a more specific proposal for review by Merton's superiors.[21]

Merton responded in April, with a copy to Heidbrink, that not only was he "all for it," but his abbot had approved such a gathering, though "with reserve." Rather than invite Peachey to forward a proposal, however, Merton laid out his own vision for what should transpire based on abbatial restrictions and his own schedule limitations. While agreeing it should include key people, it would need to be informal and small with no publicity. Gethsemani would not be prepared to host a "formal and organized sort of thing with special talks and 'exercises,'" he reported. What would work instead might be for a group of about ten to spend three or so days "in the quiet of the monastery, in meditation, attending such offices as they would like, and devoting most of the afternoons to discussion and exchange of ideas . . . But if any one wanted to stay longer, that would be all right." Such an agenda would permit Merton as novice master to attend to morning sessions with novices and would otherwise fit his typical afternoon schedule. Participants could stay in the monastery retreat house, provided vacancies permitted, and Merton had a "suitable place" for the afternoon discussions, which he supposed he would guide. Due to scheduling and summer heat considerations, Merton proposed the fall sometime after September. "I do hope it materializes," he closed, "in the informal sort of way I have outlined above."[22]

Hosting a scheduled retreat at Gethsemani that included Protestants was something of a departure for Merton and the abbey. They occasionally offered programmed events for lay Catholics anchored in the monastery retreat house. In addition, Merton sometimes received Protestant groups as guests, originally at the retreat house and eventually at his hermitage, but they would be one-day affairs for which the visitors did not stay overnight.[23] Therefore, given the unique character of this extended interfaith

21. Peachey to Merton, 13 Mar. 1963, TMC.

22. Merton to Peachey, 9 Apr. 1963, TMC.

23. Fr. James Conner, 17 Apr. 2010, conversation with author. Fr. Conner, a junior monk then undermaster with Merton, noted that the hermitage was justified in part as a venue to receive Protestant visitors. Fr. Conner identified Southern Baptists from Louisville, "Disciples of Christ" from Asbury, and Baptists from Nashville as visiting groups during this time; Merton biographer Michael Mott also mentions Episcopalians. Mott, *Seven Mountains*, 389.

conversation, the abbot's requirements for informality and no publicity are understandable.

In the following weeks, Heidbrink forwarded a brief memo to Peachey asking, "what shall we do with Merton's invitation for the fall?" and suggesting a few names to invite for discussion on three or four papers addressing "*The Agony of Christianity* (Redemption and Grace) or anything which [Roman Catholics] need pushed on and Protestants need enlightened."[24] Peachey responded in mid-May, noting other pressing priorities and the need to pin down dates for other pending CPM events tentatively set for October before a Gethsemani date could be set.[25] A few days after receiving Peachey's note, Heidbrink wrote to Merton about his upcoming tour of Eastern Europe and concerns over the need for an assertive Catholic peace advocacy group. He also mentioned efforts of Peachey and himself in collaboration with "a group of Catholic scholars" to "congeal conference time . . . under your roof," noting that "Peachey will let you know about this."[26] Merton replied that he looked forward to the event and hearing more of the program, again reminding that "it should be kept very small and informal." While prohibited from offering formal "talks, lectures, exhortations, what have you," Merton assured that "informal conversations can be of great value," provided they were offered in the context of "recollection and thought, and the exchange of ideas."[27] Heidbrink's prompt acknowledgment indicated that preparation for the fall was in the hands of Peachey, who was fully aware of Merton's limits and parameters.[28]

Peachey eventually responded directly to Merton in late June, attributing his tardiness to preoccupation with planning a "consultation for leaders of the nonviolent civil rights movement" and developing a proposal for a "commission to work on a reconstruction of Christian ethics in relation to war" that would involve both Catholic and Protestant scholars and require major grant funding. Peachey's mention of civil rights as a CPM theme demonstrates the degree to which peace advocacy and racial reconciliation efforts intertwined at that juncture and the degree to which peace groups had donned the civil rights mantle. Agreeing that a weekend in October seemed the most feasible timing, Peachey injected his own vision as to the retreat's focus: "the kind of encounter, exploration, and exhortation which the interfaith context affords" and "something oriented outward toward

24. Heidbrink to Peachey [assumed], n.d., F/4, CPM Records, SCPC.

25. Peachey to Heidbrink, 10 May 1963, D/4, FOR Records, SCPC.

26. Heidbrink to Merton, 15 May 1963, D/38, FOR Records, SCPC.

27. Merton to Heidbrink, 20 May 1963, Merton, *HGL*, 412.

28. Heidbrink to Merton, 24 May 1963, D/38, FOR Records, SCPC.

the crucial tasks of Christian witness in our world today." He cited "the responsibility of every Christian to bear witness to Christ" as an example of potential ecumenical focus in their current culture, and offered Heidbrink's suggested theme of "The Agony of Christianity (redemption and grace)." Peachey hoped to piggyback on his preparation for the interfaith ethics commission by selecting five Protestant participants from its yet-to-be-developed roster. He deferred to Merton regarding potential Catholics, but named Gordon Zahn[29] and Dan Berrigan as candidates.[30]

Merton's reply in late July affirmed Peachey's suggestions and noted that he was holding the two October weekends that Peachey had proposed. He also offered several Catholic names, noting that Berrigan would be in Europe at that time and suggesting Fr. George Dunne, SJ,[31] as an alternate. In addition to Dunne and Zahn, Merton named Dr. Justus G. Lawler, editor of *Continuum* magazine, and philosophy professor Leslie Dewart[32] of the University of Toronto. As a fifth suggestion, he proposed his friend W. H. "Ping" Ferry of the Center for the Study of Democratic Institutions. Merton reiterated his caveat that "my Superiors have decided that I am not in the future to 'conduct retreats' in the sense of preparing a series of formal talks to which a group more or less passively listens." Given the informal and interactive nature of the event, however, Merton saw his role as hosting rather than "conducting," and he felt those parameters would not interfere with proceeding as planned. He concluded, "I hope very much you will be able to iron this out and be with us in October."[33]

29. Sociologist Gordon C. Zahn (1918–2007) was a Catholic conscientious objector in WW II who served in a Civilian Public Service camp. He worked with sympathetic Vatican II cardinals to support conscientious objection and critique nuclear arms in a formal Council statement on the Church relationship to the world, *Schema XIII*. He also wrote the Franz Jägerstätter biography, *Solitary Witness*, which was referenced at the retreat (Shannon, *America*, 4).

30. Peachey to Merton, 25 June 1963, TMC.

31. George H. Dunne (1906–1998) was a pacifist Jesuit priest. After returning from missionary work in China in the 1930s, he taught at Saint Louis University's Institute for Social Order, where he was fired for opposing segregation. He marched with Martin Luther King Jr. in Alabama ("Father George H. Dunne; Jesuit Led Pacifist Efforts." *Los Angeles Times*, July 11, 1998. Online: http://articles.latimes.com/1998/jul/11/local/me-2693).

32. Leslie Dewart (1922–2009), born Gonzalo Gonzales Duarte to a Spanish father and Cuban mother, taught philosophy at the University of Toronto. See "Deaths: Ph.D. LLB Professor Emeritus University of Toronto Professor Leslie Dewart." *Globe and Mail*, Jan. 2, 2010. Online: http://v1.theglobeandmail.com/servlet/story/Deaths.20100102.93218183/BDAStory/BDA/deaths.

33. Merton to Peachey, 28 July 1963, TMC.

Despite this promising late July outlook, the event failed to materialize that fall for unclear reasons. Peachey was indeed a busy man during the last half of 1963, which no doubt contributed greatly to preventing it from coming together. He organized a conference of evangelical scholars in August at Winona Lake, Indiana; assembled about twenty-five Catholic and Protestant theologians in October at Wesley Theological Seminary in Washington, D.C.; and coordinated a gathering of thirty civil rights and church leaders in December at Black Mountain, North Carolina near Asheville. In addition, that May Peachey had begun editing a CPM publication, the *War-Nation-Church Letter*. Besides such distractions, and perhaps more significantly, signing of the partial nuclear test ban treaty on August 5 no doubt deflated the enthusiasm of Peachey for this event as it had with the antinuclear peace movement in general.[34]

Perhaps noting that the original "peace dialogue" idea for a Gethsemani retreat had fallen dormant, Heidbrink contacted Merton in early September with a different request—could Merton and the abbey host an FOR National Council meeting, numbering forty to sixty people? This group needed the "judgments and certainly the faith of those outside our traditional fold" that the monastic community could provide, and it would recognize the "necessity of going further into our life together." Heidbrink anticipated that "being in the atmosphere of the Abbey [with] access to you" would offer "a real turning point in our national purposes." It would also, he suggested, help nurture Catholic participation in the FOR.[35]

Ultimately, Merton's own health proved a deciding factor against either event, had one or the other in fact been scheduled. Heidbrink's September note reached Merton as he lay in the hospital, where he would spend two weeks to address pain associated with a fused cervical disc.[36] While recuperating there, Merton penned a short response to Heidbrink that the FOR National Council would represent "too big a gang" as "we could not handle so many."[37] A month later—the time Merton and Peachey had originally considered for the event—Merton shared with Heidbrink that he was "feeling better and able to get my work done to a great extent." He remained open to some kind of gathering, again with limited numbers, but by now the current year was no longer convenient. "But next year is free. What about sometime during the spring?"[38]

34. Peachey, *Usable Past*, 114.
35. Heidbrink to Merton, 9 Sept. 1963, D/38, FOR Records, SCPC.
36. Mott, *The Seven Mountains*, 388.
37. Merton to Heidbrink, 14 Sept. 1963, TMC.
38. Merton to Heidbrink, 15 Oct. 1963, TMC.

Apprehending Protest—A Gathering to Study Dissent

Discussion of a gathering ceased over the winter; at least no communication on the topic from these months survives. In his April 1964 report on Church Relations to the FOR board, however, Heidbrink could report that during the past year, "The FOR has maintained an intimate contact with Thomas Merton at the Abbey of Gethsemani, Trappist, Kentucky. Visits by other staff members, regular correspondence, Merton's membership in the FOR now, his willingness to supply us with many forms of writing has resulted in numerous developments. Father Philip Berrigan, SSJ, and Father Daniel Berrigan, SJ, have contributed enormously to the FOR's work in the Roman Catholic community."[39] By late April, though, Heidbrink had once again revived this thread with Merton, proposing a fall gathering.[40] Merton's response in early May offered that "we could certainly discuss 'spiritual roots of protest' in a very informal way."[41] This comment signals a notable shift in tone away from a venue for academic dialogue among competing religious viewpoints on disarmament, as Peachey had sought the previous year, to consideration of spiritual motives for direct confrontation with those who held decision-making power. Merton's response also implies that Heidbrink first coined the phrase that would become the retreat name and theme.

It is surely no coincidence that John Heidbrink suggested this topic just as he had begun seriously engaging with Jim Forest to establish the Catholic Peace Fellowship as an FOR affiliate. Close interaction with Catholic Worker sensibilities can certainly turn one's thoughts toward the realm of protest. In fact, it seems plausible that Forest played a hand in formulating the emphasis. In letters to Merton that spring, Forest also hinted that Merton might ponder actions that confront those who hold power. Late in March Forest shared with Merton his response to an article by Hannah Arendt on a play, *The Deputy: A Christian Tragedy*, that critiques Pope Pius XII's role during the Nazi era. He felt the play raised questions about how people in positions of religious authority speak against evil, and likened it to the action of Jesus clearing moneychangers from the temple: "I do not think the action [in the temple] was prompted by a consideration as to whether it would succeed ultimately in abolishing the evil. Nor do I think he was concerned with the danger to himself that might result. This is a difficult attitude of course, but

39. Heidbrink, "Church Relations. Annual Report to the F.O.R. National Council," Apr. 1965, D/37, FOR Records, SCPC.

40. Merton to Heidbrink, 9 May 1964, *HGL*, 414–5, mentions "your letter of April 29"; no longer extant.

41. Ibid.

we must strive for it, and hold it up to our leadership."[42] More to the point, in mid-June Forest strongly encouraged Merton to consider writing on the spirituality of nonviolence:

> In the past we have both mentioned the need for spiritual development in the nonviolent movement . . . The [nonviolent activist] often feels compelled to reject and reject strongly much that is associated with spirituality: certainly any form of "organized" religiousness . . . Gandhi, our great genius in modern times, is unquestionably rejected to a very large measure by the majority of those who have bodily (in this country and in the west in general) committed themselves to the search for nonviolent methods of problem solving. So what I am getting at . . . is a book which explores the implication spiritually of nonviolence, written by an American and frankly I think best by a monk . . . Much can be offered by monasticism to the formation of a true nonviolent structuring of society . . . and one which inevitably links east and west.[43]

Not surprisingly, both Forest and Heidbrink sought to draw on Merton as a spiritual resource for the kind of engagement they anticipated as they partnered in organizing the CPF.

When it came to hosting a gathering toward that end, however, it became apparent that Merton's reticence had grown since the previous fall. That May, in responding to Heidbrink's revival of the retreat idea, Merton confessed that "I had more or less counted on closing up shop after a rather busy summer, and was not going to take on anything more this year." Further, he had concluded that he held "too many irons in the fire and that a lot of them would have to come out. Chiefly this one of having groups down for discussion." As he had the year before, Merton emphasized his inability to provide for formal, planned, organized sessions, as such efforts are "just alien to this kind of life here." But he did not dismiss the request, indicating that under such terms he would nonetheless "go along" with the idea, setting the maximum attendance at six and targeting November. But he wondered if "just coming down for a visit would meet the expectations of the group."[44]

Perhaps something in Heidbrink's renewed proposal that April prompted Merton to once again insist so pointedly on minimal structure and intentionality for the retreat. Or perhaps the image of forty or more

42. Forest to Merton, 30 Mar. 1964, TMC.
43. Forest to Merton, 14 June 1964, TMC.
44. Merton to Heidbrink, 9 May 1964, *HGL*, 414–15.

FOR leaders descending at once on Gethsemani lingered from Heidbrink's proposal the previous fall and continued to haunt him. Regardless, Merton's own increasing turn toward solitude seems to have influenced his reserved responses. His long-standing dream of spending significant time alone was gradually approaching fruition. Within a year he would receive permission to live at the hermitage constructed for his needs; already that spring his comments to Heidbrink betray a growing desire for that transition into solitude.

FIGURE 1. Thomas Merton's hermitage in 1964.
Photograph by Jim Forest, courtesy of Boston College, John J. Burns Library.

This agenda became more explicit in a letter several days later to Daniel Berrigan—then away on his European "sabbatical"—which shared Merton's need to have a "very clear position on solitude" and reiterate limits to Heidbrink, who "wanted to organize the visit of the peace guys as a formal sort of conference. If they come in November, it would just be for a visit." Merton hoped that Berrigan could be among their number. But in general, he felt that "keeping contacts with the outside on a certain informal plane and always non-organized and off beat" were necessary to sustain his vocation.[45]

Berrigan's reply to Merton is noteworthy. He first commended Merton's expressed need to "have a very clear position on solitude and so on," offering two reasons. For one, "it is the form the Spirit is inviting you to," and the other "perhaps selfish" reason was that "in solitude . . . you began to speak to all of us in a way that no noise, and not even the audible wisdom of good men, could have reached." Then he added a third, quite prescient observation: "I think too it is an idea that will continue to tease and invite our Protestant brethren." As evidence he cited the series of retreats for priests

45. Merton to Daniel Berrigan, 18 May 1964, *HGL*, 81–82.

and ministers that he and John Heidbrink had inaugurated a couple of years earlier, reporting that they had "developed to the point where now they are being held at a Protestant retreat house."[46] In a word, Berrigan insightfully anticipated the ecumenical potential of traditional Catholic contemplative disciplines in an emerging postmodern culture. Perhaps Paul Peachey, in his sense that "at a deep level . . . there is a fruitful urgency about these dialogues," had intuitively perceived something similar on his wintery visit to Gethsemani.[47] From such a vantage, Berrigan could affirm "with all my heart" that at the anticipated gathering:

> . . . our best contribution to one another is simply to come and be ourselves and let the chips fall where they may. I am so damn sick of trying too hard to do the wrong things; what Heidbrink and the rest of us, in measure need, is precisely a change of [pace] that will plunge us into some silence and direct sharing; the kind of thing we had there last time, and that I have been drawing on since. Please don't allow anything formal, and please keep it small.

When confirming his strong desire to participate, along with hopes his brother Philip could join them, Berrigan asked Merton to "scratch around" for a reason suitable to justify his participation to Berrigan's superiors. "Maybe I could wrap hams or something."[48] Their exchange suggests that informality had now soundly defeated any organizational impulses toward a structured, academic dialogue for the retreat agenda. Not only was such an approach required by the abbot and personally preferred by Merton, Berrigan's like-mindedness seemingly conferred to it a sense of timely appropriateness.

Berrigan shared these thoughts on the eve of another event that undoubtedly helped shape the composition and dynamics of the retreat: a mid-June to mid-July "travelling seminar" of church leaders to Europe, co-led by John Heidbrink and Paul Peachey. Included in their company were Daniel Berrigan and Jim Forest who would participate in the November retreat. While on this trip, in fact, Heidbrink, Forest, Berrigan, and two other Catholics in the party would commit to organize formally the

46. The 1962 and 1963 retreats occurred at Mount Savior Monastery, Elmira, New York; 1964 and 1965 retreats were held at Kirkridge Retreat Center, Bangor, Pennsylvania. "Retreat," D/39, FOR Records, SCPC.

47. Berrigan to Merton, 2 June 1964, TMC. Peachey to Merton, 13 Mar. 1963, TMC. Peachey would later help establish the Rolling Ridge Study Retreat Community. Peachey, *Usable Past*, 169–82.

48. Berrigan to Merton, 2 June 1964, TMC. Dan Berrigan, Phil Berrigan, and Tony Walsh visited Merton at Gethsemani in August of 1962.

FOR-affiliated Catholic Peace Fellowship, for which Forest, Heidbrink, and others had laid groundwork in preceding months. The second All-Christian Peace Assembly—convened under the auspices of the Eastern Bloc Christian Peace Conference (CPC) in Soviet-controlled Prague—served as the tour centerpiece, which was bracketed by stops in Paris, Rome, and Zurich beforehand and afterward in Hungary, Kiev, Moscow, Leningrad, Helsinki, Oslo, and Iona, Scotland. The sojourn sought encounters with European Catholic, Protestant, and Orthodox churchmen, as well as simply with Eastern Bloc representatives of the faith.[49]

In general, the experience provided many opportunities for close and meaningful interaction with travel partners, as well as immersion in the realities of Cold War protocol. No doubt these travels helped add nuance and perspective to their understandings of what made for peace and reinforced the need for action that could nudge the inertia inherent within the halls of entrenched and self-interested power. Five years later, reflecting back on this event, Daniel Berrigan would confirm its influence:

> The impact of that trip is ineradicable upon my spirit. I was discovering for the first time, and at firsthand, the radically different social forms by which decent men and women were living. I was discovering peaceable communities of faith, surviving and even thriving in most difficult and trying circumstances. I was seeing firsthand the damage wrought to the human spirit in the West as a result of the Cold War.
>
> At Prague, I met with Christians from both Marxist and Western societies and gained some inkling of the role that churches could play in the ongoing struggles for human peace and survival. Along with my American companions, I was also exposed to the full glare of world Christian opinion with regard to our part in the Vietnam War. From Japan to Cuba, Christians were assailing us, extremely embittered at the course that even then seemed to be written in our stars.
>
> I returned to the United States in the autumn of 1964 convinced, as I now recall, of one simple thing. The war in Vietnam could only grow worse.[50]

A couple of weeks after the tour ended, Merton sent another missive to his Jesuit confidant, revealing that despite his earlier caution, he still

---

49. Peachey, *Usable Past*, 133–40; Berrigan, *To Dwell In Peace*, 161–62; McNeal, *Harder Than War*, 140; Polner and O'Grady, *Disarmed and Dangerous*, 109. The other two Catholics were James Douglass and Hermene Evens. Forest to Merton, 30 Mar. 1964, TMC.

50. Berrigan, "These Many Beautiful Years," 45.

expected the event to occur and especially wanted Berrigan to participate. By way of "scratching around" for a pretext Berrigan might use to justify the Kentucky trip to his Jesuit overseers, Merton suggested he report to novices on a trip to South Africa that Berrigan had taken earlier in the spring and then visit the nearby Sisters of Loretto motherhouse. Ham-wrapping was not on the list. Merton obviously looked forward to the upcoming event and the opportunity to interact with friends, but he continued to voice concern over its tenor. His reflections help illuminate Merton's growing pessimism and internal conflict about the potential to effect lasting social and religious change—only months before the retreat intended to equip participants for that very purpose.

"Let's make [the retreat] purposeless and freewheeling and a vacation for all," he began, "and let the Holy Spirit suggest anything that needs to be suggested. Let's be Quakers and the heck with projects." From there, his tone shifted as he shared more deeply of the inner tension that colored his outlook. "I am so sick, fed up and ready to vomit with projects and hopes and expectations," he asserted, and then proceeded to explain at length, "even at the risk of being neurotic about it." In the extended paragraph that followed, Merton confided with his fellow priest a sense of disillusionment in his vocation, one where he risked expending his efforts "in frustration and defeat over the most important issues that face the church." He feared that he now approached "the end of some kind of a line," a "trolley . . . called a special kind of hope" that anticipated things would get better, grow clearer, become more ordered. Instead, he sensed that things would actually grow worse, and he must accept that "I don't need to be on the trolley car anyway." Searching for another analogy, he added, "You can call the trolley a form of religious leprosy if you like . . . The leprosy of that particular kind of temporal hope, that special expectation that monks have, that priests have," concluding that, "as a priest I am a burnt out case.[51] . . . I am sick up to the teeth and beyond the teeth, up to the eyes and beyond the eyes, with all forms of projects and expectations and statements and programs and explanations of anything, especially explanations about where we are all going, because where we are all going is where we went a long time ago, over the falls. We are in a new river and we don't know it."[52] His was not then a frame of mind prepared to engage in strategies for social transformation.

51. Two weeks prior to writing this letter Merton had read Graham Greene's book, *A Burnt-Out Case*. Merton, *DWL*, 21 July 1964 and 23 July 1964, 130. The term "burnt-out case" refers to a leper whose disease has diminished their sense of touch, resulting in loss of digits and other mutilations. The novel's main character works in an African leper colony after leaving Europe to seek anonymity, and he likens his emotional and spiritual state to that of a "burnt-out" leper.

52. Merton to Berrigan, 4 Aug. 1964, *HGL*, 83–84.

Despite his pessimism of the moment, Merton continued to assume the retreat would occur. But the damper Merton had put forth the previous spring may have worked too well; John Heidbrink had not in the meantime pursued the matter further with Merton. By mid-September, having heard no more from Heidbrink, Merton wrote him to ask for clarity "about the possibility of you and some others coming down this fall" so he could plan "one way or the other," and offered three sets of dates in late October and mid-November.[53]

Heidbrink leapt at the opening and responded immediately, asking Merton to hold the two November dates while he checked further with Paul Peachey and Daniel Berrigan. For whatever reason he had by now taken Merton's insistence on smallness and informality to heart, asking, "Can we be seven?" Heidbrink then deferentially laid out a lengthy stream of thoughts regarding purpose and content, which in significant ways echoed Jim Forest's thoughts that past June when encouraging Merton to write a book on the theme. Heidbrink suggested that they might "push around[,] within whatsoever context or pattern of hours you say[,] the subject of spiritual roots of the US peace movement" and the "superstructure of protest and non-conformity building up daily in nearly every country." He followed with his concerns that the movement's underlying foundation was "torn loose from cultures . . . feeds off of pragmatic bits of political analysis and organizational genius," and is "restricted to elements which are rationally explainable." Further, it was "justifiably anti-church" though not necessarily "anti-religious" in the sense of broad "moral patterns of the Judeo-Christian tradition." In contrast, Heidbrink expressed, the discipline of "metaphysics[,] by way of its boring in the ascetical thought of the tradition you represent and articulate . . . can ask the questions that need to be asked regarding . . . protest and political analysis. In other words the roots of war are to be found within man." In particular, the connection of reason and intuition, matter and spirit, mind and body needed to be sought when considering such questions, as did the role of a faith that could "transform stony hearts into hearts of flesh." A recent papal encyclical on the church, *Ecclesiam suam*, had not adequately incorporated the role of "repentance," he feared. After extended paragraphs of such reflections, Heidbrink concluded, "but I have not given up and retired to a garden spot *to think alone*. I still wish to think with others."[54]

Merton's likewise immediate reply confirmed that, "Yes, I will be thinking about all those things. The great thing we can all try to do is get

53. Merton to Heidbrink, 14 Sept.1964, *HGL*, 415.
54. Heidbrink to Merton, 17 Sept. 1964, TMC.

to those spiritual roots. My part is to offer whatever the silence can give." Attending the offices could offer refreshment, since "Gregorian is good and it heals" (though he lamented that "the dopes here are thinking of getting rid of it and singing hymns"). He would keep the November slots open, have his hermitage available for meeting, and hopefully offer good weather. Seven would be optimal. They would "camp around with the idea of roots," he agreed, adding, "about all we have is a great need for roots, but to know this is already something." About all to be done in connecting with non-Christians in the movement is "to get with them and stop emphasizing that we are different . . . We are all concerned with man living and surviving . . . The word of God reaches us somewhere in the middle of all that."[55] The same day Merton dashed a letter to Daniel Berrigan confirming that the event was on and his novices and the sisters at Loretto were expecting him mid-November.[56]

With this brief flurry of letters—three in six days—the event solidified from a questionable unknown to a firm commitment. Peachey's original thoughts on including non-pacifist academics—along with Heidbrink's original suggested title of "The Agony of Christianity" and efforts to expand participation—had mostly fallen away. Instead, a contemplative focus and tone had emerged around a theme exploring the "spiritual roots" of engagement toward social and political change. Heidbrink would later report to Merton that he had "made it clear to everyone that if there is one point from which to begin the ferment and exchange, it will be through examining the spiritual basis of protest and the adequacies of the inner life for the world knocking at our doors. Now just what this means will be up to the ones who come." All that remained was to set the date and confirm participation.[57]

A couple of weeks later Heidbrink penned a brief note saying the earliest Berrigan could arrive was November 18, which made choosing the later set of dates, November 18–20, seem a foregone conclusion.[58] But it was not so simple. Heidbrink previously had been appointed to the governing council of the Christian Peace Conference—the body that had convened in Prague the past June—and they had scheduled a meeting in London over these same dates. As the only U.S. representative to this first council meeting ever held beyond the iron curtain, Heidbrink needed to attend. As he described it, he felt obligated to "[care] for this work we have underway between the churches in the East and West blocs as we plan further de-

55. Merton to Heidbrink, 19 Sept. 1964, *HGL*, 416.

56. Merton to Berrigan, 19 Sept. 1964, *HGL*, 84.

57. Heidbrink to Merton, 29 Oct. 1964, TMC.

58. Heidbrink to Merton, 26 Sept. 1964, TMC.

velopments, exchanges, study conferences, faith and order meetings, etc. Only this and family emergencies would take precedent [sic], believe me, over the chance to be with all of you; but the situation in the Eastern bloc countries now regarding the churches is acute and we should not lessen our efforts to be with the brethren from these areas whenever we can."[59] Unless Merton could arrange something after November, Heidbrink must miss the retreat. Since seven other retreatants had already confirmed those days, and a change might jeopardize their participation, moving it seemed unwise. Heidbrink's assessment? "Rot!"[60] Merton concurred that locking in November 18–20 would be the prudent thing to do. The date was set, but without Heidbrink on the guest list.[61]

As it happened, though, Heidbrink could not have attended even had the CPC council meeting not been scheduled. Hindered by numbness in his left leg, Heidbrink checked in with his doctor on Friday, November 5, only to learn that his own chronic back problems were leading to a collapse of his neural system in the leg, a situation that required immediate spinal surgery. He entered the hospital that Sunday evening, and following extensive testing, underwent the operation on Thursday morning, November 12. The procedure would immobilize him for an extended period. In response to the circumstance, he called upon Paul Peachey the weekend before entering the hospital and invited him to serve as his substitute at the meeting in London. Peachey accepted. Ironically, therefore, neither retreat initiator would be able to attend.[62]

Sorting the Final Roster

When John Heidbrink laid out his mid-September musings on formalizing retreat plans, he had also shared that "A. J. so much wants to come," asking Merton, "Can we be seven?"[63] Exactly which seven he had in mind at that

59. Heidbrink to Merton, 29 Oct. 1964, TMC.

60. Heidbrink to Merton, 26 Sept. 1964, TMC.

61. Merton to Heidbrink, n.d. [archival notation "1964/10/00?"], TMC.

62. Heidbrink to Al Hassler, 23 Nov. 1964, D/38, FOR Records, SCPC. Speaking thirty-four years after the event, Heidbrink noted that because of his condition, "I had to stay, but Jim brought it off," implying that Forest was responsible for executing the details in his absence. Given that no documentation of Forest's planning involvement survives, and Forest no longer recalls planning involvement, Heidbrink's interview comment may reflect later assumptions rather than a specific memory. "Interview of John Heidbrink," conducted by Richard Deats," 11 Sept. 1998, D/37, FOR Records, SCPC.

63. Heidbrink to Merton, 17 Sept. 1964, TMC.

point remains somewhat unclear, however. Heidbrink considered himself a participant at that point, and mentioned a need to check with Dan Berrigan and Paul Peachey regarding which of two open weeks might work. He also added that in addition to Muste, Martin Luther King and his civil rights collaborator Bayard Rustin wanted to come, which suggests that by then they at least had been apprised of plans for the event and expressed interest. Heidbrink did not mention who he had in mind for the seventh person; perhaps he referred to Merton himself. If not, most likely the seventh was Philip Berrigan, mentioned by Heidbrink in a letter to Paul Peachey several days later. As early as June Daniel had expressed the hope to Thomas Merton that his brother Philip could join when they met,[64] and that summer Heidbrink had recruited him for Catholic Peace Fellowship involvement.

Though disappointed at his scheduling conflict created by the meeting of Eastern Bloc church leaders, John Heidbrink put the retreat's success above his own desire to attend. In a postcard to Merton on September 26, he indicated they should not change the retreat date on his account and thereby "jeopardize the response we have from the 7 who can come Nov. 18–20," this time mentioning no names.[65] Merton's answer confirmed that the date should remain fixed and ended with the query, "Who is coming?"[66] It appears that Heidbrink still had work to do in that regard.

Despite his September 10 assurance of A. J. Muste's desire to participate, Heidbrink apparently failed to establish firm plans with Muste until an October 21 letter. Perhaps Muste's cataract surgery and recuperation interfered. The operation had occurred late September,[67] and following his release from the hospital Muste convalesced at the home of his daughter Nancy for some weeks into late October.[68] During this time his secretary

64. Heidbrink to Peachey, 26 Sept. 1964, D/4, CPM Records, SCPC. D. Berrigan to Merton, 2 June 1964, TMC.

65. Heidbrink to Merton, postcard, 26 Sept. 1964, TMC. In his letter to Peachey the same day Heidbrink said: "Dan can go and so perhaps A. J. as well as Phil Berrigan on this date." Heidbrink to Peachey, 26 Sept. 1964, D/4, CPM Records, SCPC.

66. Merton to Heidbrink, n.d. [archival notation "1964/10/00?"] in response to Heidbrink's 26 Sept. 1964 postcard to Merton.

67. Muste to Henry Richardson, 18 Sept. 1964, Supp. #1/4, microfilm reel 89:34, Muste Papers. Muste wrote, "I am dictating this note on the eve of going to the hospital to have cataracts removed from my eyes."

68. Muste to Ax Nelson, 20 Oct. 1964, Supp. #1/4, microfilm reel 89:34, Muste Papers. Muste wrote, "Your letter has just been read to me by my secretary, Beverly Sterner, at the home of my daughter, Nancy, in Thornwood, New York." A September 30 letter from Sterner to Heidbrink indicated Muste was "in the hospital recovering from surgery for the removal of cataracts from his eyes" at that point. Supp. #3/3, microfilm reel 89:38, Muste Papers.

periodically shuttled correspondence back and forth on a limited basis. He managed to attend an FOR conference on October 24, but he would not return to his office routine until November 6, less than two weeks before the retreat.[69]

Whatever the reason, Heidbrink's letter suggests that he was not entirely confident of Muste's inclination to meet with Merton and felt that persuasion may be in order. He opened, "Tom Merton has time and again asked if it were possible for certain people within the more radical nonconformist movements of the United States to meet with him and others in a small three-day retreat at his hermitage on a hillside overlooking the Abbey of Gethsemani, the Trappist monastery." He then proceeded to explain Merton's significance "in turning loose the pent-up oftentimes Irish-laced Catholic protest movement," asserting that "he needs us badly for his own formulations as he moves in high gear to a louder and more dynamic level of writing as he feels called upon to lead a generation of people out of the cloister into which he has led them initially." Muste's effort to attend would "be more than repaid not only by an association with Merton and this rather bizarre community in which he lives but it will reach out by way of fermentation and provocation" through Merton's writing and training of novices. Merton was "a hot potato and ready to orbit with encouragement and feeding." Further, "he has especially asked that you and Bayard Rustin be invited since you both represent two people he most wants to meet."[70] At first glance, Heidbrink's apparent tactic of separately expressing to Merton and Muste the mutual eagerness of each to meet the other—prior to explicitly inviting Muste—may seem a bit duplicitous, as do the hints of deference to classic Protestant biases regarding Catholic monasticism. But Muste would later confirm Heidbrink's claims by sharing with an acquaintance that, "I have been looking forward to this opportunity to meet Merton for several years."[71] Besides, Heidbrink who was acquainted with both Merton and Muste, understood the Protestant world's general unfamiliarity with Catholics in 1964, and was no doubt justified in his approach.[72]

69. Edward Falkowski to Muste, 27 Oct. 1964 and Muste to Falkowski, 6 Nov. 1964. Both in Supp. #1/4, microfilm reel 89:33, Muste Papers. "The Triple Revolution: Values and Goals in a Cybercultural Society," flier, 49, microfilm reel 89:29, Muste Papers.

70. Heidbrink to Muste, 21 Oct. 1964, "Supp. #3/3, microfilm reel 89:38, Muste Papers.

71. Muste to J. Nevin Sayre, 1 Dec. 1964, dictated 16 Nov., Supp. #1/4, microfilm reel 89:34, Muste Papers.

72. Heidbrink to Muste, 21 Oct. 1964, Supp. #3/3, microfilm reel 89:38, Muste Papers.

Whatever Heidbrink's reasoning, it worked, for in the first week of November he dictated a note to Muste that expressed appreciation for a recent visit they had enjoyed—presumably the occasion when Muste verbally accepted the invitation—and shared that "Tom Merton is terribly pleased (after waiting many years) that you will consider coming to Kentucky with the two Berrigans (one a Jesuit priest, the other a Josephite priest, in the FOR), plus Rustin, if he can swing it." He also confirmed the timing of the event and laid out some travel possibilities, which Muste further clarified with FOR secretary, Mildred Nelson.[73] Heidbrink did not fill Merton's late-September request for a list of who would come until nearly a month later, just three weeks before the event. By then he could share a roster that included A. J. Muste ("just out of the hospital"); Bayard Rustin ("yet to finalize the change of plans required if he is to come" but "doing his darnedest"); Paul Peachey; John Howard Yoder ("a young Mennonite brain"); John Oliver Nelson ("founder of the only serious corporate discipline Protestants have in this country . . . Kirkridge Center"); Dan Berrigan; Phil Berrigan; and John Grady ("if his son recuperates properly following brain surgery next week"). The number on Heidbrink's guest list had now grown to eight.[74]

Unknown to Heidbrink, however, a total of nine actually planned to come at that point. As early as the first week in June Merton had invited his unchurched friend, Wilbur H. "Ping" Ferry, sharing that "John Heidbrink is plotting something for the fall" and suggesting that "perhaps you might be able to get here with a few others (I want to keep it small) in November."[75] He repeated the suggestion a month later,[76] and again in mid-October asked if Ferry wanted to join him in November when "a group of Peace-niks from FOR is coming."[77] Ferry responded, "I would like to take part in the FOR thing at Gethsemani, though I am not worthy . . . but I'd do my best to arrange [my] schedule to permit me to be on hand for a bit."[78] Merton's response to Ferry shared the scheduled dates and expressed hope he could join them and meet Daniel Berrigan, "a very lively young Jesuit with great potentialities," and his brother Philip, "the only priest I know who managed to get himself on a freedom ride."[79] Otherwise he was not at that time

73. Heidbrink to Muste, 6 Nov. 1964, Supp. #1/4, microfilm reel 89:33, Muste Papers.

74. Heidbrink to Merton, 29 Oct. 1964, TMC.

75. Merton to Ferry, 8 June 1964, HGL, 217.

76. Merton to Ferry, 14 July 1964, TMC.

77. Merton to Ferry, n.d., TMC. The note has "10/15" written on it, but appears to reflect Ferry's notation of receipt.

78. Ferry to Merton, 15 Oct. 1964, TMC.

79. "Freedom ride" might pertain to various activities. Polner and O'Grady

sure who was coming. But his message did offer an explanation why the
renowned civil rights leader had dropped from Heidbrink's list: "There was
a possibility that Martin Luther King might [come], but now that he has the
Nobel Peace Prize and is just out of the hospital I suppose his time will be
taken up getting ready for Sweden [sic]."[80] Ferry promptly replied that he
would come, probably arriving in Louisville late on the 17th and joining
them the following morning.[81]

The Heidbrink/Muste and Merton/Ferry exchanges represent two of
the few instances where an invitation to participate remains documented.
Most likely Heidbrink had similarly contacted John Oliver Nelson, the CPM
chair, after plans were finalized, but it remains a mystery whether he or Paul
Peachey would have initiated Nelson's invitation. It would seem that, in
typical movement fashion, the word got out to most rather casually. The
reported interest of Martin Luther King Jr. may have emerged from informal interaction, too. King had worked closely with FOR staff for some time
and could easily have learned of it from one of them. He had previously
met Heidbrink at the University of Oklahoma, where Heidbrink served
as campus pastor.[82] Bayard Rustin, as one-time FOR staff and King's close
colleague, also began interacting with these men long before and therefore
would easily have been party to such discussions.

Merton had apprised Daniel Berrigan as early as mid-May of both
his exchange with Heidbrink about the event and his hope that Berrigan
would join them.[83] No doubt Heidbrink had himself broached the subject
with him during their European travels that June or through their ongoing
collaboration regarding interfaith clerical retreats. Then in early October,
following his rapid exchange with Merton to confirm the event would happen, Heidbrink reached out again to his ongoing Catholic collaborator,

---

comment regarding his New Orleans work: "Figuratively and in fact, Phil had become
the church's first 'Freedom Rider'" (*Disarmed and Dangerous*, 103). Near this time Merton was writing a preface to Phil Berrigan's book about his civil rights and integration
experiences, *No More Strangers*.

80. Merton to Ferry, 17 Oct. 1964, *HGL*, 219. King received his award and delivered
his acceptance speech in Oslo on 10 Dec. 1964. "In mid-October, [King] had checked
into Atlanta's St. Joseph Infirmary for a rest. Coretta said he was 'simply exhausted' and
needed a few days away from his crushing burdens" (Oates, *Let the Trumpet Sound*,
303).

81. Ferry to Merton, 20 Oct. 1964, TMC.

82. International Thomas Merton Society, "John C. Heidbrink (1926–2006)." The
obituary mistakenly indicates King encouraged Heidbrink to apply for the FOR position, but in his 1998 interview with Richard Deats, Heidbink indicated Glenn Smiley
played that role. "Interview of John Heidbrink," D/37, FOR Records, SCPC.

83. Merton to D. Berrigan, 18 May 1964, *HGL*, 81–82.

sharing that it had been set for "the suppertime of November 17th through the 20th." He had "already written to Phil" and expected his confirmation soon, adding "we should not have more than eight." It was John Heidbrink, therefore who provided the formal invitation to Philip Berrigan.

In the same letter, he also conceded that he "would give anything for a Catholic layman." Seeking Daniel's advice, he also offered his own suggestion of a third brother, Jerry Berrigan.[84] Berrigan opted for an alternative option to fill that spot, however, for in a letter the following week Heidbrink responded that Berrigan should "by all means invite John Grady to come to the Merton retreat." He added that he needed definite confirmation, though, to "congeal the roster" and repeated that they "must not have over eight people." Though he sought an equivalent lay/clergy mix, he asserted that he did not "give a damn about any balancing between Protestant and Catholic."[85] Both of the Berrigan brothers knew John Peter Grady well; Daniel was the source of Heidbrink's later knowledge that Grady's attendance would hinge on the condition of his six-year-old son, who had been hit by a car and suffered a fractured skull that required brain surgery. In his support of Grady, Daniel would periodically visit their home and surreptitiously conduct a private Mass for the Grady family. Daniel's later update indicated that Grady "hopes beyond hope to be with us at Gethsemane [sic] but the decision must wait on the boy's brain operation which has been put off another week."[86]

We know with confidence, though, that Paul Peachey provided the impetus for John Howard Yoder's participation. As Yoder recalled, after learning from Heidbrink that the event dates and topic were set, Peachey informed Yoder of the retreat in an oral conversation.[87] Peachey then followed up with a handwritten note explaining that "for the past year a few of us (John Heidbrink, Thomas Merton and I) have talked of a possible retreat with Merton in his monastery." Perhaps not fully aware of the extent to which Merton then called for informality nor the shift in focus toward "protest," Peachey suggested it would function "at a fairly sophisticated level, both Protestants and Catholics participating, 8–10 persons, to reflect on the awakening of the Church to her vocation of peace. We consider this extremely important, at a step removed from our organizational tasks, to probe the deeper moving of the Spirit in our time."[88] Peachey was well

84. Heidbrink to D. Berrigan, 5 Oct. 1964 (dictated 2 Oct.), A/130, Berrigan Collection, CUL.

85. Heidbrink to D. Berrigan, 13 Oct. 1964, A/130, Berrigan Collection, CUL.

86. D. Berrigan to Heidbrink, 16 Oct. 1964, D/37, FOR Records, SCPC.

87. John H. Yoder, "Merton document backgrounds: Entities and People behind the narrative of the Nov 1964 Gethsemani 'retreat,'" fall 1994, 2, Yoder Papers, TMC.

88. Paul Peachey, handwritten note, n.d., 13, Yoder Papers, TMC.

acquainted with his fellow Mennonite. He had served for a time with Yoder doing relief work in post-World War II Europe, where Peachey had been ordained as a minister in 1950, and participated with him in the "Concern" group of Mennonite scholars who strived to rethink the denomination's twentieth-century role.[89]

With Peachey's willingness to fill in last minute at London following the onset of Heidbrink's spinal crisis, his name also dropped from the roster. Upon learning of Peachey's last-minute departure for London, Dan Berrigan dispatched a note to "convey my greetings and gratitude as you leave for England . . . I was so grateful that you and John [Nelson] were able to get here the other night; I know it was at great personal sacrifice on your part, but one has come to expect that of you . . . We will be thinking of you and John [Heidbrink] at Gethsemane [sic]. We all lean on you more than we could tell you."[90] The meeting with Peachey that Berrigan referenced had occurred in New York City on November 9. It included a handful who had gathered at the apartment of a Berrigan friend, and it sought to invite the growing community of New York Catholic activists more deeply into the CPM's program as part of Peachey's larger initiative to broaden input into CPM's agenda. Berrigan's first reference to "John" in this case surely referred to John Nelson, CPM chair and eventual retreat participant, who had also attended the New York meeting. Retreat participants Phil Berrigan and Jim Forest had been invited to this meeting, as well.[91]

Merton would continue to anticipate the arrival of Bayard Rustin up until the gathering convened. When meeting with his novices on November 15, the Sunday before the retreat, Merton shared that he had "one last group of retreatants this week," adding that "they are very important people, so please pray for them." Reflecting the intertwined nature of peace and civil rights protest at that juncture, Merton described them as "civil rights movement" people. He shared further that "Martin Luther King . . . was going to [come], but one of his close associates is coming [instead], a man called Bayard Rustin," who "runs the civil rights stuff in the northern cities."[92] Then two days later, the evening before the retreat, Merton listed in his journal nine of the thirteen who ultimately came, adding, "Maybe also Bayard Rustin, I am not sure."[93] But Rustin failed to join them. Following

89. Peachey, *Usable Past*, 55–61.

90. Berrigan to Peachey, 13 Nov. 1964, E/10, CPM Records, SCPC.

91. Peachey to Phil Berrigan, 3 Nov. 1964; Peachey to Dan Berrigan and Deitmar Schaefer, n.d.; "Persons Interested in the Peace Witness of the Church," open memo from Peachey, 20 Oct. 1964. All in E/10, CPM Records, SCPC.

92. Recording 131.4, 15 Nov. 1964, TMC.

93. Merton, *DWL*, 17 Nov. 1964, 167. The four not mentioned were Cunnane,

the retreat, Merton would tell his novices that this was because Rustin had accompanied King to receive the Nobel Peace Prize in Oslo.[94]

The gap created by the loss of four from Heidbrink's original roster was more than filled, though, since a total of thirteen other than Merton ultimately participated. It appears that Daniel Berrigan initiated the attendance of Tony Walsh. In a late October letter to Peachey, Berrigan shared his need to "get this [note] off in a hurry before leaving for Montreal for the weekend [for] some talks to teachers and people interested in the works of mercy in a little house of hospitality," no doubt referring to Walsh's Benedict Labré House—an ideal opportunity to extend an impromptu invitation for Walsh's second pilgrimage to Gethsemani.[95] Berrigan's role in Walsh's plans is confirmed in a letter the Canadian wrote to Berrigan the week before the retreat, which shared Walsh's plans to meet him in New York for the trip to Gethsemani. For Walsh, the excursion served mostly as a needed respite rather than an intellectual adventure. He had to scramble to arrange for others to fill his role at Benedict Labré House, making it seem there was "very little likelihood that I would be able to take advantage of your very generous offer. For I am still weary and bone-tired." Once arrangements had fallen into place, though, he could report that his "committal is now made to Gethsemani." But he added, "I hope that something happens to me before Tuesday, as far as sluggishness and barrenness of thought is concerned . . . It will be good to see you."[96] Robert Cunnane, whom Phil Berrigan helped mentor into the movement, credited his inclusion to an invitation by the younger Berrigan. "He was always introducing me to new things, so in a sense I think he wanted me to come to Gethsemani to hear bigger and better things," he recalled.[97] Charlie Ring also made the journey at Phil Berrigan's request. They had hit it off well when Berrigan visited their retreat house near Boston, and he asked Cunnane to bring Ring along to the abbey.[98]

The participation of Jim Forest and Tom Cornell logically would have flowed from their work as FOR staff on behalf of the Catholic Peace Fellowship, as well as Forest's longstanding relationship with Merton, who knew in advance he would come. When speaking to novices about King, Rustin, and the event in general, Merton had added that "Jim Forest . . . is coming,"

Grady, Jean, and Ring.

94. Recording 132.1, 22 Nov. 1964, TMC.

95. D. Berrigan to Peachey, 23 Oct. 1964, E/10, CPM Records, SCPC.

96. Walsh to D. Berrigan, 11 Nov. 1964, A/145, Berrigan Collection, CUL.

97. Cunnane, 17 Apr. 2010, email to author; Cunnane, 31 May 2010, conversation with author.

98. Cunnane, 27 Oct. 2012, conversation with author.

followed by an admonition to "pray for [the retreat] especially, and pray that it will be worthwhile, it will work out, it will be good."[99] The source of Elbert Jean's invitation and the manner in which it was communicated remains a greater mystery. Jean recalled that he was contacted because of his role with the Committee of Southern Churchmen, but it is unclear who would have contacted them.[100] Perhaps Rustin took it upon himself to find his own replacement from within civil rights activist circles. Or, since as early as 1963 Merton had been in contact with Will Campbell,[101] the Committee of Southern Churchman chair, the monk may have initiated this contact. Then again, Peachey had coordinated a major CPM convocation of civil rights leaders in North Carolina during December of 1963 that both Jean and Campbell had attended,[102] so Peachey could have issued the call, as well. Given that Heidbrink seemed initially unaware Jean had attended,[103] in the end, Peachey seems the most likely source of Jean's invitation.

The Evolution of an Idea

As thoughts of a retreat emerged from their embryonic state over these months, an original focus pointing toward academic discussions on international "peace" eventually coalesced around a theme of activist-oriented "protest." This transition was both prompted by and mirrored in the evolution of the peace movement itself and its interface with civil rights activism. Given the acceleration of turmoil and violence that had ensued since John Heidbrink's Gethsemani visit, there is little wonder that Merton had grown increasingly weary of "all forms of projects and expectations and statements and programs and explanations"—perhaps another reason for the event's evolving agenda. Students of Merton's life have observed that although he maintained his commitment to nonviolence as a faithful response, he remained cautious about managing it as a tactic to effect social change.[104]

99. Recording 131.4, 15 Nov. 1964, TMC.

100. Jean, 23 Apr. 2010, email to author.

101. Campbell to Merton, 27 Nov. 1963, TMC.

102. Peachey to Campbell, 18 Mar. 1963, D/3, CPM Records, SCPC.

103. In his 23 Nov. 1964 letter to Al Hassler chronicling his spinal ordeal, Heidbrink mentioned only eight of the attendees, omitting Yoder (invited by Peachey), Cunnane and Ring (both invited by Philip Berrigan), Walsh (invited by Dan Berrigan), and Jean. He also assumed Bayard Rustin had attended. Heidbrink to Al Hassler, 23 Nov. 1964, D/38, FOR Records, SCPC.

104. Various Merton writings support nonviolence as a discipline and a response to injustice rather than as a tactic to force outcomes. See for example: *Conjectures*, 86; Merton to Jim Forest, 21 Feb. 1966, *HGL*, 294; "Blessed are the Meek," 18; Forest, *Living*

Seeking correct motives and understandings of *why* one engages in non-violent confrontation of evil therefore became a crucial matter to him. Do our actions emerge from spiritual depth, integrity, and grounding? Or from conformity to the times and uncritical embrace of a secular movement grounded in faulty assumptions of human effectiveness, power, and control?

A third, related reason for the shift in focus reflected a shift in organizing impetus. The initial discussions between Paul Peachey and John Heidbrink emerged from a Church Peace Mission planning session and therefore envisioned an academic dialogue intended to coax established church leaders into advocating for disarmament. As such, planning fit best under the CPM umbrella, and Heidbrink was appropriately content to let Peachey pursue the necessary details. But during subsequent months, as the Partial Test Ban Treaty dissolved their sense of urgency, momentum stalled and Peachey's energy became absorbed elsewhere. John Heidbrink then assumed the prominent role in sustaining the idea. With this shift, ideas and plans naturally began to revolve around FOR agenda, with a particular eye toward leveraging the event to secure and solidify Roman Catholic participation under the FOR umbrella. That path required Heidbrink to navigate among the complexities of existing Catholic peace groups, traditional Roman Catholic reluctance for theological collaboration, and long-standing Protestant skepticism of Roman Catholic belief and practice.[105]

Those dynamics of Heidbrink's agenda help illuminate his efforts after the summer of 1963 to promote a gathering. Heidbrink's frustration over efforts to form a Catholic FOR branch had grown, and he had solicited input from leaders of the more successful British Catholic PAX association. As he had confided to Merton earlier that April, "I have about given up on [the U.S.] PAX. I have always been interested in developing a Catholic guild of radical peace workers within the FOR. Dorothy Day and others have not been interested since they wanted the *Catholic Worker* to remain the focal point for this work . . . It has been my hope that the FOR in the United States could claim the stature and provide the matrix for such a radical peace witness . . . The British PAX will make their materials available."[106] Then a month later, on the eve of a visit to London seeking the Archbishop's input about how they might "come to terms with the infertility of the PAX group in this country," Heidbrink added: "I nearly perish when I think of creating another group for some sort of unique work or witness, but someone has got to begin a strong wedge in terms of materials, retreats, conferences,

---

With Wisdom, 186–90; O'Connell, "Nonviolence"; and O'Connell, "Peace."

105. See also McNeal, *Harder than War*, 139–40, 189; Dekar, *Creating*, 205–7.

106. Heidbrink to Merton, 15 Apr. 1963, D/38, FOR Records, SCPC.

symposiums and visiting firemen amongst the Roman Catholic folk of this country."[107] In his September 1963 request that Gethsemani host a meeting of the FOR National Committee, Heidbrink explicitly considered it "a time when we could draw together more Catholic participation." He was then "on the verge of getting Phil Berrigan on the [FOR] Executive Council" just as FOR members were growing "more involved in Catholic social action in the New York City area," and opportunities were increasing for FOR facilities to "be more and more available to Catholic groups for retreats and conferences."[108]

By the next spring, when Heidbrink resumed his pursuit of a Gethsemani gathering, Jim Forest had already begun exploratory work on the CPF.[109] Their collaboration no doubt further exposed Heidbrink to sensitivities of Catholic radical pacifists. He could see much potential to realize this long-sought Catholic affiliate by gathering FOR leaders with a cadre of dedicated Catholic activists in the presence of this well-known monk for a dialogue on protest.[110] Whatever the reasons and motives may have been, John Heidbrink, more than any other player, refused to let the idea of a Merton-hosted retreat die. So as the autumn of 1964 progressed, it became apparent the event would in fact finally occur. All that remained was to prepare an agenda and begin the conversation.

107. Heidbrink to Merton, 15 May 1963, TMC.

108. Heidbrink to Merton, 9 Sept. 1963, TMC.

109. Forest to Merton, 30 Mar. 1964, TMC.

110. In his April 1965 report to the FOR National Council on "Church Relations," Heidbrink shared, "Perhaps the most exciting development in the church work of the F.O.R. this past year has been the formation of an informal and free-wheeling agency through which contacts with the Roman Catholic community are made by the Catholic members of the F.O.R . . . The Catholic Peace Fellowship began in April 1964 . . . It represents the beginning of a Roman Catholic denominational affiliate for the F.O.R." A bit later he named "Participation in . . . the November 1964 retreat with Thomas Merton on the 'Spiritual Roots of Protest'" among the CPF's activities. Heidbrink, "Church Relations," Apr. 1965, D/37, FOR Records, SCPC.

3

Thomas Merton's "Planning to Have No Plans"

Now that dates and the guest list were set, it remained for Merton as host and convener to provide a discussion agenda. He had pushed hard to assure it would not be organized as an academic conference with formal papers and presentations. Still he recognized the need for an element of structure if they would spend their time well, and as the event approached he began to think about how their days together might unfold. While tying down some last-minute logistics with Daniel Berrigan, Merton added to a November 9 letter: "I have been planning to have no plans and to go along quite informally. I hope they are all in a position not to be disconcerted at this and to expect a very free wheeling and unorganized approach. However if you and I are both prepared with ideas it will do no harm. I hope however that it will be a real and authentic opportunity of awakening and new direction for us all and am praying for that."[1] Then two days later on a follow-up note to Berrigan he added a postscript asking that the Jesuit prepare to lead a discussion on some aspect of the "spiritual roots of protest." He would do likewise from a "monastic desert viewpoint."[2]

The extent of Berrigan's advance preparation remains a mystery. Fortunately, though, journal comments and reading notebook entries supply glimpses of Merton's thoughts on what he might bring to the conversation as the gathering neared.[3] They suggest that as he prepared Merton drew heavily from writings of two French scholars: Jacques Ellul, who articulated theories about the social impact of technology, and Louis Massignon, a mystic and scholar of Islam who had actively protested his government's

1. Merton to Berrigan, 9 Nov. 1964, *HGL*, 85.
2. Merton to Berrigan, 11 Nov. 1964, *HGL*, 85.
3. Merton, Notebook.

conduct toward their Algerian colony. Merton's friend Ping Ferry had introduced Merton to Ellul by forwarding his book, *The Technological Society*, in
late October. In reading Ellul, Merton became captivated with the power of
a technologically focused culture to channel our discourse and define our
priorities. This struck him as highly relevant to the retreat's agenda. Merton had become personally acquainted with Louis Massignon, on the other
hand, through their correspondence prior to the Frenchman's 1962 death.
For this gathering, he sought inspiration from some of Massignon's writings
to develop his material on a monastic posture toward protest.

Merton's correspondence and journal entries also suggest a timeframe
for his preparatory work. He most likely drafted a rough outline of key
points on technological influence as he read Ellul's book during the first
week in November. During the following week, he appears to have drafted
a second outline to organize his comments about protest. Then just two
days before his guests arrived, Merton journalized impassioned sentiments
against the technological character of a "new holiness" that some champi-
oned, sentiments that echoed a Massignon essay he had just read and that
also reinforced insights gleaned from *The Technological Society*. This trail of
references left by Merton in his journal and notebook permits close scrutiny
of material read and ideas recorded as he planned not to plan. The perspective gained from following this trail proves essential for unpacking the
record that survives of comments he later shared at the gathering.

Ping Ferry, Jacques Ellul,
and the Social Influence of Technology

Thomas Merton's intuitive distrust of technology long predated his reading
of *The Technological Society*. His natural awkwardness with things mechanical, for instance, surely contributed to his skepticism of them.[4] Beyond
that, as William Shannon suggests, various innovations of Gethsemani's abbot, a Harvard Business School graduate, helped alert Merton's antennae to
the intrusions of modern gadgetry early in his monastic career. "Replacing
horses and wagons with motorized vehicles troubled Merton, as he saw the
silence and quiet of the monastery being invaded by noise and busyness."[5]
On occasion he mentioned modern society's technical and technological
traits as troubling. In particular, his increasing dismay over atomic weapons
in the early sixties also led Merton to reflect on the role technology played
in nuclear proliferation. For example in his introduction to *Breakthrough to*

4. See for example, Reardon, "Many-Storied Monastic," para. 9–11.
5. Shannon, "Technology," 467.

Peace, the 1962 anthology that addressed impending nuclear extermination, Merton listed an "unquestioning belief in machines and processes" as one of several forces that unconsciously influence our decisions, and he cautioned against a loss of traditional human reason and wisdom that would otherwise lead us into a "post-historic world of technological animals."[6] His own essay in the book observed that "an entirely new dimension is opened up by the fantastic processes and techniques involved in modern war,"[7] and another version of this essay published in early 1962 mentioned the planning and execution of war by computers.[8] Then in a January 1963 letter to E. I. Watkin, a writer he had considered including in his anthology, Merton noted:

> The question is much greater than simply eliciting a declaration for or against nuclear war. We have to come to grips with the great facts of our time and see where we are in the midst of this colossal revolution. It is not primarily a political revolution, or even an economic one . . . it is the great technological revolution which began in the late Middle Ages and is turning man's whole life inside out, which is all very well, I am not opposed to genuine progress. But no one seems to recognize that the roots of all this are spiritual, or non-spiritual, depending on how you look at it.[9]

Just one day later, in a letter to pioneer environmentalist Rachel Carson, Merton linked the concerns she expressed in her book *Silent Spring* with nuclear proliferation. To Merton they both reflected symptoms of "the same portentous irresponsibility" within our "technological civilization" that threatens life itself. Humans both belonged to nature and transcended it, and they needed to understand their position in relation to the source of all life. But in "gaining power and technical know-how," humans had lost this understanding. In this regard, nuclear war and Carson's revelations about pesticides were closely related because they both relied on "exactly the same kind of 'logic.'"[10]

In terms of providing a sustained focus of concern, though, Shannon also observed that for Merton "it was not until 1964 that technology became

---

6. Merton, *Breakthrough to Peace*, 11, 12.

7. Merton, "Peace: A Religious Responsibility," in *Breakthrough to Peace*, 106.

8. Merton, "Nuclear War and Christian Responsibility," in *Passion for Peace*, 43. The initial essay was published in the February 9, 1962 issue of *Commonweal*. See *Passion for Peace*, 37–38.

9. Merton to Watkin, 11 Jan. 1963, *HGL*, 581.

10. Merton to Carson, 12 Jan. 1963, *WF*, 70–72.

a subject of serious reflection."[11] He further noted that at this juncture of Merton's life his close relationship with Ping Ferry played a significant role in singling out technology as a unique social force to be reckoned with. Though it may not seem to be an obvious focus for a convocation on peace and protest, it nonetheless reflects Merton's keen sensitivity to the trends and forces that affected postwar American society and influenced its militarization. Following its entry into World War II, U.S. investment in science and technology had accelerated, surging even more following the Soviet launch of Sputnik satellite in 1957. As policymakers ramped up their financial support of U.S. technological advancement during those years, they also cultivated popular assumptions that national interest and security demanded technological superiority.[12]

Ping Ferry had tapped into the significance of this trend during the early sixties. In his role as vice-president of the Center for the Study of Democratic Institutions, he pursued and advanced publication of *The Triple Revolution*—a manifesto of sorts naming technological "cybernation" as the pivotal force it was becoming. Though not central to retreat conversation, it nonetheless was discussed that November. The document's initial content emerged from Ferry's interaction in the summer of 1963 with labor leader Ralph Helstein and economist Robert Theobald,[13] and they later hammered out a first draft in collaboration with Students for a Democratic Society (SDS) leaders Todd Gitlin and Tom Hayden along with a few others. Ferry's biographer observed that "the document . . . carried Ping's title, the stamp of his tone and phrasing, and dealt with issues he had expounded for years," suggesting Ferry was central to its authorship. Ferry also worked to gather thirty-five signers, including A. J. Muste, by its release in March of 1964.[14]

This eight-page narrative critiqued social forces and transitions then in play and called for organized action in response. It particularly focused on social "revolutions" they perceived as emerging in three areas: human rights, manifested in the civil rights movement at home and various colonial liberation movements abroad; weaponry, where modern potential for mass destruction was nudging humanity toward a warless world; and cybernation, where automated decision-making was rapidly eliminating reliance on human labor. The manifesto focused not so much on countering these forces—it mostly accepted them as inevitable—but instead on adapting to

11. Shannon, "Technology," 467.

12. Solberg, *History*, 87–93.

13. Helstein, Ralph, and Robert Theobald, "A Proposal from Ralph Helstein, Robert Theobald, and W. H. Ferry," 15 July 1963, C/33, FOR Records, SCPC.

14. Ward, *Ferrytale*, 93–96.

them in ways that preserved human dignity and averted social chaos in their wake.[15]

Though expressing concern for the interaction of all three revolutions, the authors chose to primarily address cybernation. This revolution inaugurated "a new era of production" that held core assumptions that were as foreign to the industrial era as recent industrial assumptions differed from those of the agricultural era. Although they cited "reordering of man's relationship to his environment" as a consequence of cybernation and predicted it would usher in an epoch that required little human effort, their main concerns were not spiritual. Cybernation would replace human labor at an increasing pace and accelerate unemployment, poverty, and, consequently, racial unrest. It would provide for nearly unlimited productivity that was "already reorganizing the economic and social system to meet its own needs." Cybernation also affected the weaponry revolution, which was making war obsolete through its massive destructive potential, by elimination of employment in defense industries. It in turn affected the human rights revolution by frustrating expectations for employment opportunities and adequate household incomes. To address these revolutions the United States must first grasp an understanding that the primary economic concern was not to increase production but to distribute the surplus goods and services that cybernation would provide.

The solutions it offered centered on ways to manage these impending changes. The key, they felt, required radical shifts in attitude, policy, and legislation to sever the traditional link between employment and material well-being, establish a basic guaranteed annual income for all regardless of employment status, and begin to restructure social and economic systems. The means for these changes, in accord with liberal democratic optimism, consisted of public works, revised tax and regulatory policies, and other tools at the government's disposal, such as "use of the licensing power of government to regulate the speed and direction of cybernation to minimize hardship." It therefore sought not so much rejection or limitation of technology, but ways to appropriately embrace and channel it. Because democracy required public planning for the welfare of all, it followed that cybernetic advances should also be pursued in public sectors. The Triple Revolution ultimately advocated a quest toward idealized "democratic vistas" that would enable citizens "to understand, express, and determine their lives as dignified human beings" and that would require greater human freedom from "social forces and decisions beyond their control." But as a

15. A copy of The Triple Revolution with related documents is in 49, microfilm reel 89:29, Muste Papers.

secular and political document it remained largely silent on the impact that technological processes of themselves might have on human hearts, minds, and souls.[16]

The Ad Hoc Committee on the Triple Revolution released their document in March with much fanfare, sending copies to President Johnson and the leaders of both Congressional houses. The radical pacifist monthly *Liberation* published it in full in April and offered it as an offprint shortly thereafter. *Liberation* would also publish numerous articles during the following year that addressed various aspects of its proposals, and the November issue of the Marxist *Monthly Review* would provide significant commentary, as well. The Fellowship of Reconciliation dedicated the theme of its fall conference that October to "The Triple Revolution: Values and Goals in a Cybercultural Society." A series of surveys conducted that year showed considerable use of the document in various educational and public discussion venues, as well.[17]

Ferry had forwarded a copy to Merton immediately upon its release in March. Merton responded promptly, favorably assessing it as "urgent and clear." But he added pessimistically, "if it does not get the right reactions (it won't) people ought to have their heads examined (they won't). (Even if they did it would not change anything.)" Rather than engaging the document's specifics, however, Merton shared his skepticism that people would relinquish faith in political remedies and place hope in God:

> We are in for a rough and dizzy ride, and though we have no good motive for hoping for a special and divine protection, that is about all we can look for. I have recently been accused again of pessimism because I refuse to equate hope in God with an unbounded trust in our economic structures. How is it that so-called Christians (and they are perfectly sincere, even devout, nay holy) are totally convinced that the promises of God to Abraham are now totally invested in our spiritually and mentally insolvent society?[18]

His response fails to reveal that at least this particular reading of the mostly economic manifesto had sparked his interest in the theme of technology per se and its human and spiritual impact. Merton does not mention it in subsequent correspondence with Ferry, and it makes no explicit appearance in

16. All quotations from *The Triple Revolution*, 49, microfilm reel 89:29, Muste Papers.

17. Related documentation, including *Monthly Review* offprint, from 49, microfilm reel 89:29, Muste Papers. Muste signed the document..

18. Thomas Merton to Ping Ferry, 23 March 1964, *HGL*, 216.

his published journals. But the document nonetheless would be referenced during the retreat's discussion of technology and it therefore entered into their conversational mix.

Another publication Ferry shared with Merton that year elicited his sustained interest, however, and Merton apparently sought Ferry's aid in prompting discussion about it at the November gathering. Some twenty-nine years later in a letter to fellow retreatant John Howard Yoder, Ferry mentioned that, "Tom, in inviting me, asked that I enlarge on the main points in Ellul's *Technological Society*; and I seem also to recall sending around before or after our meeting the text of a paper I gave at about that time in 1964 on those themes."[19] Ferry's "paper" may have been *The Triple Revolution* itself, but he possibly referred to his own follow-up paper in circulation that fall, "Further Reflections on the Triple Revolution."[20] Regardless, his note to Yoder confirms that Ferry and Merton conspired to assure that technology in general and these two documents in particular would surface in retreat discussion.

Ferry played no role in writing *The Technological Society*, of course, but he proved crucial in bringing the book to English-speaking audiences. As early as 1962, Ferry and his Center had begun to cast about for material on the role of technology. Through the recommendation of Aldous Huxley, they encountered an obscure 1954 French treatise by Jacques Ellul titled, *La Technique*, and began to underwrite its translation. This major work of over 450 pages was completed by early 1964 and published that year under the title of *The Technological Society*.[21] Ferry had sent mimeographed copies of portions to Merton at some point in the middle of the year, but Merton later reported that he "did not have the energy to go through it in that form, as I do a lot of my reading walking around outside." But in mid-October, when Ferry offered to send a recently published copy in book form, Merton expressed strong interest in receiving one, as he wanted to read "this important book."[22]

In this work, Ellul analyzes the origin and impact of "technique," which he describes as, "The totality of methods rationally arrived at and having absolute efficiency . . . in every field of human activity"[23]—a more subtle and complex concept than what typically comes to mind with the word

19. Ferry to Yoder, 29 July 1993, 13, Yoder Papers, TMC.

20. Ferry, "Further Reflections on the Triple Revolution," 49, microfilm reel 89:29, Muste Papers.

21. Alfred A. Knopf, "Statement from the Publisher," in Ellul, *Technological Society*, iii–iv.

22. Merton to Ferry, 17 Oct. 1964, TMC; Ferry to Merton, 15 Oct. 1964, TMC.

23. Ellul, *Technological Society*, xxv.

"technology." He does not refer simply to a particular method or process, but to a collection of assumptions about reality and how to approach life in general that has grown dominant in modern society. It represents a system of integrated cultural processes that channels and limits possible outcomes. It homogenizes individual differences as it seeks efficiency above all else. This unconscious reliance on "technique" posed the greatest challenge to effectively resisting and protesting assumptions and activity within modern U.S. society, which had embraced it.

FIGURE 2. Jacques Ellul.
© International Jacques Ellul Society. Used with permission.

Ellul's book traces the evolution of technique through the history of human development and applies it toward understanding modern economic and political conditions. He illustrates its presence in such realms as education, propaganda, sport, and medicine. This hefty, dense tome in the end offers no solutions. As Ellul explained in his foreword to the American edition, the book sought only to thoroughly understand the phenomenon as a foundation to better address it. Solutions must come not from elite specialists, but "each of us, in his own life, must seek ways of resisting and transcending technological determinants . . . We must not think of the problem in terms of a choice between being determined and being free," he cautioned, "We must look at it dialectically, and say that man is indeed determined, but that it is open to him to overcome necessity, and that this *act* is freedom."[24]

Late October and early November journal entries track Merton's encounter with *The Technological Society*. On October 29 he logged the book's arrival from Ferry,[25] and the following day's entry captured his initial impressions. It was, "Great, full of firecrackers. A fine provocative book and one that really makes sense." He went on to comment that such reading might benefit those participating in the Second Vatican Council, then in its third of four annual sessions and considering its *Schema XIII* titled "The Church and the Modern World." He pondered, "I wonder if the Fathers are aware of all the implications of a technological society? Those who can only resist it may be wrong, but those who want to go along with all its intemperances are hardly right." Then, upon hearing a military airplane in the distance he asks, "I wonder if it carries bombs? Most probably. They all do, I am told. The technological society! I will go out and split some logs and gather a basket of pine cones."[26]

Three days later, Merton's next entry referencing Ellul reflected on the human dilemma his thesis implied. "I am going on with Ellul's prophetic and I think very sound diagnosis of the Technological Society. How few people really face the problem! It is the most portentous and apocalyptic thing of all, that we are caught in an automatic self-determining system in which man's choices have largely ceased to count. (The existentialist's freedom in a void seems to imply a despairing recognition of this plight, but it says and does nothing.)"[27] A week after he began the book, however, on a day he had visited Louisville and invested in a Coleman lamp and stove for his hermitage, his journal entry registered greater caution. "I think Ellul is too pessimistic," he noted:

> Not *unreasonably* so—but one must still have hope. Perhaps the self-determining course of technology is not as inexorably headed for the end he imagines. And yet certainly it is logical. But more is involved, thank heaven, than logic. All will be brought into line to "serve the universal effort" (of continual technological development and expansion). There will be no place for the solitary! No man will be able to disengage himself from society! Should I complain of technology with this hissing, bright green light with its comforts and dangers? Or with the

24. Ibid., xxxii, xxxiii.
25. Merton, *DWL*, 29 Oct. 1964, 159.
26. Merton, *DWL*, 30 Oct. 1964, 159–60.
27. Merton, *DWL*, 2 Nov. 1964, 161.

powerful flashlight I got at Sears that sends a bright hard pole of
light probing deep into the forest?[28]

At some point in November Merton also found time to write a brief,
seven-sentence review of *The Technological Society* that he submitted along
with four similar reviews for publication in the Catholic weekly, *The Commonweal*. Merton had obviously not fully dismissed Ellul's work despite
its pessimism, referring to it as "one of the most important books of this
mid-century" that addresses "our most crucial problem." He explains how
"modern technology has produced a world in which means determine ends
and becomes ends in themselves," that (directly quoting Ellul), "'destroys,
eliminates or subordinates the natural world and does not allow this world
to restore itself or even to enter into a symbiotic relationship with it.'" Though
Ellul fails to claim technology cannot be controlled, Merton suggests Ellul
nonetheless considers the situation desperate with no real attempts having
yet been made to address it.[29]

Together, these early November reflections reveal that Merton's encounter with *The Technological Society* had struck a deep chord. His dawning awareness of the pervasive extent and power of modern "technique"
over humans and their relationship to the natural order set off immediate
alarms. He began to hear its background drone more clearly in the nearby
flight of warplanes and noted it at work in the prolonged death throes of a
wasp he had poisoned with insecticide.[30] And most significantly, he sensed
its potential—if Ellul's reading of the matter were correct—to impinge on
his contemplative space in particular and human freedom in general. Regardless whether Merton may have considered aspects of this book overly
pessimistic, Ellul had gained the monk's attention. His analysis seemingly
offered Merton some helpful concepts with which to explore his suspicion,
shared earlier that summer with Daniel Berrigan, that humanity had somehow gone "over the falls" and was now "in a new river and we don't even
know it."

The pages of Merton's reading notebook, however, provide the most
explicit clues linking Merton's reading of Ellul with his planning for the
retreat. Merton dedicated about three undated pages of this notebook to
citations from the first half of Ellul's book. These references articulate Ellul's
understanding of how technique had evolved from primitive expressions
to its modern manifestations. As Merton's notes reflect, for Ellul humans
are technological animals that invent by their very nature. Historically, the

28. Merton, *DWL*, 6 Nov. 1964, 163.
29. Merton, Review of *The Technological Society* by Jacques Ellul, 358.
30. Merton, *DWL*, 2 Nov. 1964, 161.

ancient East nurtured the emergence of technology, but as it seeped into classical Western cultures, the Greek value of harmony and the Roman value of discipline imposed limits on pursuing technique as an ultimate priority. Over time, however, as reason replaced spontaneity and tradition, and productive means grew more important than ultimate ends, technique began to dominate human interaction with each other and with their environment. This involves "the translation into action of man's concern to master things by means of reason, to account for what is subconscious, make quantitative what is qualitative, make clear and precise the outlines of nature." With the rise of modernity and its trends to isolate the individual and atomize society, human efficiency became the operative paradigm and penultimate value, contributing to a social axiom that "what can be produced must be produced." It presented a dynamic where the sheer necessity of production— not the controlled intent of producers—forces its products on consumers. The invention of anesthetics, for example, resulted in "useless operations." And, as Merton would cite later in his *Commonweal* review of the book, this logic leads the technical world to destroy and repress the natural. There is no accommodation with technique, for it "automatically eliminates every nontechnical activity or transforms it into technical activity" and leads to our current "stage of historical evolution in which everything that is not technique is being eliminated."[31]

Merton also jotted comments by Ellul regarding the disintegration of moral judgment under the advance of technique, which obscures distinctions between moral and immoral applications and instead creates its own autonomous morality. In such a world, "not even the moral conversion of the technician could make a difference. At best they would cease to be a good technician." When it came to law enforcement, Ellul believed technique creates uniform processes applied to all regardless of the crime and generates, as Merton paraphrased, "a milieu in which *control of everyone* is possible and necessary." In sum, according to Ellul, technique is totalitarian by its very nature.[32]

Merton then ends his reading notes on Ellul with two extended quotations that skip several pages deeper into *The Technological Society*. The first was taken from a chapter on "Technique and Economy," copied under Merton's heading of "'progress' and 'resentment.'" The section in which it

31. Material in this paragraph originates from pages R25, L25, R26 in Merton, Notebook. Corresponding material in Ellul, *Technological Society* appears on pages 19–23, 28–31, 43, 51, 79–84, 93, 100, 193.

32. Material in this paragraph originates from pages R26 and R27 in Merton, Notebook. Corresponding material in Ellul, *Technological Society* appears on pages 97, 100, 125.

lies, subtitled "The Great Hopes," describes the expectation and promise
that technological society holds out to its members if they will adhere to
its logic. It assures them that the culmination of mechanical progress will
be prosperity and plenty. According to Ellul, humans then respond to the
frustration of impediments to reaching this state of plenty by blaming others, and the quote Merton recorded explains that, "When man finds the foe
who stands in his way and who alone has barred Paradise to him (be it Jew,
Fascist, capitalist, or Communist), he must strike him down, that from the
cadaver may grow the exquisite flower the machine had promised."[33] The
final quote from Ellul that Merton cited appears in the chapter "Technique
and the State." It follows Ellul's observation that although humanity's most
important historical development has been the intersection of technique
and civic government, no one seems aware of it. "It is astonishing," Merton
transcribed, "that we still apply ourselves to the study of political theories
or parties which no longer possess anything but episodic importance, yet
we bypass the technical fact which explains the totality of modern political
events . . ."[34]

Since these pages are undated their sequential relationship to Merton's
journal entries remain unclear. Given that traces of his journal reflections
may be glimpsed in these quotes—and that Merton received the book less
than three weeks before the event—one suspects he generated the journal
and reading notebook entries concurrently during the first week in November. Likewise, it remains unclear when he began a list of ten points
written opposite the first page of his Ellul reading notes and placed under
the heading "Notes for Peace Meeting" (see appendix A). This notation explicitly demonstrates Merton's intent to address Ellul's concerns in retreat
conversation. Its placement and content suggest he started it at some point
after he began his notes on Ellul, however, perhaps adding to them as he
read further. Though the last couple of points do not explicitly pertain to
technological society, the first eight addressed in some way our spiritual and
social interface with technique, the first reading simply, "Technology and
its spirit (ascendency of device)." He went on to more directly connect the
dots between the retreat's theme and technology, noting that the "attitude
of [the] peace movement to technology will determine its spiritual base,"
and following with the question of whether technological society was self-
destructive at its core and might have relevance for the traditional Christian
challenge to "break with the world," or at least with a "basically corrupt"
human society. His fifth point consisted entirely of a quote from Ellul that

33. Merton, Notebook, R27; Ellul, *Technological Society*, 191.
34. Merton, Notebook, R27; Ellul, *Technological Society*, 233.

expressed the subtlety of technique's threat to followers of Christ: "Thus the development of economic techniques does not formally destroy the spiritual but rather subordinates it to the realization of the Grand Design—the whole of man's life has become a function of economic technique."[35]

These "Peace Meeting" notes also make explicit connections between pervasive technological advancement and the pursuit of war and peace. "Technology makes war almost inevitable," he asserted, since it intrinsically requires that "what is possible becomes necessary." It "changes [our] whole attitude toward killing, makes it all the more intense in [its efficiency], [and] depersonalizes, alienates." Peace on the other hand, is not similarly advanced because "there is no technology of peace comparable to that of war." This raised the question of whether a technology of peace could possibly exist. Even so, Merton insisted, "We should still ask for it," seeking not only alternatives to war, but an entire alternative "technical complex" based on an understanding of how peace has an impact on the events of our world. The challenge, however, is that war in general is more familiar terrain, a more definite and acceptable response based on human experience. Peace, though, is unfamiliar by comparison and simply "does not accord with the orientation of technological society." Perhaps we needed to pursue "ideological disarmament," as well as nuclear, a sentiment in harmony with the ancient Taoist philosopher, Chuang Tzu, who Merton would later suggest, "does not allow himself to get engaged in . . . division by 'taking sides.'"[36]

Without question, Ferry and Ellul had alerted Merton to the pervasive influence of America's technological society. The doors they had opened convinced him that technology was a required topic for their discussions on the spiritual roots of protest. In particular, Merton came to believe that the spiritual integrity of protest activity depended on awareness of technique and its mechanical expressions. As it played out in retreat conversations, Merton and Ferry in tandem showed their commitment to assuring that discussions regularly addressed the topic.[37]

35. Merton, Notebook, L24. Also Ellul, *Technological Society*, 226.

36. Merton, Notebook, L24; Merton, *Chuang Tzu*, 22. Merton would publish some Chuang Tzu writings the following year in *The Way of Chuang Tzu*.

37. Regarding some of Merton's later use of ideas on technology gained from Ellul and the retreat, see Oyer, "Machine Culture," 223–32, as well as various writings on the topic by Paul Dekar and Philip M. Thompson.

Louis Massignon and Monastic Insight

Merton ended his list of "peace meeting "points with two that shifted sharply from the technological and social toward the interior and spiritual. "The grace to protest is a special gift of God," he asserted, a gift "requiring fidelity and purity of heart." Through spiritual discernment, actions that express this gift could be distinguished from "mere human *griping*." In the end, possessing this gift would inspire the "*grace to love and to wish for the opponent a better situation* in which oppression no longer exists," and we would become freed from objectifying them as merely obstacles to the outcomes we seek.[38] This shift in tone and focus signals Merton's segue toward the second primary thrust of his preparatory energy, a thrust that revolved more explicitly around the relationship of protest to his own monastic vocation.

From his entry into Gethsemani Abbey, Merton's spiritual journey included ongoing efforts to clarify and deepen his understanding of monastic experience, its historical and spiritual roots, and its role in larger society.[39] As mentioned earlier, Merton's 1958 "Fourth and Walnut" Louisville epiphany of his profound connection to others had helped modify the trajectory of his thought and writing. While remaining grounded in monastic experience, he increasingly sought to link his own interior experience of the divine to the larger flow of human events. That his first published essay on peace, "The Root of War is Fear," had originated as a chapter in *New Seeds of Contemplation* symbolically reflects this synthesis.

His sense of the interplay between a monastic vocation and the world of human affairs, however, also sharpened his view of the monk as one whose very presence embodied an expression of protest. In 1960, for instance, Merton published a slim collection of sayings taken from the earliest Christian monks, the fourth-century desert fathers. Roughly the first third of this work consists of a Merton essay on what motivated these early ascetics within their ancient context. Their withdrawal to the desert, he felt, responded to a society they considered "a shipwreck from which each single individual man had to swim for his life." As the Western world acquired its Christian status under the embrace of Rome's imperial order, the desert fathers rejected claims that a lived Christian faith could be integrated with political power to form a fully Christian society. They resisted the era's growing pressure to lead lives "passively guided and ruled by a decadent state," and sought to carve out their own context in which "the only authority under God was the charismatic authority of wisdom, experience, and

---

38. Merton, Notebook, L.24.

39. This included a substantive history of the Trappists; see Merton, *The Waters of Siloe.*

love."[40] This understanding of what drove these first Christian monastics to their ancient desert vocation adds insight into how Merton might be predisposed to see protest as a core element of his own modern monastic calling. Merton clearly articulated this growing awareness three years later when he penned a new introduction to the Japanese translation of his autobiography:

> It is my intention to make my entire life a rejection of, a protest against the crimes and injustices of war and political tyranny which threaten to destroy the whole race of man and the world with him. By my monastic life and vows I am saying NO to all the concentration camps, the aerial bombardments, . . . the economic tyrannies, and the whole socio-economic apparatus which seems geared for nothing but global destruction in spite of all its fair words in favor of peace. I make monastic silence a protest against the lies of politicians, propagandists and agitators, and when I speak it is to deny that my faith and my Church can ever seriously be aligned with these forces of injustice and destruction. But it is true, nevertheless, that the faith in which I believe is also invoked by many who believe in war, believe in racial injustices, believe in self-righteous and lying forms of tyranny. My life must then be a protest against these also, and perhaps against these most of all.[41]

As Merton also moved closer toward a more fully eremitic lifestyle during these years, he would continue to develop his views on the meaning and purpose of monasticism as well as his place within it. In the months leading to the retreat he produced several writings and engaged the larger monastic community to further tease out more contemporary understandings of monasticism as well as advocate for hermits within in his own Trappist order.[42] It offers no surprise that a week before they gathered, Merton revealed to Daniel Berrigan that he would share material on protest "from [a] monastic desert viewpoint."

What may seem more surprising, though, is that in doing so he largely turned to writings of Louis Massignon (1883–1962)[43] for inspiration to probe the subject. Massignon was a devout Catholic intellectual with a

40. Merton, *Wisdom*, 3–5.

41. Merton, "Preface," 65–66.

42. For example, see *Seeds of Destruction*, 184–220; *DWL*, 5 Aug. 1964, 133; *DWL*, 12 Sept. 1964, 143–44. Merton also circulated different essays on monasticism in mimeograph form during 1964.

43. Louis Massignon's life and thought generally based on Gude, *Louis Massignon*; Mason, "Foreword"; Mason, *Memoir of a Friend*; Griffith, "Challenge of Islam"; Shannon, "Massignon, Louis."

strong mystical bent, but he was no monk. He held a deep respect, however, for the ascetic and contemplative orders, particularly the Trappists, and he occasionally retreated to Trappist monasteries for prayer and reflection. At the urging of Herbert Mason, a mutual colleague and friend who would later translate Massignon's major works, the French scholar initiated correspondence with Merton in mid-1959. Over the next two years, as they exchanged numerous letters, Merton gained a deep respect for the scholar, coming to view him as a spiritual mentor of sorts.

Massignon's intellect and skill had facilitated his success as a diplomat, officer, and scholar early in his life. His conversion at age twenty-five—experienced during an illness while researching Islamic ruins in the Iraqi desert—led him back to the Catholic faith of his childhood, a faith his father had rejected but to which his mother had remained quietly loyal. He would become a Franciscan tertiary and eventually a priest in the Melkite tradition, an Eastern rite in communion with Rome that permitted him to remain married and also to relate more closely with Greek and Arabic Christians.

Massignon devoted his linguistic and scholarly academic skills to the study of Islam, particularly its mystical Sufi tradition. His largest work, *The Passion of al-Hallaj*, reconstructed the life, teachings, and martyrdom of a tenth-century Sufi master, al-Hallaj.[44] Massignon attributed his own dramatic and traumatic religious conversion to the prayers and mystical intervention of four souls, living and dead, that included al-Hallaj himself. Another he believed intervened on his behalf was Charles de Foucauld—a soldier turned Trappist monk turned solitary hermit—whose own pilgrimage had also meandered through the religious and geographic terrain of Islam and Mediterranean deserts. Long after local insurgents killed Foucauld at his Algerian hermitage in 1916, "by his conversion, his passion for deeper discovery of the Absolute God and fellow man, and his exceptional courage he remained a spiritual model for Massignon."[45]

Massignon's encounter with Islam and his return to Catholicism also spawned intriguing spiritual ideas. His focus on the Abrahamic origins of Judaism, Christianity, and Islam cultivated his sense that "hospitality" represented a seminal value encoded within all three religions, and this virtue provided a fulcrum for his insistence that their members should live in harmony and foster mutual respect. He formed a Muslim/Christian prayer sodality named *Badaliyah* that led to profound interfaith expressions through the years, including publication of writings that emerged from these interactions in a journal he coedited, *Mardis de Dar-el-Salam*. His

44. Massignon, *Passion of Al-Hallaj*. The first edition was originally published in French in 1922.

45. Mason, "Foreword," xxviii.

study of al-Hallaj nurtured another key element of his religious understanding, that of "mystical substitution." He believed that certain individuals were called to express profound compassion toward others such that their prayers and devotion in effect "substituted" for the suffering and sin of others and furthered their salvation. Both Christ and the martyred al-Hallaj represented two extreme examples of such a vocation. Massignon believed his four conversion intercessors had played this role for him and that he was called to do the same for others. A third element of Massignon's spirituality, the concept of the *point vierge*, or "virginal point," also bears mention. This point represents the deepest core within the center of a human's very being, the point where God alone meets us and none other can penetrate. Massignon periodically employed the term in his writings when addressing the human experience of the divine or discussing the essential nature of something. Massignon further understood that when we encounter God—or better, when God encounters us—we experience God as a "stranger" or "other." Massignon referred to his own anguished conversion experience in the desert as a "visitation of the Stranger."

Massignon also appreciated Gandhi's teaching on nonviolence—they met on one occasion in 1931—and over time Gandhi's work strongly influenced the former soldier. His efforts to reconcile the Hindus and Muslims of India served as a model for Massignon's own work to reconcile France's Catholic majority with its Algerian Muslims. During his later years Massignon increasingly interacted with the poor and marginalized Muslims of Paris, especially North African émigrés. He sometimes responded to political developments with an activism that drew on Gandhian priorities to confront the oppression of Muslims and advocate for their interests. At different times he would speak out regarding Israeli-Palestinian conflict, Western intervention in Moroccan politics, and especially French brutality toward Algerians during the colony's war for independence. This Algerian advocacy, which followed his retirement from academia, exacted a toll of diminished public acceptance during his last years.

Louis Massignon's unique combination of mysticism and public engagement on behalf of others profoundly influenced Merton as he came to know more of Massignon. Shortly after Massignon's death Merton would reflect that the former "was a man of great comprehension and I was happy to have been numbered among his friends, for this meant entering into an almost prophetic world, in which he habitually moved."[46] Their brief but rather intense interaction through letters and transmissions of Massignon's writings occurred at a time when the aging Massignon's activism was at its most radical. He took to the streets of Paris in protest against French

46. Merton to Abdul Aziz, 26 Dec. 1962, *HGL*, 52–53.

atrocities, experienced arrest, and faced hostility that at least once included public physical assault. On another occasion he unsuccessfully attempted to retrieve the bodies of Algerians that Paris police had shot and discarded in the Seine River, hoping to provide them a proper Islamic burial. According to scholar Sidney Griffith, "It was not only pacifism and non-violence that motivated him" to act in these ways. Rather, "to resist the war, to give aid to its victims was a religious act for Louis Massignon, and every demonstration or 'sit-in' where he appeared was an occasion to practice the mystical substitution that was at the heart of his devotional life."[47] Herbert Mason put it like this: "[Massignon] didn't believe demonstrations could stop the war, but only that they could bear witness to the truth in honor and friendship," and that such "bearing witness was not a judgment, but an act of invitation to see reality through another's eyes."[48]

Massignon's efforts and motives moved Merton, inspiring him to join those efforts, if only in spirit. In the spring of 1960 Merton shared in correspondence that Massignon "has been writing about all the causes in which he is interested and I am going to try to do a little praying and fasting in union with him on the 30th of the month when there is to be a demonstration outside Vincennes prison . . . This is one way in which I can legitimately unite myself to the *témoignage* [testimony] and work of my brothers outside the monastery."[49] In their correspondence Massignon described to Merton not only his actions but his motives, writing that "Peace could not be gained by rich means, but through the outlawed, and it was required of us 'to assume their condition' (spiritually I mean), in 'substitution' as our dear Lord did in Gethsemane."[50] Merton resonated with such views, sharing with mutual acquaintance Jacques Maritain that he felt "quite close to [Massignon] with his mystery of suffering Islam, its flint-faced rejection and mad sincerity. I want to understand all the people who suffer and their beliefs and their sorrows. Especially the desert people."[51] Just a few weeks later he also reflected to Herbert Mason, "I want to say how deeply moved I am at this idea of Louis Massignon's that salvation is coming from the most afflicted and despised. This of course is the only idea that makes any sense in our time." Continuing, he then characterizes a Latin American statue of the Virgin Mary with the Christ child as presenting an insight "precisely that of Louis M." Merton interpreted the mother as an indigenous Andean who re-

47. Griffith, "Challenge of Islam," 158.

48. Mason, "Forward," xxxvii.

49. Merton to Jean Danielou, 12 Apr. 1960, *HGL*, 134.

50. Massignon to Merton, 2 Aug. 1960, as quoted in Griffith, "Challenge of Islam," 161.

51. Merton to Maritain, 17 Aug. 1960, *CT*, 32.

flected "a great mystery of poverty and darkness and strength" and the child as "the Resurrection to be born from the despised peoples of Mexico and the Andes" who holds a "mystical bit of fruit" that represented salvation. He added that "it makes me able to tell you that I am in complete solidarity with you and Louis Massignon on this point and that I want to badly go ahead as God may permit, in somewhat the same direction, but over here."[52]

Given such a comment, some observers understandably credit Massignon as an influence that nurtured Merton's own turn toward engagement with the world and with other faiths during the last decade of his life. William H. Shannon, for example, writes that he "proved to be an important influence leading [Merton] to the study of Sufism . . . Massignon's willingness to speak out, to take risks, may well have been part of what influenced Merton to do the same in the 1960s."[53] Following Massignon's death, Merton remembered him to Ernesto Cardinal as "a great organizer of non-violent action in Paris and [he] also did much for Christian Moslem dialogue."[54] No doubt Massignon's introduction of Merton to the life and thought of Charles de Foucauld, the one-time Trappist and eventual desert hermit, offered encouragement and validation for his own persistent pursuit of solitary life, as well.

FIGURE 3. Statue of the Virgin Mary commissioned by Thomas Merton from Ecuadoran sculptor Jaime Andrade. Merton describes its imagery as "precisely that of Louis M[assignon]" in her depiction as "the Indian woman of the Andes" who represents "all that is most abject, forgotten, despised, and put aside."

Photograph by Thomas Merton. Used with permission of the Merton Legacy Trust and the Thomas Merton Center, Bellarmine University.

52. Merton to Mason, 9 Sept. 1960, as quoted in Mason, *Memoir*, 122–23.

53. Merton, *WF*, 275–76.

54. Merton to Cardenal, 17 Nov. 1962, *CT*, 137.

Although Merton's November note to Daniel Berrigan suggests he had settled on "desert monastic" and "spiritual roots of protest" themes at least a week before the retreat,[55] exactly when he began to prepare his actual comments on the topic is less clear. His journal and reading notebook entries suggest he was processing the material upon which he would draw right up until the retreat began. He headed the reading notebook page that immediately followed his Ellul entries with, "Further notes—on Spiritual Roots of Protest." While John Heidbrink may have first jotted that phrase in a letter to Merton the previous April,[56] it had not stuck as a working title during the exchanges that followed. When planning revived with a flurry in mid-September, Heidbrink referred to the "roots of war" and a movement "torn loose from culture,"[57] which inspired Merton to "camp around with the idea of roots" and our "great need for roots."[58] In October Heidbrink described to invitees the event's focus as "examining the spiritual basis of protest."[59] But the retreat title does not resurface in correspondence until Merton's November 11 comment to Berrigan. Together with his journal and notebook entries, this suggests that he began to sharpen his focus on protest within a week of when they convened.

The reading notebook entries that follow Merton's Ellul excerpts reveal that for inspiration regarding protest he had tapped at least six Massignon essays, then accessible only in French. In a letter to Jim Forest earlier that May, Merton had mentioned he was "reading some fantastic stuff on Islam by Louis Massignon."[60] Then four days later he elaborated to Jacques Maritain that he was reading "the big volumes of Louis Massignon's *Opera Minora*, so much more 'majora' than most other people's masterpieces." Continuing on to express his renewed appreciation for the Frenchman's work, Merton shared that he "never realized what a profound poetic mind he had; the rich poetic orchestration of his material, always inexhaustible, is something unequaled. And what spiritual implications in everything!"[61] Several pages before his November reading notebook retreat entries on Massignon Merton had recorded some undated references to volume 1 of *Opera Minora*. It suggests that he to some degree mined those three recently published, massive volumes during 1964, focusing on the end of the final volume in

55. Merton to D. Berrigan, 11 Nov. 1964, *HGL*, 85.

56. Merton to Heidbrink, 9 May 1964, *HGL*, 414.

57. Heidbrink to Merton, 17 Sept. 1964, TMC.

58. Merton to Heidbrink, 19 Sept. 1964, *HGL*, 416.

59. Heidbrink to Merton, 29 Oct. 1964, TMC.

60. Merton to Forest, 20 May 1964, *HGL*, 280.

61. Merton to Maritain, 24 May 1964, *CT*, 45.

November as he prepared for the retreat. In this effort, he appears to have sought hints to Massignon's own spiritual roots for the nonviolent protest in which he had engaged on behalf of Algeria's Muslims. Five of the six essays Merton now tapped appeared in the latter pages of *Opera Minora* volume 3.[62] The sixth appeared in a different anthology of Massignon's writings, *Parole donnée*, gathered and published during his last year of life.[63] Four of these essays provided a considerable amount of the material Merton would record in his journal or notebook and incorporate into his monastic protest outline. A summary understanding of their content therefore becomes essential to appreciate fully their impact on Merton's preparation.

Massignon Essays on Abraham, Islam, and Charles de Foucauld

Four "monastic protest" essays that Merton drew from overlapped somewhat in content, but taken together they covered several of the key elements of Massignon's spirituality outlined above. They supply glimpses of his understanding about God's self-revelation among humanity, as well as how humanity in turn responds and comes to know God. More specifically, they illuminate how those relationships have played out through the biblical patriarch Abraham, among the real-world experiences of Islam, and in the life of Charles de Foucauld. But interpreting those glimpses is not simple.

Louis Massignon was a recognized master of language, and, as Merton alluded, he constructed these essays with poetic but complex phrasing. His primary translator, Herbert Mason, asserts that the man was himself "not esoteric or ethereal."[64] But he also notes that his writing style was "very idiosyncratic, with sentences in some instances extending to two pages in length." Further, the "meanings" in Massignon's texts "were often implicit and required my intuition and remembrance of our conversations to understand. [Sentences] were always long and suggestive of more than was said."[65] Mason adds that, "His originality . . . was drawn from his exceptional linguistic gifts and his passion to understand from his kindredness with his subject. [But] as a guide he is almost impossible to understand."[66]

---

62. Massignon, *Opera Minora*. Page numbers cited by Merton correspond with the 1969 reprint. The original was published in Beruit by Dar Al-Maaref Liban S.A.L. in 1963. *Opera Minora* translates as "Minor Works."

63. Massignon, *Parole donnée*. "Parole donnée" translates as "Given/Pledged Word."

64. Mason, *Memoir*, 1.

65. Mason, "Unexpected Friendship," 9.

66. Ibid., 11.

Given such challenges, attempting to summarize these essays and suggest how they may have inspired Merton proves daunting. Even when carefully translated, they yield their import grudgingly. Yet in reading them with some knowledge of what Merton sought to communicate on monastic protest, certain ideas and comments uttered by Massignon become significant. In general, we can sense how the worldview that emerges from these writings would have encouraged Merton to position his own vocation within the mystical flow of human history and consider how the relationship God initiated with Abraham continues today not just in the great Abrahamic traditions writ large, but in his individual role as a Trappist monk living in the midst of twentieth-century American society.

Two essays that Merton referenced focus almost exclusively on Father Charles de Foucauld (1860–1916), the desert-based hermit that Massignon counted among those four mystical intercessors who facilitated his conversion. One, "Foucauld in the Desert before the God of Abraham, Hagar, and Ishmael," originated as a presentation during Ramadan in May 1956, the fortieth anniversary of Foucauld's death and two years into Algeria's war for independence from France.[67] Massignon used this occasion mainly to dispute the reputation Foucauld had acquired in some circles as a spy and advocate of France's colonization of northern Africa and subjugation of its Islamic population. The second essay on Foucauld was titled, "An Entire Life with a Brother Who Set Out on the Desert: Charles de Foucauld."[68] This material originated from an address given at the Sorbonne on March 18, 1959, as the centennial of Foucauld's birth approached. After giving a brief nod to Foucauld's academic accomplishments, Massignon spends most of the essay elaborating on his "deeper level of intelligence"[69] as an explorer who pursued discovery of the sacred in others.

Understanding the life of Foucauld helps to also understand both his significance to Massignon and Merton's references to him regarding monastic protest. In 1886, following several years in military service, Foucauld converted to Christianity. Four years later he joined a Trappist monastery in the Syrian desert, where he spent the next seven years. After leaving the monastery, Foucauld embarked on a solitary life of prayer unaffiliated with a particular order, initially near a Nazareth convent and then, following

67. Massignon, "Foucauld in the Desert." Dated based on internal evidence referencing Ramadan 1956. Griffith, "Challenge of Islam," 165, indicates initial publication in the 1958–1959 issue of *Mardis de Dar-el-Salam*. English quotes and paraphrasing are based on the unpublished Virgine Reali translation.

68. Massignon, "Entire Life." Originally published in Massignon, *Parole donnée*, 63–72. All quotes and paraphrasing are based on Herbert Mason's translation.

69. Massignon, "Entire Life," 21.

ordination as a priest, to hermitages in the Algerian desert, first near Morocco and eventually in southern Algeria not far from Niger. He was shot and killed in 1916, supposedly by a nervous youth who guarded him as a band of local tribesmen confiscated weapons that the French army had deposited within his dwelling during World War I.

Massignon first made contact with Foucauld prior to his own conversion. When embarking on a 1904 expedition to map obscure regions of Morocco, Massignon relied on Foucauld's 1883 study of the region, undertaken while disguised as a Russian Rabbi. When Massignon sent a letter of appreciation to Foucauld, the hermit replied in kind, adding a note that he would keep Massignon in his prayers. This reference would later convince Massignon of Foucauld's role in his own 1908 conversion, and through later correspondence they developed a close spiritual friendship. Foucauld encouraged Massignon to join him in the desert and succeed him among the local indigenous Muslim population, an invitation with which Massignon wrestled up until his eventual marriage in 1914. Foucauld wrote a letter to Massignon, dated the day he was killed, in which he includes the comment, ". . . if God preserves your life, which is what I am asking with all my heart." Foucauld was killed just a few hours after writing it, a sequence of events that played out while Massignon was stationed in harm's way on the Balkan front lines of World War I. Massignon interpreted Foucauld's final appeal and death as a sacrificial substitution of the hermit's life for his own. He remained fiercely loyal to Foucauld and his ideals and spiritual aspirations. Massignon later sought papal approval for publication of Foucauld's *Directoire*, a rule that inspired a handful of monastic orders, including the Little Brothers of Jesus and Little Sisters of Jesus. He would later also convey his loyalty in public speaking engagements that recounted his memories of the hermit in tribute to him, two of which resulted in these essays studied by Merton the week of the retreat.[70]

A third essay Merton referenced, "The Three Prayers of Abraham," was published as such in 1949 and elaborates on themes he had explored since the 1920s.[71] It addresses the patriarch's lingering imprint on the three great religious traditions that trace their origins to him. Massignon opens, though, with several paragraphs that explain how human awareness of God's transcendence since Abraham has been preserved and passed to future generations through the witness of a few select individuals. The fourth of these essays, "Respect for the Human Person in Islam, and the Priority of

70. Foucauld's life and interaction with Massignon from Gude, *Louis Massignon*, 18–20, 62–69, 80–87.

71. Massignon, "Three Prayers." All quotes and paraphrasing are based on the Herbert Mason translation.

the Right to Asylum over the Responsibility to Wage Justified Wars,"[72] was written in 1952. Using linguistic analysis, Massignon provides intriguing reflections on hospitality and intercession, asserting that Islam's unique view of the human person inspired Islamic legal requirements to offer foreigners hospitality, even in times of war.

One key idea that Merton extracted from these readings pertains to Massignon's understanding of the special human "messengers" who play a key role in linking the whole of humanity to a transcendent God. This especially comes through in the opening pages of "The Three Prayers of Abraham." He suggests that the ascetic disciplines embodied in monasticism, particularly the silence and prayer of the Trappists, now provide a vital gateway through which these witnesses might gain the awareness needed in their role. Massignon goes so far as to connect the collapse of French and Russian societies through revolution to a weakened monastic presence within them. For Massignon, asceticism is practiced by these special messengers for the sake of others rather than for themselves.

Once they have embraced their role, a central function of these messengers is to embody Massignon's idea of substitution, through which they assume the suffering of the oppressed and the sin of the oppressor into themselves. This enables God to simultaneously resolve both within the messenger's own being. God often veils these messengers from recognition, however, sometimes even from themselves, which often renders them ignored and despised. But their veiled rejection "enables the witness to substitute for others in order, unbeknown to them, to bear their sins and to deflect from them their punishment."[73] It also permits them to enter the pain of others through participation in their suffering. Such words surely encouraged Merton about the vitality of his own vocation, its mystical role in holding together American society, and a potential to extend the chain of witnesses for his own generation. The messenger's key posture toward others will reflect hospitality that welcomes the stranger, because God typically assumes the form of a stranger when encountering humans.

As far as individuals who have historically filled this role, he names Gandhi as an example from outside the Abrahamic traditions. But it was Charles de Foucauld who served as a particularly important witness for Massignon. Alluding to Christ, he observes how Foucauld had communicated "by his life and above all by his death, that the priest is the repository for an eternal alms of hospitality that was passed to him by a man sentenced

72. Massignon, "Respect for the Human Person in Islam." All quotes and paraphrasing are based on the unpublished translation by Dr. Hollie Markland Harder.

73. Massignon, "Three Prayers," 5–6.

to death at the very moment he was betrayed, handed over, and executed."[74] Massignon testified that through a "living experience of the sacred in others, Foucauld . . . helped me find my brothers in all human beings, starting with the most abandoned ones."[75] Foucauld lived out his role as witness in southern Algeria among the indigenous Muslim population, who "in the most symbolic metaphysical sense"[76] were among the most oppressed and abandoned of all. He shared their humble life and revealed to them "the real spiritual bread of hospitality that these humble people themselves had offered to him."[77] The life and death of this "mystic in the wilderness," his "profound vocation of victim and intercessor,"[78] were offered up in sacrifice for these desert Muslims. Foucauld's death passed on his "sacerdotal testament," bidding us to emulate his "Christian loyalty toward Muslims, for whom the guest is precious, for whom the confidences of the guest are the most precious deposits."[79] We must not strive to conquer Islam through domination, rather we must adopt Foucauld's "spirit of participation" in relating to them. Foucauld would remain a "militant saint, inasmuch as his spirit of substitution lives in us."[80]

The patriarch Abraham, however, provided for Massignon the ultimate model of a special messenger of God, one to whom the three great monotheistic religions that he spawned look for guidance. His "three prayers" echo through the ages and continue to both bless and chasten us. His first prayer emerged from Abraham's hospitality to three angels who visited him and revealed that Sodom—"the city of self-love which objects to the visitation of angels, of guests, of strangers, or wishes to abuse them"[81]—would be destroyed due to its sins of inhospitality. Abraham pleaded with God to spare the city if enough righteous men could be found within it. When not even ten could be found, however, the city was destroyed and his prayer went unfulfilled. For Massignon, this unfulfilled prayer still "hovers forever over societies doomed to perdition . . . that they . . . might be spared the heavenly fire."[82]

74. Massignon, "Foucauld in the Desert," 3:780.

75. Massignon, "Entire Life," 22.

76. Ibid., 22.

77. Ibid., 23.

78. Massignon, "Foucauld in the Desert," 3:778.

79. Ibid., 781.

80. Ibid., 779.

81. Massignon, "Three Prayers," 10.

82. Ibid., 12.

Abraham's second prayer asked for the survival of Ishmael and his descendants following their exile into the desert, an exile which prefigured "the penitential life of hermits, of solitaries."[83] Abraham's wife, Sarah, had prompted this exile to secure her own son Isaac's birthright from his half-brother, Ishmael, born of Sarah's slave, Hagar. God's fulfillment of Abraham's prayer for Ishmael eventually nurtured the emergence of Islam, with its "vocation to the sword" against idolatry in defense of Abraham's transcendent God. Through Islam, this prayer yielded a people who understand the utter inscrutability and inaccessibility of God, one who approaches us, if at all, "as a Stranger who interrupts our normal life . . . and then passes on."[84] Abraham's third and final prayer reflects his willingness to sacrifice Isaac, an act which God interrupted and left unfulfilled until Mary sacrificed her own son centuries later.

As each of Abraham's prayers has played out through the ages, however a shadow side also emerged among the three traditions that claim him. Though each originally enjoyed some element of privilege before God, they have often taken that blessing for granted to their detriment. For example, Abraham's Jewish descendants failed to live up to the special priestly character he conferred to them through his willingness to sacrifice Isaac. Their legalism and scorn of the uncircumcised became embodied in pharisaic literalism and resulted in "fossilization" of their privileged character. Still, beneath this fossilization "smoldered an unknown purity, a compassionate resurgence of grace"[85] perpetually nurtured among select Jewish women. That grace ultimately penetrated Judaism's fossilized privilege and culminated in Mary, who "offered herself to the Stranger"[86] in spite of the scandal and suspicion it evoked. As for Christianity, Massignon laments how as the main beneficiary of Abraham's third prayer it historically took up arms to force Jewish conversions, embarked on anti-Islamic crusades, and relegated to Jewish financiers the sin of usury in promotion of Christians' own economic self-interest. Further, the very existence of Islam, the offspring of Abraham's second prayer, embodies a reproach of Judaism for "believing itself privileged to the point of awaiting a Messiah" that has in fact already arrived, and it reproaches Christianity for not recognizing the "full significance of the Holy Table [hospitality], and for not yet having achieved that rule of monastic perfection . . . which alone creates the second birth of Jesus within them." For Massignon, the presence of Islam as a divine reproach to

83. Massignon, "Entire Life," 22.

84. Massignon, "Three Prayers," 14.

85. Ibid., 16.

86. Ibid.

both Jews and Christians, "who abuse their privileges as if they belonged to them by right and of themselves,"[87] should inspire their respect of Islam and their revival of Abraham's second prayer for the survival of Ishmael's descendants.

Massignon saw this theme of regrettable and impudent conflict among the children of Abraham continuing to play out in his own era. For example he noted how Foucauld had helped him transcend the classic tension between "science and faith . . . ending in what I have observed and lived of the clash between the opposing monolithic monotheistic faith of the Muslims and the perforating technology of Western culture's colonial penetration."[88] This comment helps explain what Massignon sees as the source of Muslims' metaphysical oppression and abandonment: the relentless imposition of Western priorities upon Islamic culture. He even confessed the complicity in this of both Foucauld and himself prior to their conversions. Through their incognito desert excursions and encounters with Islam, "both of us had entered their home protected by the . . . sacred hospitality [of Islam]; both of us had abused it, we used it, in disguise, in our layman's passion to understand, to conquer, to possess. But our disguises had given them to us unspeakably by that right of asylum that no man of honor, especially no outlaw, can betray, for it is his last virginal point: his honor as a man."[89]

Massignon voiced this idea of an Islamic right of asylum loudly in "Respect for the Human Person in Islam, and the Priority of the Right to Asylum over the Responsibility to Wage Justified Wars." He suggests that Islamic personhood emerged from Islam's focus on the inner nature and character of an individual, which he contrasts with our Western inclination to instead anchor personhood in one's external or social orientation. For Islam, one's status as an individual believer in the one true God, Allah, lies at the core of what distinguishes a true person from the "barbarian foreigner." But Islam also grants a degree of personhood to Christian and Jewish foreigners who imperfectly acknowledge this one God, and Islam requires hospitable protection of them. Muslims ground this benevolence in the model of Abraham's hospitality toward the three visiting angels—an incident referenced on three separate occasions in the Koran. The power of this story also led Muslims to view strangers as visitors who are likewise due special hospitality, and ultimately owed a right of sanctuary and asylum, even in times of holy war. To illustrate, Massignon recounts the story of a Bedouin woman who for three days protected and fed a fugitive claiming

---

87. Ibid., 14–15.
88. Massignon, "Entire Life," 22.
89. Ibid., 30.

the right of asylum, later helping him escape—even though she recognized him as the man who had murdered her husband. He likened this to the Christian story of St. Jean Gaulbert who, upon meeting the murderer of his brother by chance, granted the perpetrator's plea for mercy. To Massignon, Islamic sacredness of hospitality toward the stranger and its assumption that they are sent by God is also intrinsic to many primitive cultures as reflected in their diverse rites of offering gifts, "peace pipes," and other tokens of respect to strangers they encounter.

In contrast, however, the sacredness of hospitality is far from intrinsic to modern western cultures in general, and Christianity in particular has failed to retain this Abrahamic mandate. He lamented how the international administration of displaced persons following World War II failed to base its decisions on a respect for the human person such as Islam's. Rather than protected as foreign "guests," they were "nationalized" and either forced to serve in the host country's armies or deported, which in many ways followed Nazi Germany's ethnic cleansing model. Such observations from within the Arab world led him to conclude that "the biblical, Abrahamic religious meaning of Muslim hospitality toward foreigners [has diminished] because of contact with us, and increase[d] a dreadful belief in the inevitable advent of war between the rich and poor . . . [such that] I would not guarantee that [Muslim hospitality] can last a long time."[90] If it does not, a gift offered by Islam to the West for the West's salvation will have been lost. It is a gift that ironically had been preserved up to then by Islam's reluctance to embrace aspects of Western rationalism, a gift that serves as "a sign of salvation for humanity in danger" and which "emancipates the human person from idolatry, from the slavery of technique performed by our hands."[91]

Through these four "Islamic" essays of Louis Massignon, Merton extracted several themes that would recur in his reading notebook and speaking outline, and they would surface in the notes of those who listened to his retreat presentation. These themes suggest that God's voice may be found in those rejected and despised, that social privilege may be misused, and that assumptions of our own privilege may "fossilize" us to prevent our recognition of God's voice in others. They also encourage an embrace of strangers and enemies and participation in the lives of those rejected, perhaps to the point of substituting our suffering for theirs. Massignon looked toward those living outside the privileges of Western culture, naming not only Muslims but Hindus and others we may consider "primitive." His images of withdrawal into the desert, the role of Trappist asceticism, and the

90. Massignon, "Respect for the Human Person," 3:545.
91. Ibid.

life of one-time Trappist Charles de Foucauld all affirm that Trappist monks reside at a pivotal intersection between God's presence on earth and human society. These writings suggest that perhaps monks are ideally suited to serve as God's transcendent witnesses. This helped Merton conclude that Massignon's insights captured essential elements of what constitutes a monastic protest.

Merton's Notes on Monastic Protest

Merton began to organize these insights within the pages of his reading notebook under the heading of, "Further notes—on Spiritual roots of protest" (see appendix B). Next to this heading he added a Latin epigraph taken from the Virgin Mary's Magnificat proclamation that anticipated Christ's birth: "*Deposuit potentes de sede,*" or "[He] took down the mighty from their thrones."[92] It offered an apt reminder of New Testament views on how God relates to agents of power and domination. Under these headings, Merton began to log a series of eight points to organize these further notes. His debt of inspiration to Massignon becomes apparent in this outline, but the essays he read mainly provided Merton a frame of reference for adaptation to his own agenda. His usage of them did not always directly replicate Massignon's main intent.

Merton's first point, echoing his subtitle of the "voice in the wilderness," raised questions on "judgment and privilege in the prophets." He noted both a "sense of responsibility of the 'privileged nation'" and an awareness of "the danger of privilege." This danger stems from the paradox that mere possession of human privilege automatically brings one under the scrutiny of judgment, an inherent tension heightened by our tendencies to "protect privilege as an absolute by belief in legalism and technology." Merton's second point expanded the first and folded in elements of Massignon's identification with the humble and his faith in substitutionary suffering on their behalf, asking, "[Can one] use one's privileged means to heal the ills of others? To meet those needs?" In response Merton noted that while we can attempt to do so, ultimately "the important thing is a detachment from the privilege which enables one to recognize the higher value of sharing the suffering and struggle of others [in order] *to heal the visible nihilism of which it is a symbol.*"[93] Point three further reinforced the dangers of indifferent

92. Quotes for this outline are from Merton, Notebook, L27, R28, L28.

93. Emphasis in original. The idea of sharing the suffering of others in order to heal their spiritual condition also appears in Massignon's essay, "A New Sacral," examined in the following section, "Harmonizing Ellul and Massignon."

privilege, lifting up the need to look for God in the other as revealed in a biblical dialectic. Through it, God's presence emerges in "the stranger, the underprivileged, the 'younger son,'" where "the one who 'has not' comes with the message and the love of God." In whom might this presence of God manifest? It varies across time and circumstance: "The Jew, the gentile, the Negro, the Greek philosopher (the Buddhist)" are all possibilities for Merton. According to his fourth point, this dynamic requires a response in us that puzzles those who possess human privilege, one that echoes Foucauld's influence in freeing Massignon from the constraints of his academic and empirical training. We must maintain a "readiness to abandon theory before the unjust demands of experience [and before our encounter of] meeting the 'other' who has an 'answer.'"[94] Ultimately, (point five) the purpose of doing so is to provide a sort of "recapitulation," one that embodies the broken condition in its fullness and enables a substitutionary "conveyance of it all in Christ."

FIGURE 4. Louis Massignon.
Photograph courtesy of Bérengère Massignon.

Whereas Massignon mostly whispered in the background of Merton's first five comments, point six explicitly introduces him. With it, Merton reveals the circumstance that he sees as the core of what prevents this

94. Massignon also expresses the idea of abandoning theory in favor of experience in "A New Sacral."

detachment and recapitulation—"the privileged collectivity and privileged institution stands in the way, not by warfare but by abuse of privilege," or as in the quote of Massignon that he registered: "Certainly, it would be desirable in these days of social action to be able to rely on the public testimonies of communities constituted and consecrated for this purpose. But it is precisely the abuse of their privileges which fossilizes them and deprives us of their help."[95] Taken from "The Three Prayers of Abraham," this citation falls within Massignon's opening discussion of special witnesses who convey a sense of God's transcendence, the role of Trappist asceticism in their call, and their veiled status as unrecognized and hateful to others. In direct relation to Merton's use of the citation, the essay went on to observe that often these messengers function outside of institutional structures. Even Foucauld "became a priest only at age forty-three and as such remained secular and alone."[96] What Massignon in essence asserted in the context of this quote, with which Merton apparently concurs, is that God often speaks most clearly through those free of institutional constraints. By implication, fulfilling a monastic—especially an ascetic Trappist—legacy involves rejecting whatever privilege might muffle or garble the message God intends his witnesses to communicate.

Merton's seventh point contrasts this fossilized privilege with "the privilege of Abraham and his witness," which was exercised on behalf of Sodom through his belief that he might find honorable men within Sodom's walls. This allusion would also hold implications for a monk's position in society. Massignon had characterized this first Abrahamic prayer as unfulfilled, and one that "hovers forever over societies doomed to perdition in order to raise up in their midst those ten righteous men in order to save them despite themselves. And we must believe that at times Abraham's prayer finds ten righteous men so that they . . . might be spared the heavenly fire."[97] It requires little imagination to suppose that a monastic calling that embodies protest could involve becoming one of those ten just ones whose presence might save an otherwise doomed society. This example also might invoke powerful cold war imagery linking nuclear destruction to the fiery fate that heaven had visited upon Sodom. The "real root" of spiritual protest, as Merton concludes in his final point, is then "identification with the underprivileged [and] dedication to their 'universe' as 'epiphany' . . . [and] as intercessory for us."[98] The integrity of this root corresponds to how

95. Merton quotes this verbatim from Massignon, "Three Prayers," 5.
96. Massignon, "Three Prayers," 5.
97. Ibid., 12.
98. "The Universe as Epiphany" is the title of a review Merton wrote in 1960 of

strongly we embrace the "reality of this belief—in suffering, in refusal of privilege and protest against the arrogance and stupidity of the privileged." The strength of our embrace is measured by the degree of our "true *hope* in the spiritual privilege of the poor."

Merton appended to this definition a contrast of "inadequate roots," which consisted of "the 'official policy' of any church or party." A problem we face in seeking roots is that "we think that our protest will be meaningless unless we are clearly identified with this or that group," thereby expressing our "servility to 'orthodoxy,' as in liberal ideas, etc." He cross-referenced this observation to an obituary Massignon had written of Jules Monchanin, the fifth of the six essays Merton cited in his notes. This priest, monk, and hermit had in 1938 established an ashram in India and helped pioneer Christian-Hindu dialogue. Merton linked his own caution against inadequate roots to a line taken from Massignon's eulogy: "Among so many theologians who are indifferent and so many missiologues who seek personal, material gain, Monchanin had assumed his place in a sort of 'no man's land,' exposed to attacks on both sides."[99] Adequate spiritual roots therefore lead us out of safe camps and into the crossfire between them.

The two notebook pages that immediately follow these points provide additional comments that draw on Massignon's treatment of Charles de Foucald. The first of these pages, also headed "Spiritual roots of protest," begin with three short excerpts from the *Directoire* of Charles de Foucauld that emphasize nourishing our interior life to cultivate integrity: "The first thing to do to be useful to souls is to work with all our strength and continually on our personal conversion . . . One is good not because of what one says and what one does, but because of what one is . . . the extent to which our acts are acts of Jesus working in us and through us."[100] Merton follows this with a summary statement of what Massignon might have us learn from Foucauld's sense of sacred hospitality: "Man must be a spiritual and intellectual refuge for his fellow man by compassion and understanding, not only giving to him but seeking in him and from him the presence of the word."[101] Then on the following page, under a heading of "compassion and understanding—Massignon on Foucauld," Merton jotted three phrases

---

Teilhard de Chardain's *Divine Millieu*, rejected by Trappist censors, but eventually published in 1979. The essay addresses Teilhard's views on God's manifestation, or "epiphany," in the material world around us. Thanks to Mark Meade of the TMC for helping connect Merton's notation to the essay title.

99. Taken from Massignon, "Abbot Jules Monchanin."

100. As quoted in Massignon, "Foucauld in the Desert," 3:778.

101. Merton, Notebook, R29. This is assumed to represent Merton's own words since it is not attributed or presented as a quotation.

from "An Entire Life of a Brother Who Set Out in the Desert: Charles de Foucauld." They express Massignon's appreciation of the Algerian hermit's experiential knowledge "of the sacred in others and, in response, of holiness in oneself." It provided him "a real understanding of the human condition . . . which drew him and committed him to the most abandoned of human beings," something that "cannot be communicated by external means but by acceptance through the transfer to ourselves of the sufferings of others."[102]

The next two pages after the Foucauld references contain notes on "Respect for the Human Person in Islam." Merton's comments focus on the historical origins of an Islamic view of personhood, particularly its sense of the central role played by "testimony" and unification with God in establishing personhood, and how this contrasts with Western ideas. Merton also highlighted comments about Islam's reluctance to embrace modern technical processes in order to preserve God's mystery and action in our world. Massignon's critique of the West's disregard for the sacredness of hospitality in Islam and primitive cultures—as well as abandonment of its own tradition of hospitality—was not lost on Merton either, as he noted that such disregard was "marked by forgetfulness and contempt of the Bible." In referencing primitive hospitality, Merton inserted a side reference to South Pacific cargo cults, which see "the colonizer as the divine emissary bringing treasure."[103] And in alluding to "the case of the Bedouin woman" and her uncompromising commitment to Islam's right of asylum, he noted, "by contrast: *Dresden!*" Then, after commenting on Massignon's concern with refugee policy, Merton summarized the gist of the essay as capturing Islam's insistence on waging war when Allah's rights are ignored, while at the same time recognizing the "'right of Asylum' even in Holy War."[104]

The fact of Merton's immersion in these Massignon essays as the retreat approached is also reinforced in his personal journal, which indicates he encountered them not simply as a source of theory to construct a persuasive presentation. He also drew on them for his own spiritual enrichment. On November 17, the eve of his guests' arrival, he briefly mentioned Jules Monchanin and his "prayer for 'all the dead of India.'" Merton then copied into the journal two additional Massignon quotes in their original French. The first of these came from "Foucauld in the Desert" and reflected words spoken by French sociologist Charles le Coeur in reference to Foucauld:

102. Merton, Notebook, R30; *Massignon*, "Entire Life," 21, 22, 23.

103. This appears to be one of Merton's earlier references to cargo cults. He recorded a conference on it in 1967, which was transcribed and is the basis for his essay "Cargo Cults of the South Pacific." Thanks to Mark Meade of the TMC for assistance with this background. See also Merton's mention of cargo cults in chapter 4.

104. Merton, Notebook, L30, R31, R32.

"For a mystic the souls of the dead count as much as those of the living; and his particular vocation was to sanctify the eternal Islam—that which has been and is forever—in helping it to give a saint to Christianity."[105] In the essay, this passage concludes le Coeur's summary of Foucauld's intimate association with his Islamic neighbors, one in which he would remind the negligent among them when it came time to offer their daily prayers. The second journal quote originated from "The Three Prayers of Abraham": "Asceticism is not a private luxury preparing us for God, but is rather the profoundest work of mercy: that which heals broken hearts by its own breaks and wounds."[106] This comment is integrally tied to Massignon's claims in the essay's opening for the metaphysical role of Trappist discipline in preparing witnesses and messengers of God's transcendence and in averting the implosion of entire societies. With it Massignon offered a profoundly social vision for the rigorous ascetic practice of individuals specially called.

Merton's preparation for his "monastic protest" presentation did not stop with these reading notebook pages or journal entries—he would build on them to prepare a more organized outline from which to speak. But these initial notes confirm how he approached his task, and they accentuate ideas of Louis Massignon that served as a reservoir from which he drew. The ultimate objective of Merton's protest would not focus superficially on opposing particular actions of a person or government, but would instead target the presumptions from which those actions emerged—particularly assumptions held by those with power and privilege about others who had neither. For Merton, the spiritual roots of protest lay with our ability to accept an intercessory gift through our encounter with the stranger, the abandoned and despised other. For these encounters to yield fruit, he recognized that we must resist inclinations to preserve our privilege. Instead, healthy spiritual roots will lead us into an ongoing personal conversion that empowers us to offer spiritual and intellectual refuge to our fellow humans.

Harmonizing Ellul and Massignon

Massignon's influence on Merton's retreat preparation was not limited to reflections on monastic protest, however. Through his readings Merton also discovered that his French mentor held views in harmony with Ellul's *Technological Society* that could help bridge the themes of technique and monastic

105. Merton *DWL*, 17 Nov. 1964, 166, Robert Daggy translation, originally from *Opera Minora*, III, 775.

106. Merton, *DWL*, 17 Nov. 1964, 166–67, Robert Daggy translation, originally from *Opera Minora*, III, 804.

THOMAS MERTON'S "PLANNING TO HAVE NO PLANS" 87

protest. A few obscure lines in Massignon's four Islamic essays hint that he associated technology with Western culture's penetration into and pressure upon Islamic society, to the detriment of Islam's integrity. Clear evidence that Merton had in fact recognized this and begun to synthesize the skepticism that both French writers felt toward technology comes through in both journal and notebook entries. Regarding the former, Merton's journal had remained silent on technology for ten days after expressing a certain pause toward Ellul's pessimism. But then on November 16 Merton journalizes an emphatic return to that theme with an endorsement that couples the minds of Ellul and Massignon on the matter:

> Technology. No! When it comes to taking sides, I am not with the *beati* who are open mouthed in awe at the "new holiness" of a technological cosmos in which man condescends to be God's collaborator, and improve everything for Him. Not that technology is per se impious. It is simply neutral and there is no greater nonsense than taking it for an ultimate value. It is *there* and our love and compassion for other men is now framed and scaffolded by it. Then what? We gain nothing by surrendering to technology as if it were a ritual, a worship, a liturgy (or talking of our liturgy as if it were an expression of the "sacred" supposedly now revealed in technological power). Where impiety is in the hypostatizing of mechanical power as something to do with the Incarnation, as its fulfillment, its epiphany. When it comes to taking sides I am with Ellul, and also with Massignon (not with the Teilhardians).[107]

Merton ends this reflection with a quote in French from the sixth Massigon essay Merton is known to have consulted while preparing for the retreat, "Un Nouveau Sacral"—"A New Sacral" or "A New Way of Relating to the Sacred"—which translates as: "We cannot fail to denounce the so-called 'harmlessness' of the 'apostles' of these technologies, which subject the spiritual to the temporal and soil life at its source in such a hypocritical way."[108]

---

107. Merton, *DWL*, 16 Nov. 1964, 166. Ending quote as translated by Daggy, from *Opera Minora*, III, 802. Daggy translates "beati" as "blessed ones." "Teilhardians" alludes to those who view human achievement as development toward a more divine state of being that reflects the expression of Christ in the world. In a later journal entry Merton noted: "My own opposition is to Teilhard*ism*—not to Teilhard de Chardin because I have not studied him enough. I like the *Divine Milieu* and find him personally a very sympathetic figure" (*DWL*, 23 June 1965, 260).

108. Merton, *DWL*, 16 Nov. 1964, 166. Ending quote from "A New Sacral" in *Opera Minora*, III, 802, translated by Dr. Hollie Harder.

Massignon wrote this particular essay in 1948 for publication in *Dieu vivant*, a journal he helped initiate and co-direct and to which Merton had occasionally contributed in the early 1950s.[109] His essay on the "Three Prayers of Abraham" was also published here one year later. Structured as a lay initiative, the journal grew from the atmosphere of disillusionment and devastation that Europe experienced following World War II. The initial issue, published in 1945, explained its genesis as "born in a period that recalls the darkest pages of the Apocalypse because of the violence and extent of the cataclysm unleashed, and likewise because of the atmosphere of spiritual death that is suffocating the world."[110] It distrusted applied science and technology, taking the position that a fate of human diminishment and self-destruction could not be averted through "more refined and subtle techniques," but only through an inbreaking of the transcendent.[111] Massignon, the father of a physicist, was a scholar who valued academic inquiry, and Herbert Mason recalled him as one who appreciated the contribution science made to human understanding.[112] But Massignon had also observed the damage Western culture inflicted on Muslim societies, not to mention the havoc and misery that engulfed postwar Europe, and he shared *Dieu vivant's* skepticism of how technology and technocracy had grown to dominate the West's worldview.

In the journal's seventh issue, Massignon had published an article that questioned "The Future of Science."[113] This essay was reproduced in *Opera Minora*, sandwiched between "Foucauld in the Desert" and "A New Sacral."[114] Though not cited in Merton's notebook, its position within *Opera Minora* suggests that as he prepared he would surely have noted and perhaps read it. The gist of the article critiques how science, in its claims to answer human needs and questions, seemingly usurps the role of God in modern society. As an imperfect and fallen human construction, however, science in the end remains vulnerable to serving as a tool of evil. Humanity's hope rests in its embrace of a transcendent "liturgical cosmos" acknowledged within church tradition, a cosmos that expressed the movement and mind of its Creator. The subsequent issue of *Dieu vivant* printed a letter that criticized this idea of a liturgical cosmos, and Massignon responded to those criticisms in the essay that became "A New Sacral," published in the

109. Griffith, "Challenge of Islam," 153.

110. Gude, *Louis Massignon*, 156–57, quoting *Dieu vivant* co-founder Marcel Moré.

111. Gude, *Louis Massignon*, 157.

112. Mason, *Memoir*, 35–36.

113. Massignon, "Future of Science."

114. Ibid.

journal's tenth issue.[115] It strongly rejected human pretensions to control its own fate through science and technology while ignoring realities of evil and a fallen human condition. A transcendent and living God, not human ingenuity, would ultimately heal the ills and overcome the dangers that permeated their postwar world. Its denunciation of the scientific community's role in unleashing nuclear weaponry unsettled many at the time, including his own physicist son.[116] The quotes from this essay that appear in Merton's journal and reading notebook confirm he in fact read it as he prepared.

"A New Sacral"[117] opens by citing examples of a secular worldview that rejects the call of *Dieu vivant* to rely on a God that transcends human knowledge in our efforts to overcome evil. A 1946 statement titled "One World or None," issued by leading physicists, asserted that preventing humanity's self-destruction relied on formation of a world government and international oversight of nuclear facilities. Albert Einstein had stated that, "Ignoring the realities of faith, good will and honesty in seeking a solution, we place too much faith in legalisms, treaties, and mechanisms," a comment Merton thought worthy of copying into his notebook. Massignon viewed such plans that place great trust in human potential to be inadequate measures that ignore spiritual causes of evil and our need to rely on a living God. Also disconcerting to Massignon, Emmanuel Mounier cautioned that too great a reliance on a transcendent God would encourage humans to welcome apocalyptic events as vehicles to hasten the end of history and thereby inaugurate a prophesied union with God. For Mounier, this view devalued human accomplishment and inhibited our embrace of "science's explosive liberation, moving freely along a linear trajectory through the space of an infinitely open destiny." Massignon found even greater objection, though, with comments by a letter writer who had reacted to *Dieu vivant*'s view of nature as sacred. In its place the writer proposed "a broader sacral view that integrates science and technology" and transforms humanity into "a very close collaborator with God." Massignon's response to this sentiment is noteworthy, especially since Merton copied the French passage verbatim into his reading notebook under an English caption that read, "Collaboration of man with God in technology?" Translated from the French the copied passage reads:

> The inappropriateness of this sentence irritates anyone who knows, through prayer, that God is at the root of our actions,

115. *Dieu vivant* issue number confirmed in Marcel, "Life and the Sacred," 115.

116. Mason, 17 Feb. 2013, email to author.

117. Massignon, "New Sacral." All quotes and paraphrasing in the following summary are based on the unpublished translation by Dr. Hollie Markland Harder.

and that he is in no way an external "occupier" who requests the "collaboration" of his creation. We have felt the call from God, and we resent the ridiculousness of this condescending proposal to use technical tricks in order to perfect the work of the Creator, something to which we are united through our awareness of our own imperfections that led to our downfall.[118]

The remainder of this essay elaborates on the "pure absurdity" of this call for a new and broader way of relating to the sacred. "The truly sacral unveils natural landscapes that are common to all times and to all places," and therefore the symbolism of those landscapes is accessible to all humans and finds expression through a universal church. Massignon acknowledges that such claims draw laughter from students of science. The *Dieu vivant* sacral does not offer pragmatic, physical cures to suffering, but appears to offer empty promises that merely divert attention from it. To Illustrate, Massignon cites the example of Father Damien, "the Saint of Molokai," who worked among the lepers of Hawaii, contracted their disease, and died of it. He sought to share their leprosy rather than cure it, and in doing so, he helped deliver them from a greater spiritual disease, as Christ had. The saint's offer of the only true cure—love—would in the end heal the sick person through eternal life, the life that matters most. Merton also saw this interpretation of Damien's work as worthy of copying into his notebook.[119] In following Christ's example, Massignon's *Dieu vivant* community seeks to learn through daily experience rather than rely on scientific systems, which are "perishable sketches . . . temporary cradles, architectural scaffolding." This community reaffirms "the importance of the fear of God . . . over all sciences" and embraces God's leveling "divine tactic," which "lowers the older ones next to the adopted ones of the eleventh hour, will have the under-privileged judge the privileged, supports the arguments of women over men, and lifts the servant, who lives the most humble of all human experiences, above the most well established theory."[120]

Although it is not a journal of social action, the intellectual friendship that *Dieu vivant* provides encourages its readers to reject what might be considered "affordable" technologies that profit some and impoverish others. In the statement Merton used to cap his November 16 journal entry,

118. Merton, Notebook, L26, from Massignon, *Opera Minora*, 3:798. Dr. Harder notes that Massignon's use of "occupier" and "collaboration" would have carried strong emotional impact when written in 1946 France, immediately following Nazi occupation.

119. Merton, Notebook, L27, from Massignon, *Opera Minora*, 3:799.

120. Massignon, *Opera Minora*, 3:801.

Massignon urges them to denounce "apostles" of such a technology that subjects the spiritual to the temporal and hypocritically corrupts life at its source. Massignon closes the essay by calling for readers to "mentally substitute" themselves for others and enter into their mental structures. Doing so will induce suffering, but it will also lead to greater understanding and truth.

His reading of "A New Sacral" proved significant for Merton's views on technology as the retreat opened. Jacques Ellul was a lay Protestant theologian as well as a trained sociologist, but he tended to segregate these worlds in his writings such that some books were primarily theological and others primarily sociological in nature. So although *The Technological Society* presented a powerful critique and analysis of technology's impact on human society, it reads as a secular treatise lacking explicit theological content. As such, though Merton deeply connected with its themes, he could still question its pessimism as incomplete and inadequate, since, as he had noted, "more is involved, thank heaven, than logic" when it comes to the inevitability of technology's influence. In "A New Sacral," however, a Catholic mystic who revered Trappist spirituality, one he had personally interacted with and counted as mentor, had critiqued twentieth-century technology in a way that did not simply question its impact from a humanist agenda. Massignon had named it as an idolatry that sought to replace the very presence of God in human experience. Merton's spirited journal entry of November 16 reads like a synopsis of key points in "A New Sacral." It echoes aspects of the essay's imagery, such as humanity's self-perception as collaborators with God in a life scaffolded by technology, and our pursuit of a "new holiness" that evokes its own liturgy. This entry exudes a sense of conviction not fully matched in his earlier entries on Ellul. Even his concession here that technology is "simply neutral" seems unconvincing, as he also cautions that there is "nothing to be gained by surrendering to technology." Why would Merton discourage surrender to technology if he remained confident it was simply neutral?

Merton's placement in his notebook of the "New Sacral" quote on humanity's technological collaboration with God is also telling. Rather than including it among his other notes from Massignon on monastic protest, Merton backtracked to place it on the back of the page opposite the last of his notes on Ellul. This placement further supports that the essay helped harmonize these two French writers for Merton. He had already noted in the essays on Foucauld, however, that Massignon viewed technique skeptically. This is demonstrated by two other short quotes added to the final page of his Ellul entries. The first of these hearkened back to 1960 as Merton first came to know Massignon through correspondence. In the spring of that year Massignon had forwarded a copy of the *Mardis de Dar-el-Salam* issue that included "Foucauld in the Desert before the God of Abraham, Hagar, and Ishmael." That May, Merton journalized: "Mardis de Dar-es-Salam [sic]. Deeply moving prayer of Louis Massignon on the Desert, on the tears of Agar, on the Moslems, the '*point-vierge*' of the Spirit seemingly in despair, encountering God."[121] Then in July Merton penned his gratitude for the material, writing to Massignon that "I cannot thank you too much for the latest issue of the *Mardis of Dar el Salam* [sic]," and offered an extended reflection on what he had read within the issue, which was:

> ... full of the most wonderful things, and I was above all deeply moved by your own short meditations on the desert and the God of Agar and Ishmael ...
>
> Louis, one thing strikes me and moves me most of all. It is the idea of the "*point vierge, ou le désespoir accule le coeur de l'excommunié*" ["the virginal point, the center of the soul, where despair corners the heart of the outsider"]. What a very fine analysis, and how true. We in turn have to reach that same *point vierge* in a kind of despair at the hypocrisy of our own world. It is dawning more and more on me that I have been caught in civilization as in a kind of spider's web, and I am beginning to say "No" louder and louder, though surrounded by the solicitude of those who ask me why I do so. There is no way of explaining it, and perhaps not even time to do so.[122]

As he gathered thoughts on monastic protest four years later, though, Merton chose a more extended quote that better explains his 1960 desire to say "No" to civilization's hypocrisy. His 1964 notebook citation as translated reads: "Under pressure from a so-called Christian civilization, and technically superior, the Muslim faith reached the virginal point, the center of the soul, where despair corners the heart of the outsider."[123] This virginal point was important not simply as an ethereal object of reflection. It served as the last refuge from the oppressive forces of modern technological society.

Following this entry, Merton added a brief phrase from "An Entire Life with a Brother Who Set Out in the Desert: Charles de Foucauld" stating,

---

121. Merton, *TTW*, 30 May 1960, 5. Merton reworked the entry to include in *Conjectures of a Guilty Bystander*, 151.

122. Merton to Massignon, 20 July 1960, *WF*, 278.

123. Merton, Notebook, L27. Merton attributes the quote to "LM" in this notebook without citation. These words appear in "Foucauld in the Desert," later published in *Opera Minora*, 3:780.

". . . vitiation of the word by technocracy."[124] It appears within Massignon's explanation of Foucauld's impact on his own spiritual life and Massignon's experience of Muslim peoples as "the most abandoned of human beings." Foucauld did not seek their evangelization, but served as "a messenger in our perverse times in which every expression is corrupted by technocracy" and one who "came to share the humble life of the most humble."[125] The idea that technology interferes with genuine communication therefore caught Merton's attention as another concern about our technological society. For Merton, these brief references to Foucauld's encounter with Algerian Muslims as they faced western intrusions support Ellul's portrayal of technique as a presence that demands submission to its own logic.

Read together, these French writers highlight the potential for Western technology to replace an awareness of our Creator's "liturgical cosmos" with its own agenda. It impinges upon and dominates both the freedom of individuals and the integrity of non-Western cultures. More specifically, these writers support the notion that pressures exerted to conform us to technology's efficiencies also erode an innate and divine hospitality often found among societies considered to be more "primitive," including Islamic culture. From this, Merton would conclude that access to the real spiritual roots of protest—our detachment from privilege and embrace of the underprivileged—requires detachment from the technological excess that our society relies upon in its quest to penetrate, convert, and subsume other cultures.

Thanks to his discipline of journaling and recording notes from readings, Merton granted us access to his thoughts, priorities, and resources as he anticipated his retreat with makers of peace. He would continue to refine his material right up until his guests' arrival in hopes of framing a successful dialogue. These refinements led to the final speaking outline that would guide his comments on "monastic protest" and a mimeographed handout that set the retreat's tone and suggested themes of discussion. Merton probably did not expend undue effort in his preparation for the retreat, basing it on readings at hand without extensive added research. He did not craft a formal paper to present nor did he solicit any from others. But neither did he completely follow his original "plan to have no plans" during the week or two before they gathered. Merton invested the limited time his monastic schedule permitted in considerable forethought on what he might

124. Merton, Notebook, R30. Merton's writing is not fully legible, but he cites "*Parole donée*, p. 64" as the source, which includes the phrase, "*viciée par la technocratie.*"

125. Massignon, "Entire Life," 22.

contribute and how the group might best spend their time together. His investment proved profitable from the moment he and his thirteen guests first assembled on the retreat's opening day.

4

Opening Day—*Quo Warranto*, Technological Society, and the Monastic Protest

STILL RECOVERING FROM CATARACT surgery, the aged eyes of A. J. Muste gaped through thick lenses at the rolling Upland South landscape that unfolded before him. The veteran activist sat comfortably as the car cruised along the roadway, his gaze turned toward the window, soaking in the crisp colors and forms the disease had once all but hidden. He had arrived in Louisville the day before, and earlier that morning he gathered with others at the Albert Pick Motel just off the city's north-south expressway at Arthur Street. There Daniel Berrigan, commissioned by Merton to assure they found their transport to the abbey, had shepherded them to a car that Merton had arranged. In due time the monastery complex rose before them, and the car pulled into the tree-lined driveway that signaled their approach to the enclosure's gatehouse. Upon arrival the travelers collected their bags, and monastery staff ushered them to their retreat house rooms for a brief respite before they launched their opening session that morning.[1]

Arriving at Gethsemani's Gate

It originally fell to John Heidbrink as the event coordinator to iron out final arrangements that would enable these guests to make their way to the retreat during this week before Thanksgiving. No doubt distracted by his revised plans to meet with Eastern Bloc colleagues in London, though, Heidbrink seemingly applied Merton's vision of freewheeling informality

---

1. Chapter opening based on details in Cornell, "Merton on Peace," 23; Merton to Berrigan, 11 Nov. 1964, TMC.

to these details, also. His late October communication to the monk naming participants and recapping administrative specifics essentially placed any needed follow-through in Merton's hands. After naming those he believed would come, Heidbrink requested special attention to the needs of John Nelson, who apparently warranted such consideration because he was making considerable effort to arrive for a truncated visit wedged into his hectic schedule. He suggested, however, that the others "can jolly well manage on their own wind and most likely by renting cars, etc."[2]

When confirming Muste's participation the first week in November, Heidbrink indicated to him that the Berrigans originally planned to leave Tuesday, November 17, and rent a car to take themselves and Muste to the abbey.[3] Muste's subsequent call to the FOR office for more details had revealed that Jim Forest and Tom Cornell would arrive on a flight from Kennedy Airport at 11:00 a.m. on Tuesday,[4] and Muste ultimately acquired reservations to embark on November 17 as well.[5] His notes on the arrangements suggested that the Berrigans originally intended to arrive in Louisville at 4:00 a.m. Tuesday morning on a flight from Newark, but by November 11 those plans had changed. In a note to Daniel Berrigan that day, Tony Walsh confirmed that he would fly to Kennedy airport, "not the other as [previously] mentioned," to "be met by Pope Paul's representative for the Gethsemani conference"—in other words, by Berrigan himself. At JFK they would have lunch and then catch a 2:25 PM flight for Louisville.[6] He makes no mention of being joined by Philip Berrigan, who by then apparently had made plans to travel with John Peter Grady.

Heidbrink's expectation for others to "jolly well manage on their own" apparently caught Paul Peachey off guard however—he had not been copied on Heidbrink's summary. He perhaps assumed closer management of details for an event so remotely situated. A week after Heidbrink had passed the logistical baton to Merton, Peachey wrote to his own invitee Yoder, sounding a bit frustrated and perhaps embarrassed at the open-ended state of affairs. "Apparently there will not be too much coordination on the arrangements," he noted. "I have not been told how we are to get from Louisville to the Monastery which is a distance of 60 miles. Jack Nelson tells me that he is to be met Wednesday morning, since he is unable to make it Tuesday evening

2. Heidbrink to Merton, 29 Oct. 1964, TMC.

3. Heidbrink to Muste, 6 Nov. 1964, Supp. #1/4, microfilm reel 89:35, Muste Papers.

4. Handwritten note of flight arrangements, Supp.#1/4, microfilm reel 89:33, Muste Papers.

5. Muste to J. Nevin Sayre, 1 Dec. 1964, dictated 16 Nov., Supp. #1/34, microfilm reel 89:34, Muste Papers.

6. Walsh to D. Berrigan, 11 Nov. 1964, A/145, Berrigan Collection, CUL.

. . . I would expect that we would be met."[7] Having no instructions to offer, Peachey suggested that Yoder communicate directly with Merton. Yoder did so only three days before his own departure from northern Indiana, stating he assumed plans were not altered by the fact that his contact Peachey now would be in Europe. He added that when he landed in Louisville at 1:00 p.m. Tuesday he would check at the airline desk for a message from Merton as to how he would arrive at the monastery.[8]

Peachey had copied both Daniel Berrigan and Merton on his letter to Yoder, which motivated Merton to reach out to Berrigan for logistical assistance. Could his Jesuit confidant "keep a general eye on the whole situation in that regard as I presume you will be driving out from the airport"? If he needed backup, Merton said he would "get some friend in town to take care of it."[9] Two days later Merton dashed another note to Berrigan confirming the monastery would send a car to the Albert Pick Motel on Wednesday morning. He affirmed Berrigan's apparent suggestion that all on hand would simply meet there at 9:00 a.m. that morning to make the trip as a group, though some might arrive the evening before. By now, John Heidbrink's original hope that all might gather for supper on Tuesday night had faded, though some did arrive that day. Jim Forest and Tom Cornell, having landed in Louisville late Tuesday morning, found their way to the abbey that same afternoon and took their extra time on site to roam the abbey grounds and visit Merton's hermitage, casually snapping some photos as they walked before spending Tuesday night in the abbey retreat house. After Phil Berrigan cancelled his original Tuesday morning flight from Newark, he eventually accompanied John Grady to Kentucky, apparently by car. Elbert Jean drove up from his home in Nashville, and Ping Ferry made his own way as well. It took a bit of last-minute scrambling, then, but in the end a cast of thirteen retreatants would arrive at the abbey to join Merton in probing the spiritual roots of protest. It was an impressive turnout for an event under consideration for over two years but formally scheduled only two months earlier.

Getting Started—The Opening Session

Merton's late note to Berrigan had added that he would "look forward to seeing you all [the] morning of Wednesday" after the 9:00 a.m. departure of several from Louisville. He may have simply referred to their anticipated arrival at Gethsemani, but more likely he had in mind their initial assembly

7. Peachey to Yoder, 5 Nov. 1964, 13, Yoder Papers, TMC.

8. Yoder to Merton, 14 Nov. 1964, 13, Yoder Papers, TMC.

9. Merton to Berrigan, 9 Nov. 1964, TMC.

to open the retreat. It seems unlikely that they gathered as a group much before 11:00 a.m. given the sixty mile or so drive from Louisville and the need to settle into their retreat house rooms. This facility ran lengthwise south to north, where it abutted the abbey church, as it still does. It had a conference room in the basement and its own refectory and dining area. As demand for guest space at the abbey had increased over the past decades, the monks had subdivided retreat house quarters to accommodate more visitors. Consequently by 1964 the guest rooms where Merton's visitors slept were quite narrow, perhaps six to eight feet wide, and sparsely furnished with only a bed, table, sink, and pegged wall rack to hang clothes. Guests shared common lavatories and showers. The facility was managed by a lay Catholic who lived across the road from the enclosure and was the father of two Gethsemani monks. At the time, he organized the lay Catholic retreats that were hosted by the abbey and conducted by a monk serving as retreat master.[10]

Merton's earlier offer for good weather had fallen through when the group first assembled late on the morning of Wednesday, November 18. Rain was falling, so rather than seek out Merton's hermitage, they remained in the monastery compound to convene their introductory session. Those on hand assembled in a meeting room located in the southwest corner of the nearby gatehouse. After each had found a place on one of the chairs or couches that ringed the room, Merton produced his mimeographed handout bearing the title "Spiritual Roots of Protest" (see appendix C) and distributed it to guide their initial conversation.[11] He obviously intended for this sheet to set the tone and frame their time together, though as Tom Cornell recalled, it was not closely consulted in subsequent sessions.[12] It did, however, reflect the priorities Merton had processed in letters with John Heidbrink and Daniel Berrigan. "We are hoping to reflect together these days on our common grounds for *religious dissent and commitment* in the face of the injustice and disorder" that characterizes our world. "What we are seeking is not the formulation of a program," he asserted, "but a deepening of roots." The handout articulated the event's focal question as: "*By what right* do we assume that we are called to protest, to judge, and to witness? . . . Are we simply assuming such a 'right' or 'mandate' by virtue of our insertion in a collective program of one sort or another? An institution? A 'movement'?" This deepening of roots sought to plant them solidly "in the

10. Br. Patrick Hart, 16 Apr. 2010 and 3 Nov. 2012, conversations with author; Fr. James Conner, 17 Apr. 2010 and 3 Nov. 2012, conversations with author.

11. Reproduced in appendix C. Mimeograph originals are found in 13, Yoder Papers, TMC and A/32, Berrigan Collection, CUL.

12. Tom Cornell, 29 May 2010, conversation with author.

'ground' of all being, in God, through his word" and to align their motives with the judgment of that word. In addition to focusing on protest per se, however, Merton's document suggested other points to explore together. These included "the *nature of technological society*," posing for discussion that they consider two extremes—was it "by its very nature oriented toward self-destruction" or, drawing upon Massignon's critique, might it instead be seen as "a source of hope for a new 'sacral' order."[13] He also asked whether we are called to react or protest against the fact that "technology is not at present in a state that is morally or religiously promising." Added points he offered for them to consider addressed the impact of mass media on communication, the relevance of an interior life, and the role of personal renewal.[14]

Merton's handout also encouraged mutual receptiveness to each other's views and willingness to share one's own. Doing both would foster new insights and a new openness in each. "We will not necessarily cling to sectarian programs and interpretations," he challenged. "We will think, speak and act as brothers, conscious that one same Spirit works in us, according to the gifts of each, for the manifestation of the justice and truth of God in the world, through Christ." As far as process, it suggested that, "at each of our meetings, someone might act as leader of the discussion after himself starting off with a talk on any aspect of the question that seems relevant. For example:

> Wednesday Afternoon: T. Merton, "The Monastic Protest. The voice in the wilderness."
>
> Thursday Morning: A. J. Muste
>
> Thursday Afternoon: John H. Yoder
>
> Friday Morning: Fr. Daniel Berrigan, S.J.[15]

They apparently negotiated Merton's suggested schedule, however, since as it actually played out, Berrigan and Muste would switch their assignments, with the former leading Thursday morning's session and Muste delivering the final talk on Friday morning. Most likely they also discussed conducting the Masses they would hold the following two mornings.

---

13. Merton's use in his handout of this phrase from Massignon's essay suggests the document was created just a day or two before the event.

14. Merton, "Retreat," 259–60; emphases original.

15. Ibid., 259–60.

FIGURE 5. A. J. Muste during the Wednesday morning
opening session in the monastery gatehouse.
Photograph by Jim Forest, courtesy of Boston College, John J. Burns Library.

Once they had attended to such preparatory details, this opening session of itself prompted much discussion.[16] When posing his handout question of "by what right" do we assume a call to protest, Merton drew upon
a Medieval legal term—*quo warranto*—as his gateway to probe motives for
social protest.[17] Translated literally as "by what warrant," the phrase originated from English tradition. It referred to a mandate issued by the crown
that required a person to demonstrate they held the authority to exercise
a particular right or exert some power that they claimed to have. Merton
wanted to discuss the underlying assumptions those in the room held about
why they felt empowered to resist custom and challenge established authority in order to transform the status quo. Though Merton had not typed
this Latin phrase in the handout itself, he twice included the paraphrase
"*by what right?*" This question represented for Merton a sort of unanswer-
able, existential "Zen question" with which each person needed to grapple,

16. Discussion content from this opening session originates from Forest, "Gethsemani Retreat," and Daniel Berrigan, "Notes on handout." See "Archives and Manuscript
Sources" section of bibliography.

17. Though Merton did not use it in the handout, Cornell vividly recalled use of
this term (Cornell, 29 May 2010, conversation with author) and Daniel Berrigan recorded it in "Notes on handout."

whether protesting government action or arms manufacturers. More specifically he wondered, if we otherwise live the details of our lives superficially or in conformity with social norms, do we still retain the right—or will we even be inclined or motivated—to protest? Then to focus the question more personally and set the stage for his afternoon comments, Merton also noted that "a monk is a man of protest." When monastics initially withdrew from the larger flow of society, they were challenging accommodations made by the larger church. For Merton, "The monastic protest is primarily against a worldly Christianity, a Christianity rooted in the Establishment and contributing to the Establishment," or perhaps even "conniving with establishments," as Berrigan phrased it. Merton conceded that today, however, "We monks too contribute to the Establishment, and in a big way," although he would later add that, "From a monastic point of view, even when you're not protesting at all, your being can be a protest."

Other input helped broaden the "warrant" by which we may protest. When Ping Ferry asked, "What is the source of your personal authority?" Merton shared that according to Islamic thought "one becomes a person by his act of faith [i.e., testimony]," and therefore the "loss of capacity to protest [is] connected to a loss of personality." To push this prerogative even further, Merton suggested that "one might ask also, by what right [do] you jump out the window of a burning building,"[18] implying protest may in fact become an act required for sheer survival as a person. Tom Cornell would later recall that in addressing motives for protest, Merton also invoked Jeremiah 20:7–18 to explain that one does so in response to "a fire that is burning in my heart."[19] From the start, then, the sentiment quickly bubbled to the fore that protest represents an act of faith in response to innate or perhaps spirit-led callings to confront matters that in some way contradict how God intends humans to exist.

According to Jim Forest, Merton's opening words also acknowledged that considerable risks and challenges accompany this response—challenges that often originate from within the church itself: "The jails of the inquisition and its fires are not yet totally extinct," Forest recorded. Protest "means confrontation, encounter" and is impossible without it. As Daniel Berrigan captured it, Merton suggested that, "Having part in protest [is] incomprehensible [to the] majority," and it therefore can "at times mean opposition to other Christians and other Catholics." To illustrate how protest

18. Forest, "Gethsemani Retreat," implies Merton said this, but Yoder in his presentation the next day attributed this imagery to Ferry.

19. Cornell, 13 Apr. 2010, email to author, attributes the Jeremiah reference to Merton; it is not attributed in Cornell, "Merton on Peace," 23, and Merton did not include it in his reading notes or preparatory outline.

can be thwarted, Merton cited superficial coverage in the recently established Catholic magazine *Ramparts* on conflict between a Catholic priest, Father William DuBay, and his superior, Cardinal James Francis McIntyre of Los Angeles. McIntyre was highly conservative both religiously—he criticized Vatican II liturgical reforms—and socially—he encouraged priests to educate themselves about Communism by attending John Birch Society meetings. Earlier in 1964 DuBay had made national headlines by asking Pope Paul VI to remove McIntyre from office because he failed to support civil rights for African Americans—the cardinal had banned preaching on discrimination and civil rights and discouraged direct action demonstrations.[20] The example of *Ramparts* coverage suggests that shallow or perhaps complicit reporting can buffer or obscure the impact sought through actions and statements of protest.

FIGURE 6. Thomas Merton during the Wednesday morning
opening session in the monastery gatehouse.
Photograph by Jim Forest, courtesy of Boston College, John J. Burns Library.

Following this observation about the role of protest in modern media, Merton then turned to a related "further point" in his handout: technology and its social impact. The manner in which he first raised the topic remains unclear. Perhaps his handout questions prompted the conversation, or he

20. See *HGL*, 167 for more on DuBay, who was also listed as a sponsor of the CPF in the mid-sixties.

may also have drawn from a separate list of points jotted on the back of a cover sheet for the outline on monastic protest that he would use for his afternoon presentation. The list read:

Technology:

1) 'What can be done *must be done*'
2) It will (and must) be done before people are able to understand what it means and what its consequences must be, 50/50 chances it will be opposite to desired effect

    Proliferation of means—end vanishes p. 430

3) How in such a situation can we possibly speak of control?
4) If this is out of control can cooperation be 'moral'?
5) How can one not cooperate?
6) If one cannot help cooperating, how can ones cooperation be immoral?
7) Mystique and technology 422–423.[21]

The page notations in points 2 and 7 refer to *The Technological Society*. The latter, point 7, references Ellul's discussion of how technology reduces the diversity of religious expression and both homogenizes and diffuses "ecstatic phenomena." Point one also echoes a concept, if not a direct quote, from the book as captured in Merton's reading notes—"what can be produced must be produced."[22] It is also identical to a comment Ferry would presently inject.

The initial comments of this technology discussion that Jim Forest recorded reflect Merton conveying that our "total immersion in a machine culture, an age breathing technology," breeds alienation. Forest later recalled comments suggesting that it reduced humans to a "bio-chemical link" that served merely as "a shaky bridge between the solid-circuit perfection of cybernetic systems and moodless computers, and not a being little less than angels."[23] Within this machine culture "man becomes an idolater before the Machine," and upon assuming this idolatrous posture, "he loses his capacity to protest, establishes a mentality in which protest is meaningless and absurd." At this Ferry interjected that "computers are beyond the 'by what right' question" and proceeded to elaborate. The "basic reality of technology is this," Ferry posed, "if it can be done it must be done. What is possible is necessary." It seeks the *one best way*, where "'best' has only one

21. Merton, "Notes for F.O.R. retreat."

22. Merton, Notebook, R29; Ellul, *Technological Society*, 81.

23. Forest, "Struggle with Peacemaking," 41. Forest indicates that the term "bio-chemical link" originated in a scientific paper.

meaning—efficient!" It fails to foresee or understand consequences. Merton responded to Ferry by asking a question that echoes his speaking outline, "If it is impossible to control, is it immoral to have anything to do with it? We have gone over the falls," Merton observed, "entered into an apocalyptic situation. Technology is apparently taking over." Daniel Berrigan noted that the question then looms, "What options are left?" Merton's sense of having gone over the falls hearkens back to his comments to Berrigan earlier that August, when he used the same phrase to express fatigue and frustrations with the plethora of "projects and expectations and statements and programs and explanations"[24] that swirled around him. Here it seems that he had more explicitly identified our technological captivity as playing a central role in sending us over those figurative falls.

The insertion of Ferry's voice at this point reflects his own eagerness to promote this theme. Given that technology was not explicitly mentioned in Heidbrink's list of possible retreat topics, Ferry seemingly played a considerable role in placing—and now keeping—it on the agenda. Merton's journal entry the following night, recapping the event to date, noted that "Ping Ferry has been very helpful (he and I talked a lot at first about Ellul)."[25] Bob Cunnane confirmed that although Ferry was not assigned one of the four slots for presenting material, he nevertheless "had a lot to say. I remember him being very articulate and very strong in his opinions. I remember he'd say, 'Yes, but . . .' though I didn't feel it was ever antagonistic. He had a very different style from most of the people that were there, like a businessman with a bunch of clerics. He was a dominant member in his organization, so I think it was very hard for him not to be top fiddler."[26] For his part, Tom Cornell also remembered Ferry as essentially generous in spirit.[27] In the end, what most struck Cunnane about the views that Ferry and Merton advanced throughout these discussions was their nuanced understanding of "technique" as a cultural force—"it wasn't a kind of Luddite thing against technology per se." Comments he had heard about the manner in which technique now dominated media and removed meaningful content from communication particularly impressed Cunnane. Both communists and the West had their own standard slogans that they repeated and believed, just as the Nazis had done in World War II. "I remember Merton asking, 'Are we singing hymns while the ship sinks?'" Cunnane added that, "It was very interesting to me, because we were not brought up to consider culture,

24. Merton to Berrigan, 4 Aug. 1964, HGL, 84.
25. Merton, DWL, 19 Nov. 1964, 167.
26. Cunnane, 31 May 2010, conversation with author.
27. Cornell, 29 May 2010, conversation with author.

really." His exposure to different cultures while studying in Rome had already begun to impress on him the extent to which views in the church were culturally determined. The Rome experience demonstrated that, "In some ways I was closer to American Protestants than I was to Italian Catholics."[28]

Daniel Berrigan's brief notes on the opening session capture additional input regarding the realm of technological critique voiced during this time slot. Though for the most part unattributed, they probably reflect mostly Merton's comments. They also help tie more closely together the implications of technology for peace advocacy. One comment reinforces Merton's contention that technological awareness is a prerequisite for the integrity of protest: "Without technological understanding, we, as peace protesters, become *snob* items." Berrigan's notes also ask whether the "peace issue" might be a "pedagogical *moral* gesture," as part of a larger effort to enlighten society about their modern dilemma. In addition, Berrigan noted a concern that the "GIGO," or "garbage in, garbage out," logic of technique when applied to war would yield technology such as lasers that could kill the most efficiently while also implicating the millions of workers paid to produce them. Jim Forest would later confirm occasional reference to "GIGO" situations at points during the retreat.[29] Overall "We are in the service of technique instead of the opposite," Berrigan recorded. These comments began to turn the conversation toward such *Triple Revolution* concerns as, "What is to be done with the *time* if we get machines working for us?" Berrigan had also jotted the three prongs of Ferry's *Triple Revolution*, which confirms that document had played an explicit role in conversation. He noted the question of what an economy with adequate goods might look like and whether it would ultimately demoralize people. Berrigan then closed his notes with a question attributed to Ferry: "Will this be a bread and circuses civilization with a final act of destruction?"[30]

Following this exchange on technology, the opening session adjourned and the men broke for lunch. They had used the time well. In addition to reviewing agenda and seeking general orientation for the coming days, they had grown more familiar with each other and begun to process ideas together. Merton and Ferry had also successfully established technology as a force germane to their focus. Although they referenced both *The Triple Revolution* and *The Technological Society*, the tone they set for later exchanges

28. Cunnane, 31 May 2010, conversation with author.

29. Forest, 13 Oct. 2010, conversation with author.

30. Berrigan's two attributions to "(FERRIS)," in "Notes on handout," are assumed references to Ping Ferry.

emphasized Ellul's skepticism toward technology more forcefully than *The Triple Revolution*'s hopes to manage it.

FIGURE 7. Thomas Merton at his hermitage writing table
reviewing his speaking outline before the afternoon session.
Photograph by Jim Forest, courtesy of Boston College, John J. Burns Library.

Thomas Merton—The Monastic Protest

During the retreat, Thomas Merton maintained his monastic schedule, chanting with the other monks at appointed hours and tending to other routines. Bob Cunnane recalled that most of their interactions with him were limited to the scheduled retreat sessions, though the retreatants them-selves interacted with one another during the free hours of their stay. "We were on our own at night. Muste always went to bed early, and a lot of us joined together at night. We just talked more or less personally about what we were doing." Cunnane also noted that for the most part they enjoyed privacy and isolation during their stay. "I remember feeling good about the fact that we were there by ourselves. I wasn't feeling bad for Merton that someone might watch us and tell others we are doing this and that."[31] Oc-casionally during their discussion, Jim Forest would pause from recording his copious notes, set aside his pen and notepad, and snap a photo or two

31. Cunnane, 31 May 2010, conversation with author.

of the group listening to a presenter or engaged in conversation.[32] His images reveal they had dressed well for arrival and departure, with those of the Catholic clergy donning their clerical attire and most others sporting jackets with ties. When they gathered for their private discussions, however, several of them dressed casually in shirtsleeves or perhaps a sweater, though A. J. Muste and Elbert Jean appear to have consistently worn suit and tie. Charlie Ring kept to his priest's attire, and Merton routinely wore his monastic habit. Ping Ferry wore a jacket and bow tie even to the isolated hermitage session.

Their first full discussion session convened later that Wednesday afternoon following lunch. By then the rain had ceased, so they made their way to Merton's hermitage for this leg of the dialogue. The near-octogenarian Muste struggled somewhat in his trek over slippery leaves. He tired easily. Tom Cornell would later recount how, as they navigated the grounds beyond the enclosure, he and Ping Ferry "hovered behind [Muste] as inconspicuously as possible, arms outstretched to scoop him up if he fell, like angels commissioned lest he dash his foot against a stone."[33] Merton's hermitage stood beside a field on a wooded hillside, out of sight about a mile north of the monastic enclosure. It was constructed in November 1960 for Merton's use. He had christened the structure "St. Mary of Carmel," at first using it mainly to host guests for conversation or spend a few hours in solitude. Merton had received permission to spend his first night there just a month before the retreat, and he would soon make it his permanent residence in August 1965. This simple structure initially had no electricity or restroom. It was wired in early 1965, and a bathroom and small chapel were added in the spring of 1968. It remains today as it stood then and is still often put to good use for monks wishing to spend time in solitude.[34]

In the fall of 1964, however, Merton's hermitage consisted of only three rooms and an open front porch, all sharing the same floor of poured cement. The largest room, where Merton received his guests, spanned the width of the structure. In the front wall, next to the door granting entry from the porch, a large window in three sections faced the open field that spread along the hillside in front of the cottage. Two smaller windows were positioned on either side of it. Merton had placed a long table along the wall beneath the large window, where he would sit and look out over the field as he worked. The room's two side walls also included fairly large windows that

32. The only known complete set of Forest's photos are a set of contact prints held in Box 21, File 41 of the James Forest—Thomas Merton Collection [MS1989-02], John J. Burns Library, Boston College. The negatives cannot be located.

33. Cornell, "Merton on Peace," 40.

34. O'Connell, "Hermitage," 197–200.

admitted considerable light during the daytime, and in one corner Merton had placed wooden shelves that overflowed with books. A sizable stone fireplace dominated the back wall opposite the picture window, and the space between it and the doorway into the kitchen incorporated a large grid of ornate, open cinder blocks that allowed heat to pass from the front room into the back. Merton accessed the third room, his small sleeping quarters, from the kitchen. It contained a narrow bed, a small stand with clock, a few simple icons hanging from the wall, and a tiny closet.

**FIGURE 8. Tree roots Thomas Merton placed on the porch
of his hermitage the week of the retreat.**
Photograph by Jim Forest, courtesy of Boston College, John J. Burns Library.

Merton's aesthetic sensitivities found pleasure in the forms of nature and the landscape around him. For this particular occasion he had located an uprooted stump and some unearthed tree roots with intertwined and angular lines that apparently appealed to him, and he placed them in the center of his large front porch to greet his guests. Though these objects are not mentioned in notes from the gathering, one suspects they may have served the purpose of providing imagery to help the retreatants focus on its theme of "roots." As the walkers trickled up the hill and onto the hermitage site that afternoon they found Merton sitting inside at his table under the large front room window studying his speaking notes. After greeting them and chatting a bit, Merton excused himself to walk outside and pace the open field in front of his refuge for further preparation until all had arrived and it was time to begin. When all were present and the time had arrived they filed past the visual aids displayed on Merton's porch, through the hermitage front door, and into his large receiving room. Charlie Ring, Bob Cunnane, Phil Berrigan, and Tony Walsh all scrunched together on a bench next to the fireplace. Dan Berrigan chose to sit on a backless stool flanked by chairs holding Ping Ferry to his right and John Grady to his left. Merton pulled out additional seating to accommodate the rest, and together they formed a large circle around the room's perimeter to begin their session.

In his handout, Merton had queued himself up as the opening discussion leader with the topic of "The Monastic Protest. The Voice in the Wilderness."[35] His preparations for this session had included refining further how he might present ideas he planned to share on the topic. Toward this end he crafted a separate outline on a plain piece of paper independent of his notebook entries. This document consisted of a cover sheet inscribed "Notes for F.O.R. retreat" and "November 1964," followed by a sheet titled "Spiritual roots of Protest" (see appendix D) that contained his extensive notes from which to speak. The back of the cover sheet contained the seven talking points on technology mentioned above. The notes that Forest, Yoder, and Berrigan took on his presentation confirm that Merton indeed relied on the outline as he shared with the others that afternoon, but extemporaneously inserted other comments as well. When these four sources are read together, backed by his reading notebook entries, a rather detailed picture emerges of what he shared.

Seated at one end of his writing table under the picture window, his notebook and outline spread before him, Merton began to share. He slightly adapted his planned approach by immediately building on the morning's extended discussion of technology rather than introducing it a bit further along as he had outlined. He first asked the men gathered in his hermitage to reflect for later discussion upon how one responds to modern technological realities. A protest must come to terms with technology, he asserted, whether trying to stand outside it as protest or entering into its flow and trying to connect with it. Should the church "get control of the computer," as Forest captured it, or as Yoder noted, "get ahold of technological society and make it the millennium"? Then addressing protest, Merton asserted that the "familiar litanies" of what Catholics protest against, such as "dress," should not be their starting focus and frankly were not relevant. For Merton, a

35. Content from Merton's "Monastic Protest" session originates from four sources: D. Berrigan, "Notes on mimeograph"; Forest, "Gethsemani Retreat"; Merton, "Notes for F. O. R. retreat"; Yoder, "Transcription of Original Notes by JHYoder." See "Archives and Manuscript Sources" section of bibliography.

monk is by nature a man of protest, and he felt empowered to utter such judgments given that the historic "monastic background was originally a protest against the Church's establishment." Those monks who first withdrew had "continued to show respect for people who stayed in society, but not for the Emperor."

FIGURE 9. Thomas Merton reviewing his preparation notes in front of his hermitage before the afternoon session.
Photograph by Jim Forest, courtesy of Boston College, John J. Burns Library.

Merton then introduced a statement by novelist Graham Greene that he had flagged in his reading notes as an opening reference. He had noticed it in the current week's issue of *I. F. Stone's Weekly*, which routinely peppered its pages with excerpts from the foreign press. This particular quote had originated in the November 6 *London Daily Telegraph* and appeared reproduced at the top of page one in *Stone*'s November 16 issue. It commented on recent photographs in British media "showing the tortures inflicted on Viet Cong prisoners by the Vietnam army." What most disturbed Greene centered on his observation that early in the war, though both sides tortured enemy prisoners, at least their "hypocrisy paid a tribute to virtue by hushing up the torture inflicted by its own soldiers and condemning the torture inflicted by the other side." These particular photos, however, were obviously "taken with the approval of the torturers," and their captions "contain no hint of condemnation." Greene concluded from this that, "The long slow slide into barbarism of the Western world seems to have quickened," and he asked, "Does this mean that the American authorities sanction torture as a means of interrogation?"[36] When Merton first selected this as his likely opening, his notebook entry emphasizes its portrayal of "the gradual *deadening* of humanism." Merton saw that this deadening reflected Greene's ultimate object of protest, his effort to "resist the deadening *in ourselves*" that emerged from the "sheer mass of shocking material to which we have become adjusted."[37] It was a strategy that would easily lead into discourse on the need to heighten our sensitivity and awareness regarding those most abandoned and oppressed.

As he actually used this material that afternoon, Merton linked Greene's critique of the torture these recent photos revealed with its technological sophistication and the morally questionable but politically unquestioned methods that our culture sanctions to achieve the results we seek. He directly quoted from Greene's statement and suggested it implied that in our technological society, humanity is approaching a point where people are no longer shocked. It offers a telling illustration of our utter blindness. In response to our drift into this state of blindness, Merton invoked a Latin prayer taken from the story of Jesus healing blind Bartimaeus as told in Mark's gospel: *Domine ut videam*, or "Lord, that I might see." Without clear sight we stumble forward unaware that our technology ultimately uses us rather than we using it. Even Vatican II discussion of such noble goals as eliminating poverty "allows all sorts of domination by technology of religion."

Merton then edged closer to themes tied with Louis Massignon's views on mystical substitution for and participation with others, identifying them with a monastic understanding of vocation and giving two examples of such a call. He began by recounting the experience of St. John Gaulbert, mentioned by Massignon as offering a Christian parallel to traditional Islamic respect for human persons. This eleventh-century Florentine soldier on Good Friday met the murderer of his brother on a narrow bridge and moved to kill him in revenge. When the man fell to his knees and begged for mercy, Gaulbert forgave him, threw his sword off the bridge, and embraced him.[38] It was an act, Merton felt, through which Gaulbert essentially "left

---

36. Greene, "The Author," 1. *I. F. Stone's Weekly* was a left-leaning political newsletter; Graham Greene was an English literary critic and author critical of U.S. imperialist tendencies.

37. Merton, Notebook; emphases original.

38. According to both Forest, "Gethsemani Retreat," and Yoder, "Transcription of Original Notes by JHYoder," Merton mistakenly indicated that Gaulbert's father had been murdered rather than his brother.

the world," and became "'cloistered' by his forgiveness," as Gaulbert would eventually establish a Benedictine monastic order. Merton then added Louis Massignon's story from "A New Sacral" of St. Damien, the saint of Molakai, who contracted, shared, and died from the leprosy of those he served. He had copied in his notebook a couple of excerpts pertaining to this story that reveal how Damien's apparent failure had actually succeeded at a higher level. As Massignon had written, "St. Damien of Molokai wanted to share the leprosy of the lepers, and he did not cure them. So be it. But this physical leprosy was more than anything else the symbol, the sacred character of another disease, this one being spiritual, of which the saint came to cure them, like Christ, by sharing the other . . . When we enter the minds [of the sick] to straighten and prune them, we do this by means of our compassion until truth blossoms in their minds."[39] As Merton recounted to his audience, this story reflects a basic monastic (and ultimately Christian) priority of "participation rather than efficacy." Using this reference, Merton drove home the idea that compassionate participation with those who suffer is the primary monastic response of engagement, as it allows "divine mercy to strike across the tangle of ends and means set up by infidelity."

Merton expanded his portrayal of the monastic vocation, noting that over time in practice it often falls short of its ideals. Formally, monks are called to follow "inefficacious" means and behaviors, and this non-worldly mandate has even been canonized. For example, canon law initially exempted and then forbade monks from military service, supporting the idea that "strictly speaking, priests, monks and nuns [were to be] dedicated to nonviolence."[40] However, ever since Napoleon, the church had given in to conscription of clergy by modern states. They did so on the basis of "expediency"—which Merton pointed out was an older expression of the word "technique"—to the point of now accepting military service as a clerical obligation. In appealing to the virtue of a state mandate to "get in there and do your duty," the ecclesial authorities actually sought to "preserve clerical and Church privilege." To illustrate the extent to which this post-Napoleonic logic had altered views of modern clerical obligation during war and call for a higher ideal of faithful non-cooperation with evil, Merton invoked the case of Franz Jägerstätter, an Austrian layman who refused Nazi military service. His bishop, instead of supporting Jägerstätter's position, insisted

---

39. Massignon, "New Sacral," 3:799.

40. Forest, "Gethsemani Retreat"; Merton, "Notes for F.O.R. retreat"; Yoder, "Transcription of Original Notes by JHYoder," all refer to the exemption as canon #121 and the prohibition as canon #141. The canon code was revised in 1983 and these numbers no longer refer to these provisions. See *Libreria Editrice Vaticana,* 1917 Codex, for the references in place in 1964.

that military service was his religious duty. Jägerstätter was ultimately given a military trial and promptly beheaded.[41]

From here Merton picked up on the focal theme around which he centered his remaining comments as outlined: "Privilege" and "the privileged collectivity." This was a condition that "Must be seen against the background of *choice* and *exclusion, acceptance* and *refusal*." Under this rubric he plotted five sub-points to expand upon. The first of these addressed a privileged collectivity and the topic of greed in the Bible, which he linked to the Magnificat phrase initially jotted in his reading notes: *Deposuit potentes de sede,* or "[He] took down the mighty from their thrones." Merton, it would seem, was building a case that to be "privileged" was not necessarily a good thing. He found a "consistent mysterious pattern" within biblical examples of being chosen or rejected and excluded. Those who are chosen by God are often rejected by others, while those who are otherwise thought to be privileged are in the end "set aside." One example would be the assumed "privileged elder son," perhaps referring to the biblical story of Abraham exiling his firstborn son Ishmael into the desert and instead conferring his blessing upon his second son, Isaac.[42] Another example of the privileged but not chosen would be the Pharisees, who although numbered among the social elite were judged by Jesus "less worthy than the sinners."

The reverse also holds—those chosen by God are often rejected by the privileged. In this case, the divine chosenness of the Jews also meant a temporal Auschwitz, and Ishmael was also protected by God though rejected by his chosen people. On this point, Merton parenthetically conceded that it's easy for us to name such oppression as a sign of their chosenness. In contrast, we (presumably white, wealthy Christians) in our culture assume "we've got the good news—we are the last word, the final selection [who] deserve privilege and power"—that somehow God has chosen us more for a role of "privilege and even power than for service." We also assume our chosenness is irrevocable and infallible, that "we cannot again be rejected ourselves." Consequently, Merton asserted that we fail to "test our confessions for their truthfulness," perhaps recalling Massignon's views about Islamic challenges to the assumptions of privilege claimed by Christianity and Judaism. Merton's outline offers various other examples of this paradox of assumed privilege contradicted by God's actual choice and favor: "gentiles

41. Gordon C. Zahn was in the process of publishing his biography of Jägerstätter, *In Solitary Witness,* late in 1964. In early November Ferry told Merton he had copies of the book's galleys and would share them if he was interested. Ferry to Merton, 4 Nov. 1964, TMC.

42. Abraham's prayer for the survival of Ishmael and his descendents represents the second of Abraham's three prayers as addressed by Louis Massigonon.

and Jews, white and black, the 6% [that receive] 50+% of income [in the] US."

FIGURE 10. Thomas Merton's hermitage the week of the retreat.
Photograph by Jim Forest, courtesy of Boston College, John J. Burns Library.

In his speaking outline Merton inserted a marginal addition to this list that referenced "'*Cargo*'—the white and undeveloped." As with the "cargo" notation in his reading notebook, he alludes to industrialized Western whites and the underdeveloped of the world as embodied in South Pacific cargo cults. Their belief system associated material goods introduced by Western commerce (and especially excess World War II matériel that washed up on their shore) with acts of their deities. Although this cargo cult reference does not explicitly appear in notes taken of the presentation, Yoder captured comments that suggest Merton in fact mentioned the concept: "primitives expect a stranger to bring a gift from God," and "the underprivileged thinks of the privileged as a mediator." Jim Forest also noted comments on an "African" worldview that sees "the stranger" as somehow divine, someone we are called to go and greet. Yoder also noted that when discussing this topic Merton cited *The Dark Eye in Africa*, a book by the South African Laurens van der Post, who had spent time among indigenous Africans.[43] This work laments the failure of his own countrymen and Europeans in general to appreciate and embrace the intrinsic value of indigenous Africans' world view and their connection with mystery and nature. Relying on the power of myth and Jungian insights, van der Post saw in the West's rejection and domination of "primitive" African life a denial of its own need for those

43. Van der Post, *Dark Eye in Africa*.

traits to balance and make whole its one-sided obsession with rational economic and scientific progress. Merton had corresponded with the author
between 1959 and 1961, dedicating his 1961 book *Behavior of the Titans* to
van der Post.[44] Merton periodically referred to the book and author during
his last decade of life;[45] it seemingly played an important role in shaping
his own understanding of indigenous world views. Just a few months before the retreat, for example, Merton had used van der Post's concept of
the West's entry into Africa as that of a myopic "one-eyed giant" to open
his introductory essay on Mahatma Gandhi in *Gandhi on Non-Violence*.[46]
Then in writing his Aunt Kit more than two years after this gathering he
commented, "I am working along those lines [of van der Post's books on
Africa] a little myself: interested mostly in the religious-political messianic
movements, native Churches and whatnot. Especially in Melanesia though.
The Cargo cults, etc."[47] His allusions to the topic at the retreat suggest that
Merton included indigenous cultures, their expression of hospitality and
gift, and their encounters with Western intrusion as still another reflection
of the dichotomy between chosenness and rejection.

Merton's second point under "privilege" addressed the idea of "hope
and the deformation of hope," associating it with St. John of the Cross, for
whom "Christian hope is in the final stage a hope so strongly in God as to become a sort of despair with human means." In our pursuit of hope we are in
essence "seeking an opening" for what is good to break through. But Merton
asks whether we do so "after the manner of power or of 'water,'" which seeps
into openings on its own time and in its own way. Regarding the dangers in
deformation of hope, Merton cautioned that we not become "Christians in
a Kierkegaardian sense," which leads to dissolving our unique identity into
a popular mindset and causes us to "lose our right and capacity to protest."
We "despair of everything [we think we are] capable of realizing."[48] An essay
on Christian existentialism that Merton drafted the following year sheds

44. The Thomas Merton Center holds one letter from Merton to van der Post (18
Sept. 1959) and five letters from van der Post to Merton (between Oct. 1959 and Apr.
1961).

45. For example, see Merton, *DWL*,.4 Oct. 1959, 335, and 8 Nov. 1959, 341, as well
as letters to Dona Luisa Coomaraswamy (12 Feb. 1961, *HGL*, 129), Rachel Carson (12
Jan. 1963, *WF*, 71), and Helen Wolff (19 Feb. 1960, *CT*, 101).

46. Merton, "Gandhi and the One-Eyed Giant," 3–31 was dated April 1964; it footnoted *The Dark Eye in Africa* in reference to the phrase.

47. Merton to Agnes Gertrude Stonehewer Merton, 14 Aug. 1967, *RJ*, 82.

48. Yoder, "Transcription of Original Notes by JHYoder," indicates that Merton
referred to John of the Cross when he began speaking of hope as despair.

further light on his understanding of "Kierkegaardian" Christianity.[49] In it he draws on Kierkegaard's description of a "leveling" social process where, in Merton's words, an individual has "abdicated conscience, personal decision, choice, and responsibility, and yielded themselves to the joy of being part of a pure myth." In doing so, they have "surrendered into the public void."[50] He goes on to explain Kierkgaard's disdain for a Christianity that functions to manifest this public void and perpetuate the "abstract leveling" of human identity. As Merton described it, "Instead of obeying the Word and Spirit of God living and active in His Church . . . one surrenders at the same time one's human and one's religious integrity," which is a "spiritual disaster."[51] What Merton was most likely doing in this sequence, then, was connecting the "privileged" mindset of the modern Western church with Kierkegaard's lament of the Church's embrace of collective myths concocted from a public void that absorbs one's identity and integrity.[52]

The despair that accompanies an awareness of this dilemma can bring us into a more refined hope, however, one located deep within, in the place Massignon had named and that Merton now invoked for his listeners: our *point vierge*. To reach this point, we must be pushed into a realization of our own impotence and inadequacies. In his speaking outline Merton parenthetically wrote "China, Islam" next to the phrase, offering examples of those who had been penetrated and corrupted by the West and its imposed technological priorities. In naming China, which had just detonated its first atomic weapon the previous month, he alluded to a country pressured by the world's two atomic powers onto a nuclear path out of fear for its own survival. Regarding Islam, Yoder noted that Merton commented on "Saharan tribes' dereliction when pressed by technically superior 'Christian' civilization." This reference virtually assures that Merton had inserted or paraphrased Louis Massignon's mention of the *point vierge* that so thoroughly captivated him when he first encountered it in 1960: "Under pressure from a so-called Christian civilization, and technically superior, the Muslim faith reached the virginal point, the center of the soul, where despair corners the heart of the outsider." This phenomenon of "salvation through dereliction" is also a biblical pattern. Those who had been so rejected that they are

49. Merton, "The Other Side of Despair." Typescript draft dated 1965 in Box 2, Merton Papers, SUL.

50. Ibid., 264.

51. Ibid., 272.

52. Forest, "Gethsemani Retreat," also records an illustration by Merton of the absurdity of a Kierkegaardian Christian mindset that fails to test reality, where "we can say we're going to the North Pole and we go downstairs and walk around the block and we come back and say we've gone to the North Pole and that's it—you're infallible."

"pushed to the wall" may in fact be chosen by God. And it is this chosenness by God that animates a "Christian instinct [where we are] drawn toward the man at the wall, because if we identify with this man we find God and we find Christ" in our encounter with him. In reality we are all driven to the wall and in that sense chosen, though in practice that fact is hidden from those in the West and obscured by our privilege. But our ability to break through our blindness and identify with those pushed to the wall in effect "reminds us we are all that way."

FIGURE 11. Ping Ferry, Daniel Berrigan, and John Peter Grady during Thomas Merton's Wednesday afternoon session on "The Monastic Protest" at his hermitage.
Photograph by Jim Forest, courtesy of Boston College, John J. Burns Library.

Merton's outline next named five "privations": humanity, poverty, sickness, sleep, and death. Though not referenced in Merton's reading notes, this list had appeared in yet another *Opera Minora* essay by Massignon titled, "The Meaning of the Last Pilgrimage of Gandhi." There the list is credited to a Shiite scholar named Khasibi, and Massignon viewed them as five conditions where an "instinct of the sacred that alerts us to the divine visitation" becomes awakened.[53] Merton related them to the significance of "reciprocity in spirit" and "participation in the personal life" of those who despair, a participation that we cannot evade with our paternalism over others. This is a genuine reciprocity based in true liberty, not simply falling back on "doctrinaire attitudes on liberty" or "trusting in legalism and mechanism." Rather Merton called for trust in "the unplanned encounter, risk, and breakthrough given by God," citing Massignon's "Mark of the 'spiritual encounter'" and alluding to Massignon's encounter with God as a "visitation of the stranger."

53. Marcel, "Life and the Sacred," 116.

This phrasing from his speaking outline did not appear in the notes of Yoder or Forest, however, and it appears that the direction he took the ideas of reciprocity, liberty, and spiritual encounter in the flow of his presentation focused more on avoiding legalism, particularly within the church. "There's too much religion and not enough God," Merton complained, and it has become "a matter of life and death." Our call is not one of "bolstering up religion but surrendering to God," adding that, "In the monastery we've got lots of religion and that's the trouble with the place." This image of too much religion resonated strongly with Elbert Jean, whose experiences surrounding the Little Rock school integration ordeal had fostered considerable disillusionment with the institutional church. As Yoder recorded, Jean injected comments at this point that support our need for "freedom from religion" and assert that "liberty is a mess of pottage" and "Protestants have become Johnny come lately Catholics." The mention of "pottage" alludes to Esau selling his birthright for a meal of stew, a euphemism for giving up something of great value for something lesser. What Jean communicated suggests the idea that the freedom Protestants historically claim today has been sold out for their own versions of legalism.

Merton's outline continues with a third point under the topic of "privilege," which he names "Judgment of the privileged," indicating that "to have privilege is to be under judgment." He then asks, "Can one use one's privilege to heal others?" and answers, "Not if one's privilege blinds one to relationship with others" and seeks only to paternalistically give to them. It mirrors essentially the same question in his reading notebook where he answered the question a bit differently, asserting that it is more important to detach from privilege to embrace the higher value of sharing others' suffering than to try to heal them. Paraphrasing the quotation he had copied into his notebook from "The Three Prayers of Abraham," Merton asserted that the judgment upon privilege is that it "fossilizes," and therefore, "*We cannot rely on the witness of a privileged collectivity.*" What comes through from the notes of listeners is that "we Christians are a privileged collectivity" who are "white and prosperous and [assume] we've got the right religion." We also suffer from "the illusion that we have everything to give and nothing to receive." In reality, though, "The Negro is offering us salvation, and we're not offering [it to] him." This comment echoes sentiments expressed in Merton's 1960 letter to Herbert Mason in which he interpreted the statue of an indigenous Virgin Mother with Child as offering to us the fruit of salvation.

The concept of our "fossilization," inspired by the Massignon passage from "The Three Prayers of Abraham" and captured in Merton's reading notebook, also comes through clearly in listeners' notes at the retreat. They also suggest that Merton linked this idea to the dangers of spiritual blindness he had raised at the outset. Daniel Berrigan recorded that our "position of privilege has blinded us to the fact that the lost save the saved, who in fact are lost. Privilege fossilizes; the fact of privilege means we need help the most, we persist in [our] most perilous position." Yoder phrased it that our privilege "makes us responsible to the nonprivileged, but it also makes us blind to what we get from them," just as Isaiah called his own people "blind and deaf." Forest added that an awareness of our own fossilization prevents us from being "in a position to feel secure."

Merton seems not to have lingered on the fourth sub-point in his outline, which highlighted "the privilege of Abraham." The patriarch's ultimate privilege before God did not derive from being "visited by the three Angels," but was grounded in his ability to "believe there were ten just men in Sodom"—the object of his first prayer. In comparison to Abraham, "What is our capacity to find the good among the 'worst' or hopeless? Can we plead for the just men among them?" Merton thought not: "in a certain sense we're the poorest [in] our capacity to really find the good."

FIGURE 12. Thomas Merton delivering his talk on "The Monastic Protest."
Photograph by Jim Forest, courtesy of Boston College, John J. Burns Library.

Merton's fifth and final sub-point comes through strongly, however, explicitly referenced by Yoder as "Massignon on the notion of substitution." In his outline, Merton had cited two forms of substitution, one for the "innocent victim" and another for the "oppressor" or the "enemy." He also invoked the name of Massignon's Muslim/Christian prayer sodality, the "*Badaliya*"—a term that for Massignon "bespeaks a form of mystical substitution of one person and his merits and prayers for the salvation of someone else."[54] Merton's outline also associated it with "substitution for captives" and of "the ram for Isaac" as well as "the paschal lamb—Christ." Substitution involves "prayer centered on [the] graces necessary for [the good of the] rival, the spiritual good of the 'opposition.'" In the retreatants' immediate context, Merton noted, this might mean prayer for those to the right of the social and political spectrum. He added in his speaking outline a quote proclaiming that, "No one is truly a believer until he prefers for his brother what he prefers for himself," and though unattributed by Merton, it closely matches a saying some Muslims attribute to the Prophet Muhammad.[55] Merton followed this with a further explanation of the essence of mystical substitution: "*Presenting oneself in the place of others before the judgment of God*," adding that it is accomplished "by taking upon oneself [the] consequences of their sin—their anger and hate." He ended this point and his outline as a whole with a parenthetical note, "yet the comedy of this is Catholics and (Chinese) communists." Notes of his presentation fail to explain the nature of this comedy, but perhaps it alludes to judgmental opposition toward communism promoted by the church, a contrast to offering oneself in place of another before God's judgment and conveying the matter into God's hands.

When Merton presented the idea of substitution to the retreatants he addressed the mystical nature of substitution, citing it as a "Jewish and biblical idea [where] one gives himself to free others, the innocent, the poor, etc. and also for the enemy." But Merton advocated more literal expressions of it, as well. Yoder recorded Merton's recounting of how medieval monastic orders would take the place of victims, citing St. Vincent de Paul, who "substituted for prisoners in Algeria." It is a call to "stand in for the victim but also the oppressor" choosing to "bear the burden of his sin" because one way or another, "we will have to do it anyway."[56] Yoder also recorded Merton's attempt to apply this idea to Jewish suffering in the Holocaust, insinuating that it was not their sacrificial choice to enter that horror but

54. Griffith, "Challenge of Islam," 157.

55. From Islamic hadith, Sunni collections of the Prophet's sayings compiled from oral tradition in the ninth century. Hashimi, "The Muslim and His Friends," 7, quoted it as: "None of you truly believes until he likes for his brother what he likes for himself."

56. Most stories describe de Paul as being kidnapped by pirates, sold into slavery in Tunis, and later escaping with his master after converting him. Though de Paul's "substitution" does not sound literal, it would fit as an illustration of taking sins of an oppressor on one's self in a mystical sense for their salvation.

was beyond their control: the "Jews could not avoid Auschwitz." The only thing "they could choose was to die for Sin" perpetrated by others. Yoder then cryptically added, "Only by our bearing this sin could we choose to Jerusalemize technique," no doubt suggesting that the only way to redeem such horrid outcomes of our modern, efficient, technical logic is to assume the burden of its consequences upon ourselves, as Christ had done through his crucifixion in Jerusalem. Berrigan's comments support this idea, phrasing it, "Technology may inaugurate the new earth if we can take the sin on ourselves as a result of history." Forest captured a rather similar sentiment from this section of Merton's presentation, but one with a different contemporary focus, one emphasizing how our modern, technological society makes it quite difficult to enact the substitutionary ideal. He recorded that "the technique of social living would make it impossible to become a worker in a Chinese factory or a prisoner by exchange in Cuba" and thereby to either "take upon oneself the sin of the enemy" or realize a "willingness to take upon [ones'] self the sin of a particular society."

With his return to the implications of a technological society, Merton had come full circle in his presentation. Yoder further noted that Merton expressed agreement with a perspective of Massignon and of Jean Danielou as over "against Mounier" that was published in *Dieu vivant*. Yoder's comment gives no real hint what that perspective might be, but it surely pertains to the gist of "A New Sacral" from which Merton quoted in both his journal and his reading notebook. Daniel Berrigan's record confirms this, sharing a paraphrased summary of that quote: "God does not occupy us from outside. In what way could we call ourselves his collaborator?" Massignon's essay makes no mention of Danielou, but Danielou had also contributed to *Dieu vivant* and was a personal friend of Massignon who held sympathetic views and lived next door to him in the late fifties. Danielou also served as a confessor of sorts for Merton, and corresponded with him.[57] How he fits into this point of Merton's fails to emerge in the retreat sources. But here Merton had found another opportunity to drive home the relationship of his newly strengthened skepticism of modern technological priorities to his own vocational priority of mystical and transcendent connection with others, making it clear that the former inhibited the latter.

Rather than ending here, though, Merton closed by referencing Massignon's essay on Islam's "Rights of the Human Person" to which he had devoted two of his working notebook pages. From it he shared with his colleagues that Islam grants a higher priority to the "right of asylum" or "welcome" or "at least sanctuary" of the enemy than to the principle of "just war" or

---

57. Herbert Mason, 17 Feb. 2013, email to author.

"jihad" when that enemy is a foreigner in their land. This perspective offers "an index of Islam's 'respect for the person.'"

What becomes clear in reviewing these fragmentary snapshots of Merton's talk that afternoon, is that his actual presentation did rely heavily on the material of Louis Massignon that he had read. Merton often channeled Massignon's spirit and priorities in his comments to these Christian peacemakers. A central aspect of that spirit involved not just advocating on behalf of the oppressed, but entering their world and assuming their posture as rejected and despised. One could not sustain this posture while holding onto power, a state that fossilizes hearts and induces blindness. The path to our salvation in fact requires humble encounters with the rejected, the enemy, the stranger. We the wealthy, Western, Christian privileged collectivity need them both for our own salvation and for gaining integrity in our expressions of protest. This integrity requires our willingness to substitute not only for the oppressed, however, but to express equal concern and sacrifice for the oppressor. Though perhaps not stated as explicitly as in his notebook outline, Merton's initial conclusion came through strongly—the "real roots" of protest are planted in our identification with the underprivileged as an epiphany and intercessory for us, and with refusal of our own privilege and denunciation of the arrogance expressed by those who retain theirs.

Responses to The Monastic Protest

When Merton ended his prepared comments and opened a time of discussion, his suggestion that dereliction or rejection might ultimately prove virtuous sparked the initial interchange.[58] Some Protestant participants seemed not to resonate with the mystical underpinnings of Merton's approach to those abandoned and rejected, wondering if it might not devalue pragmatic, positive action. Ping Ferry began by asking whether rejection guarantees that God will automatically assume responsibility for outcomes. We as humans can respond to conditions of poverty in three ways, he noted. We can see it as a blessing—"a vehicle of salvation"; as a challenge to do welfare work—"we can't let the nuisances die [but we must] keep it out of sight"; or we can see it as a challenge to pursue justice. Elbert Jean followed, asking whether despair is really bad if the God who "judges"—who "assigns us to dereliction"—is love, adding that, "From this base I cannot get to empathy." Perhaps he alluded to the paradox of viewing suffering as both a calling to accept for ourselves but, when imposed on others, an evil that evokes

58. Except for a couple of comments Forest added to his notes, only Yoder kept extensive notes of this discussion.

empathy and action to overcome it. Merton responded that he presupposed "the Grace of being a Christian" would permit us to embrace this dynamic without despair. Jean then asked, "Is our privileged state what it means to be a Christian? Or a fringe benefit?" He suggested that our first recourse would not automatically be "projecting program" to impose standard solutions, but rather to "wait for Pentecost" to inspire spirit-led responses. Merton replied to Jean that although there may be some "programmatic constants" we might fall back on, he agreed we also need to "hear again daily" the call of Pentecost.

FIGURE 13. Charlie Ring, Bob Cunnane, Philip Berrigan, and Tony Walsh (face hidden behind fireplace) during Thomas Merton's Wednesday afternoon session on "The Monastic Protest" at his hermitage.
Photograph by Jim Forest, courtesy of Boston College, John J. Burns Library.

John Nelson's comments next helped guide the conversation toward the realm of civil disobedience and a likelihood of conflict with authority. "If all we take to jail is our questioning," he asked, "then what is it that transforms? Is our witness just [our] being there? Or is [being there] a winding-up for a credible witness later?" He felt that to have integrity, true rejection by the establishment was something suffered because of who we are, not because we challenge the circumstances of someone else. Regarding that question, Tony Walsh suggested that in taking on suffering we influence others and he referred to some aspect of the Peace Corps as an example.

When Ferry rhetorically asked "what good did it do" to suffer for another, Muste weighed in, asking "What of it" if no obvious good was attained? "Jesus was no [apparent] success. But we must will that conditions change and be involved." He added that, "I must to all I can," which might include using instruments of power, so long as I remain attentive to the humanity of those I try to influence. Muste went on to emphasize that even those rejected are accountable to God for their responses: "The black supremacy demand is not right just because the black has his back to the wall. The one against the wall is thereby chosen and thereby under judgment," as well.

Ferry continued to goad, calling for effective actions of global impact. "What good is a pilgrimage to China except for a few? [The Russian dissident poet] Yevtushenko has more effect on people than a disarmament conference. Our age is hungry for internationalism." Yoder's notes are not clear on who spoke next, but someone offered the example of Quakers as a model for progression from rejection to activism—they went to jail in the seventeenth century and now perform relief work and lobby for legislation.[59] Muste injected the example of the first Christian martyr Stephen, against whom "authorities including Saul 'gnashed their teeth' . . . but were also 'touched in their hearts.' . . . The result of Stephen's Martyrdom was unexpected."[60]

Daniel Berrigan next entered the conversation. He furthered an emphasis on abandoning control over outcomes by emphasizing that despair might ultimately prove virtuous. "Despair is a form of hope. Can one have hope in God but despair of history?" What is the basis for affirming "the possibility of using human means to work for good? Merton can despair of good causes leading to good effects. Jägerstätter did." Berrigan seems to have been reinforcing Merton's reflection on St. John of the Cross, saying there is an aspect of giving up on accomplishing human objectives that ultimately recognizes outcomes remain in the hands of God, and that very act of relinquishing control expresses hope that God will indeed guide history. Yoder failed to attribute a string of observations that followed, but he later speculated they may have been Merton's. They all generally support the assertion that hope can indeed emerge from despair. A reference to Teilhard de Chardin coupled with support for despair as placing control with God, however, hints at continuation of Daniel Berrigan's comments. The first of

59. Yoder, "Transcription of Original Notes by JHYoder," suggests the speaker attributed the comments to church historian Roland Bainton, a colleague of John Nelson at Yale.

60. The story of Stephen, the first Christian martyr, is in Acts 7:54–60. Stephen was stoned as a young Saul of Tarsus, the future Apostle Paul, tended to the cloaks of the men who stoned him.

these suggested that Julian of Norwich's famous reassurance of "'all will be well' means that Jesus has a secret answer to hell." Likewise, the philosophy of Teilhard de Chardin suggests that "the good outcome is possible but not revealed." Confronting the logic of Marxism can also be the source of "the Christians' hope." An obscure and cryptic reference to Tennessee Williams followed, noting that "it took fundamentalism and neo-orthodoxy to enable" the playwright, followed by the phrase, "deeper then higher." This may have referred to the profound angst created by Williams's personal struggles and their relationship to his creative output. Another phrase in this series, "Neo-Protestantism has known despair," could allude to the role of modern life and questions of meaning with which twentieth-century theologians often grappled, prompting new theological insight. The final statement in this string, however, added a voice of caution as we seek hope through our veil of despair: "The trapdoor to Hell is just in front of the gate to heaven."

On that note, Ping Ferry chimed in to once more steer the conversation toward matters of technology asking, "Can we get Man to be moral with his capacities? Technology is not neutral but questionable." Then, encouraging his colleagues to probe the question more deeply on their own, Ferry offered to provide anyone interested with a copy of Ellul's *The Technological Society*. But not all were convinced that such a view of modern society held the last word. John Nelson followed Ferry's offer by suggesting that a more optimistic take on modern technique might be gained from Gibson Winter in *Creation as Metropolis*, which sought application of social science methods toward urban renewal and Christendom's service to the poor and minorities who remained there. In response to both, Merton offered that "some of us think our civilization is at the end of its rope, but there is new hope in China, Africa." This referred back to a notation in his speaking outline he placed under the theme of "Hope" and associated with Massignon's *"point vierge."* It reminded his listeners to look for hope to those who push back against western penetration and domination, rather than idolize Western technocracy as the source of our hope. Jean countered with his own response to Ferry's critique of its neutrality by agreeing that no, "technology is not neutral—when I want to get home I am glad the busses run," suggesting that it is in fact beneficial. Perhaps this exchange on the pervasive power of technique inspired the final note from this session that Jim Forest recorded: "We're treating the cybernetic society as if it were [the] empire of Charlemagne."

As the discussion neared closure, Nelson returned to Ferry's earlier challenge of "what good did it do" to enter into and challenge the suffering of others. Nelson apparently favored the power of interpersonal influence more than direct service or confrontation. "What good did the Catholic

Worker do?" he asked. "It trained [socialist activist and SDS leader] Michael Harrington, helped some Puerto Ricans. What good did the Yale students do who went to the Mississippi Delta project?" a likely reference to the Freedom Summer campaign of recent months. "What good did the WWII CO's do who went to Civilian Public Service." Nelson then challenged, "Compare [their impact] to the way John Wesley changed society." In converting and sanctifying individuals, one "reduplicates himself and all those persons go out" into society and make a difference. In defense of Catholic Worker service, Jim Forest countered Nelson's assertion. "It would be absurd to expect Bowery people to pull themselves up by their own bootstraps" after their conversion as Wesley might expect. "The ministries of the Catholic Worker are expiation for society." In contrast to Wesley's emphasis on personal change, Forest offered counterexamples of meeting material needs as a vehicle for transformation. "The Brethren of the Common Life[61] would have remade them in houses. [The past year in England], Anton Wallich-Clifford[62] developed villages for the socially inadequate, like houses of hospitality, with money from [the British charity] Christian Action." And with Forest's discourse on works of mercy, Yoder's own notes of the afternoon's discussion also end.

Their time on the wooded hillside was not yet finished, however. To round out their first day of dialogue, Merton's guests also took time to unwind and play. Ten years later Tom Cornell would recount that while "Jim Forest went out to the woods with a Berrigan [Daniel] for confession; the other Berrigan [Philip] went for two cases of beer" in the trunk of the car he and John Grady had driven. Upon his return, "the Protestants, A. J. included, looked with bewildered condescension on the Catholics in the holy hermit's [privy-less] hut swilling down their beer, belly-laughing and running out to the trees for relief."[63] Perhaps in deference to his Protestant guests, Merton refrained from imbibing, however, despite his well-known love for beer.[64] Eventually, as the afternoon ended, they made their way back to the retreat house for their evening meal, more informal conversation for those inclined, and a night's well-deserved rest.

61. A fourteenth-century lay movement that created religious communities where all shared material life in common.

62. Wallich-Clifford was a CPF sponsor in 1964. He had previously served as London's chief probation officer but had developed the Simon Community Trust in 1963 as an ecumenical Christian effort to develop housing for the underclass and homeless communities ("The Catholic Peace Fellowship, A Memorandum," D/32, FOR Records, SCPC).

63. Cornell, "Merton on Peace," 23.

64. Cornell, 13 Apr. 2010, email to author.

FIGURE 14. Charlie Ring (standing), Bob Cunnane, Philip Berrigan,
and Tony Walsh prepare to enjoy some beer at the hermitage following
Thomas Merton's Wednesday afternoon presentation.
Photograph by Jim Forest, courtesy of Boston College, John J. Burns Library.

Their first day had granted the retreat a heady kickoff. They had shared
openly together, not always agreeing, but genuinely listening to each other.
As Bob Cunnane remembered it, the men "had great respect for one another; no one seemed to dominate . . . There was fun and laughter, but serious realism, as well."[65] And in many respects, it had also been Merton's day.
The themes spread over fourteen pages of his reading notebook in the days
leading up to the event reverberated through Wednesday's conversation. He
and Ferry had succeeded at weaving into their exchange questions about the
challenges and contradictions of technology and technique's domination of
Western society. The ideas that permeated his notes from Massignon's readings about our privileged status, the call to detach from them, and the need
to identify with the underprivileged held sway over much of their closing
discussion. This opening day had encouraged a tone of humility and caution
regarding one's ability to calculate and achieve the ends they sought in their
protest. Likewise, they heard skepticism about their ability to engage social
ills from a high ground of moral superiority, free of deep entanglements
with the social dysfunctions they protested.

65. Cunnane, 17 Apr. 2010, email to author.

But the day's conversation had also affirmed their warrant to protest as something inherent, something that came from within and represented an expression of their personhood, their humanity. To protest was to respond in harmony with the Creator's intent for creation. They had also grappled with other aspects of their activity, such as one's willingness to release assumptions of effectiveness into the hands of God and an ability to balance transforming material conditions with transforming individual hearts. In the end, one's life situation and daily practice can itself embody protest, whether through monastic withdrawal, mystical substitution, participation in suffering, or a posture of visible rejection and abandonment. Living by terms the powerful set and adopting their calculations of effectiveness may send us through the trapdoor to hell rather than the gateway to heaven. On the other hand, is it enough simply for one's "being" to speak as a protest, while otherwise passively waiting for "Pentecost"? When faced with forces that dehumanize and usurp our personhood, should we not also plan and act, however imperfect and incomplete? If so, what actions are valid options in a society where a pervasive technological presence turns our best intentions on their heads and impresses them into its own self-legitimizing service rather than service to humanity?

Though it had unveiled numerous questions like these, their fellowship had not provided clear answers as the sun set on Gethsmani that evening. After all, their time together was intended not so much to gain answers as to draw upon spiritual roots together—to turn toward one another for insight, understanding, and strength when the formal structures around them seemed to obscure their questions more than clarify them. They had certainly made good headway toward that end, it would seem. But in an era when church boundaries remained rigid, could this experience of communing to tap a common spirituality of protest also embrace common spiritual *practice*? They would find out the next morning as they gathered for Mass.

5

Day Two—Christ and His Church in Protest

EARLY THE FOLLOWING MORNING, the Gethsemani retreatants gathered to prepare for worship. Guided by their host, they exited the north end of the retreat house, passed through the abbey church, and entered a silent cloister hallway. Several turns later and up another flight of stairs they emerged into a small chapel that jutted from the northernmost wall of the enclosed structure. Gethsemani's monks had added the chapel some years earlier to better accommodate their resident novices, whose ranks had swelled considerably during the past decades. The addition included two stories, with a meeting room comprising the first floor and the chapel occupying the second. This morning, however, only Merton's guests were present to share their first common worship experience.[1]

Thursday's Memorable Mass

Despite their calling as peacemakers to embody the reconciliation of Christ, their formal religious affiliations nonetheless betrayed the continuing human brokenness of Christ's body—even the Protestant groups represented that morning rejected "open" communion beyond their own denominational boundaries. Worship together had been discussed in their opening session the day before, and Merton had conferred to Daniel Berrigan the responsibility for officiating at the Mass. Merton had apparently also communicated to some of the Catholics that his abbot required any Mass involving the entire group to preclude the Protestants from participation in the Eucharist. The following morning, as Merton and Berrigan conversed about

1. Chapter opening based on details from Merton, *DWL*, 19 Nov. 1964, 167; Br. Patrick Hart and Fr. James Conner, 3 Nov. 2012, conversations with author; Cunnane, 15 Apr. 2010, letter to author.

worship details before they began, the monk's discomfort visibly grew, and he suggested that Berrigan's plans might take the celebration a bit too far.[2] Ultimately, though, he left details to the Jesuit's own discretion. Bob Cunnane recalled that their conversation ended with Merton saying, "'Whoa, you do what you want.' It wasn't nasty," Cunnane assured, "just, 'Whoa, I'm not going to be responsible for it. You do what you want.'"[3]

In the end, though Berrigan chafed, he agreed to limit distribution of the elements to Catholics. As he later recalled, "In fact, there was nothing else to do: we were guests," adding that, "Besides, the prohibition was no great departure from standard discourtesy."[4] But Berrigan made the best of options remaining. He would distribute the elements in both kinds (bread and wine) and offer the liturgy in English, a rarity in days prior to the Second Vatican Council that was just wrapping up its third of four annual sessions. Berrigan asked Presbyterian John Nelson to read the Gospel passage and Quaker A. J. Muste to read the epistle during Mass. As told by Ping Ferry, Merton had asked him the night before to share a homily. Reluctantly, Ferry stayed up late agonizing over its preparation. As they walked through the passages to the chapel that morning, Merton second-guessed assigning it to a Protestant. "If the Abbot ever heard that you had done the homily," Ferry recalled Merton saying, "there would just be hell to pay. I'd never hear the end of it," indicating he would do it himself.[5] Forest also remembered that Merton had given the homily.[6]

As the Mass progressed that morning and it came time to offer prayers for the living and the dead, Berrigan gathered them around the altar and invited others to add names to those he mentioned, also an innovation for that era.[7] Jim Forest used the opportunity to invite prayers for the monks of Gethsemani.[8] Berrigan next began to initiate the rite of Communion, apparently beginning with his brother Philip. Philip had not been a party to conversations about limiting the Eucharist, however, having missed Wednesday's opening session. The previous day he and John Grady had arrived via car. Grady had delayed his departure as long as possible to assure that his six-year-old son remained stable following head surgery that

2. Yoder to R. Daggy, 2 June 1995, 3, Yoder Papers, TMC; Yoder, "Background and editorial comments," printout fall 1994, 2, Yoder Papers, TMC.

3. Cunanne, 31 May 2010, conversation with author.

4. Berrigan, *Portraits*, 16.

5. Ferry, 210–11.

6. Forest, 29 May 2010, conversation with author.

7. Merton, *DWL*, 19 Nov. 1964, 167; Berrigan, *Portraits*, 16.

8. Merton, recording 132:1, 22 Nov. 1964, TMC.

stemmed from a fractured skull after being struck by an auto.⁹ The younger
Berrigan undoubtedly changed his original air travel plans in order to accompany Grady. According to his brother Daniel, Philip Berrigan was
characteristically "burdened with few native inhibitions,"¹⁰ and as he approached the altar that morning he instinctively began "passing the bread
and inviting everybody present to pour the cup."¹¹ In turn, all—even the
Unitarian Ping Ferry—accepted both.¹² As it happened, then, "Everybody
received communion together in spite of [the abbot's] absurd order."¹³ And
so, in Daniel's later words: "*Sic solvitur.*"¹⁴

**FIGURE 15. Exterior of Gethsemani Abbey showing the novitiate chapel where
Thursday morning Mass was held.**
Photograph courtesy of the Abbey of Gethsemani.

9. D. Berrigan to Heidbrink, 16 Oct. 1964, D/37, FOR Records, SCPC.

10. Berrigan, *Portraits*, 16.

11. Berrigan, "Berrigan on Merton," 6.

12. Cornell, 29 Mar. 2010, conversation with author.

13. Berrigan, "Berrigan on Merton," 6.

14. Berrigan, *Testimony*, 104. Berrigan translates "*Sic solvitur*" as "thus was the
matter resolved." Details of Philip Berrigan's arrival and involvement remain unclear.
Of Daniel Berrigan's three published accounts (1973, 1982, 2004) only the 2004 account attributes Philip's late arrival at Mass explicitly to an overnight drive. Berrigan's
1982 account indicates Philip arrived late (whether to the Eucharist or the abbey is
unclear) with "another priest." His 1973 account said he arrived late for the Eucharist.
All three relate the late arrival to his failure to hear instructions, though no surviving
participants today recall such instructions. Photographs from Wednesday afternoon
show Phil Berrigan present by then. He perhaps arrived Wednesday after the morning
session. Fatigue from his drive may have contributed to late arrival at the next morning's Mass.

Regarding Daniel Berrigan's ambivalence about excluding the Protestant guests, fellow priest Bob Cunnane shared, "I felt the same way . . . It's pretty hard to invite someone and say, 'Okay, you're here, but you're not here.'" In fact to the appearances of some, the elder Berrigan had intended it all along. To Yoder it appeared that once Berrigan received the assignment, he essentially "took over on his own terms."[15] For Cunnane, who knew of other occasions when Daniel Berrigan had offered the Eucharist to non-Catholics—and who had in fact done so himself on occasion—"it seemed right to me at the time, and I wasn't surprised by it. In fact, I would have been surprised if Dan had excluded them." But he understood the dilemma and sympathized with Merton, who he knew felt tension with his abbot and who, Cunnane sensed, "kind of made believe he didn't see, like 'don't ask, don't tell.'"[16] Jim Forest recalled his surprise that all took communion, but neither did he see it as out of character for a Mass led by Berrigan. "Dan was very uncomfortable with the idea of closed communion. I used to take part in very small private Masses that he did in his apartment with the Jesuits. He got in trouble with his superiors at the Jesuits because of the informal masses he was doing." Forest also assumed Berrigan had intended an inclusive event from the start. "Presumably if we were not all going to receive communion, he would go to some length to explain what the reason was, and I don't remember any explanation."[17]

In retrospect, the moment seemed almost divinely orchestrated, a blessing upon their quest, perhaps. Why else would this narrow window for all fourteen to assemble as one coalesce around this inclusive Eucharist? Wednesday's late arrival by Philip Berrigan and John Grady would be followed on Thursday morning by the departure of John Nelson to catch his noon flight from the Louisville airport, and Ping Ferry would also need to leave later on Thursday, prior to Friday morning's session. As Daniel Berrigan recognized, their communion together was "a moment of great truth and insight for us all." He would later recall that after they finished, Yoder approached him to comment that "if it's that simple, sign me up." Muste, he noted, "in a rather more quiet way echoed the same sentiments."[18] Cunnane concurred. "It was very interesting to me that when people were invited like that to take communion, it seemed they took it as a great privilege, like it really meant a lot to them."[19]

15. Yoder, "Background and editorial comment," fall 1994, Yoder Papers, TMC.

16. Cunnane, 31 May 2010, conversation with author.

17. Forest, 29 May 2010, conversation with author.

18. Berrigan, "Berrigan on Merton," 6.

19. Cunanne, 31 May 2010, conversation with author.

For Merton, reflecting that night in his journal, it had unfolded as a "way-out Mass . . . yet it was beautiful too . . . Dan's celebration of the sacrificial liturgy was simple and impressive. All in English and 'uncanonical' even to the extreme point not only of Communion in both kinds but Communion to the Protestants!!"[20] Merton's discomfort with the boundaries that had been tested lingered even after his guests had departed.[21] The following Sunday, when confiding to his novices about the Mass, Merton chuckled that despite finding certain aspects quite meaningful, "some of the other things I'm a little doubtful about"—without explicitly mentioning to them that Protestants had partaken of the elements. When coupled with other Eucharistic innovations of Berrigan's, such as saying Mass around a table in homes, Merton joked that he would not be surprised "if Dan Berrigan suddenly disappears in the Castel Sant'Angelo," a papal fortress used on occasion as a prison.[22]

Following Mass the party made their way back through the monastery and church to the retreat house. The abbey church they passed through differed dramatically from its current appearance. Originally constructed in an ornate gothic style, it featured faux plaster arches and vaulting, with dark Munich-style stained glass windows. Following Vatican II, this structure underwent a major renovation, completed in 1967. The finished work would reveal the structure's original simple brick walls and wooden roof beams and provide brighter, more contemporary windows. As one historian of the abbey put it, these renovations symbolically, "reflected liturgical reforms taking place contemporaneously in the church. The bywords of [the architect's] redesign were 'light, clarity and simplicity'—basic elements of Cistercian spirituality, but also terms that were gaining cachet as the spirit of the Second Vatican Council began to act upon the broader Catholic consciousness . . . It's impossible not to see this time of tearing down and rebuilding as a metaphor for what was happening within the Catholic Church itself at the time."[23] In some very real ways, events that transpired during this brief 1964 interfaith sojourn could also be said to anticipate that figurative renovation of Roman Catholic and monastic relationships to the surrounding world.

Because of continuing rain, the group opted to remain within the monastery compound rather than attempt a wet and muddy trek back to Merton's hermitage, and once more they prepared to gather in the abbey gatehouse. Like the novitiate chapel, the gatehouse no longer stands today,

20. Merton, *DWL*, 19 Nov. 1964, 167.

21. Berrigan, "Berrigan on Merton," 6.

22. Merton, recording 132:1, 22 Nov. 1964, TMC.

23. Aprile, *Abbey of Gethsemani*, 162–65.

but it originally comprised the cloister's southern boundary and provided
the main point of entry into the monastic enclosure. This long, rectangu-
lar, one-story building was constructed with textured concrete blocks that
lent the appearance of a stone structure. It was built in 1911 as a fireproof
replacement of its predecessor, which had burnt to the ground the previous
year. A large wooden double-sided entry door was positioned at the center,
standing between two columns under an arch inscribed with the greeting
"*Pax Intrantibus*," or "Peace to those who enter." The space to the right side
of the door as one entered from the south housed a small sleeping area for
one or two porters who attended to whoever appeared at the gatehouse
door. The large abbey postal center consumed the remaining space behind
the porters' chamber. To the left of the entryway the monks positioned a
small, plain store where abbey farm products like cheese, bread, honey,
and dried meats were sold, along with some books. The space farther to
the left, behind the store, had once served as a museum to display the array
of objects that former abbot Dom Edmond Obrecht had collected from his
many travels during the early 1900s. By 1964 the museum space had been
remodeled into three meeting rooms that provided the monks a place to
receive family and other guests in privacy for conversation. A corridor with
a washroom at its far end connected these rooms.[24]

Visitors gained access to the monastery retreat house by way of a
sidewalk on the enclosure's interior leading from the gatehouse through a
small courtyard garden and over an elevated bridge that led to the retreat
house door. The bridge spanned a sunken pathway for use by those arriving from the surrounding community to worship with the monks. This
pathway provided access from the tree-lined driveway and through a lay
cemetery to broad steps leading up into the abbey church. That morning
as the men exited the retreat house once again—this time at its southern
end—they crossed over the bridge and trod along the courtyard sidewalk to
enter the gatehouse from within the enclosure. Once inside the gatehouse,
they followed the corridor to the farthest, corner meeting room, which was
also the largest of the three and the site of all their gatehouse discussions.
It had windows on two of four walls and was furnished with lamps, potted
plants, padded chairs and couches along its perimeter. End tables sat next
to the seating and couple of small coffee tables were scattered in the middle.
A large abstract painting hung on the north wall. As Jim Forest recalled,
"The gatehouse room was big enough for the space needs of our small
group— but of course I preferred (no doubt we all preferred) the hermitage,

24. Ibid., 122; Br. Patrick Hart, 17 Apr. 2010 and 3 Nov. 2012, conversations with
author; Fr. James Conner, 17 Apr. 2010 and 3 Nov. 2012, conversations with author.

not only because it was more spacious but it had a more intimate, homey atmosphere." As the session was starting that morning, the abbot's personal secretary, Brother Simon,[25] brought a package just received in the gatehouse postal center that contained copies of Merton's newly released book, *Seeds of Destruction*. In a gesture of affection and friendship, Merton congenially autographed and distributed a copy to each. When it came time to begin, they found their places in the circle of available seating and settled in to hear what perspectives Daniel Berrigan might offer for discussion.[26]

Daniel Berrigan—The Risen Christ and the Church of Protest

Although Merton's mimeographed handout suggested that A. J. Muste might lead the Thursday morning slot, Daniel Berrigan assumed that responsibility, instead. Merton had encouraged him to "take any angle you like" in preparing to lead one of their discussion sessions. Berrigan chose, it seems, to focus not so much on protest in particular, but to elaborate more broadly on the Catholic Church and its engagement of the world. He had ruminated and written on this relationship between Catholicism and the world for some time. His experiences confronting real world poverty and other ills, as well as his interactions with insightful and dedicated laity, seemingly convinced him that his church had room for spiritual expansion. His reading of the Jesuit paleontologist Teilhard de Chardin encouraged him to look toward human development broadly understood as a source of revelation and insight from which the church might learn.

Berrigan's first book of non-poetry, *The Bride: Essays in the Church*, published in 1959, broached the topic of how church tradition interfaced with history during an era when science best explained human experience. "The task of theology," he wrote in the book's introduction, "is . . . to show the Church's compatibility with the life and action of the new world; to assert again a respect for the human uses of matter and the way in which human effort can be gathered into the Divine synthesis made known in Christ and

25. Within about a year of the retreat, Brother Simon would revert to his baptismal name of Patrick Hart, as encouraged by the Second Vatican Council. He later became secretary to Merton shortly before Merton's 1968 death (Hart, 5 Nov. 2012, email to author).

26. Br. Patrick Hart, 17 Apr. 2010 and 3 Nov. 2012 conversations with author; Fr. James Conner, 17 Apr. 2010 and 3 Nov. 2012, conversations with author; Forest, 20 Apr. 2010, email to author; Merton, *DWL*, 167; D. Berrigan, 22 Mar. 2011, conversation with author.

continued in his Church."²⁷ Later in the book he shared his vision for how the modern church might serve as agent for realizing this divine synthesis throughout creation. "The Spirit will be working toward universal unity," he optimistically asserted, "transcending nation and time . . . In the vision of heaven will reside the hope of the Church militant; it will at the same time act as stimulus to action."²⁸

Berrigan expanded this optimistic trajectory two years later in his second work of theological reflection, *The Bow in the Clouds: Man's Covenant with God*. Here he delved more into the relationship of Catholic individuals—rather than the church—to this unfolding new world. In a chapter on "Prophecy and Society" he described the prophet's function as providing a conduit between God and humanity, a role that will prove lonely and alienating, one "sent to men almost as a stranger."²⁹ In proclaiming his message to the church, however, the prophet does not offer "mere protest . . . [he] is in a sense the herald of the golden age of man." But because of humanity's fallen state, it will seek to destroy those who speak the vision of God. Therefore, in the face of such opposition, the prophetic voice in essence becomes "a strong reaction of life to the forces of death."³⁰ Near the book's end, Berrigan paraphrases St. Thomas Aquinas to imply that even if the individual Christian is not called to fill this socially prophetic role, each is nevertheless called individually to investigate and synthesize within themselves the unfolding reality at hand. God's truth had entered the world through Christ's incarnation, and in the words of St. Augustine, humans could "welcome the truth wherever it be found."³¹ Ultimately Berrigan saw humanity as now maturing to an adulthood where "man is in a process of creating a future to his own image" and "has taken in hand the forces of nature and subdued them" such that the world no longer reflected only God's power but that of man as well. God is now shaping history "with a new invitation issued to the adult race which is in the process of claiming its rightful, creaturely, rational kingship over the world."³²

The year following this book's publication, during his first visit to Gethsemani in August of 1962, Berrigan tested some of his maturing ideas in a lecture to Merton's novices, continuing some of these themes, but voicing sharper critiques of how the Roman Church sometimes failed. He

27. Berrigan, *Bride*, 3.
28. Ibid., 139.
29. Berrigan, *Bow in the Clouds*, 81.
30. Ibid., 102–3.
31. Ibid., 185–86.
32. Ibid., 216–18.

spoke of our call for the church in particular and human life in general to embrace the process of change that manifested the work of a dynamic God in the world. This embrace proved hard for Catholics to pursue, however, as evidenced through the Church's inclination to suppress new movements rather than display a more transcendent patience. Catholics needed to cultivate more sympathy and understanding for the currents swirling around them, welcome cultural diversity, and consider new philosophical concepts. The central theme of his presentation to the novices, as in his books, called for a decidedly Teilhardian embrace of human growth and development as an expression of God and the presence of Christ in the world. Only at our peril would we fail to seek out an intrinsic and fundamental unity between the "seething world of creation and the seething world of the revelation of Christ." Berrigan went so far as to equate Christianity's growth with humanity's growth, asserting that "to be a humanist is to be a Christian and to be a Christian is to be a humanist."[33]

During the period of questioning by novices that followed his presentation, Berrigan helped focus such abstractions onto the crosshairs of practice and affirmed the vital witness of the early church despite temptations to take its primitive practices too literally. But he asserted that Christ's work on earth had "set up rhythms between a living Eucharist and a time process" in which "the Eucharist was to make the Church and then the Church would [in turn] make the Eucharist." But if we now worship and practice the Eucharist as ancient relics such that the church's "liturgy is dead and distant and uninterested in becoming a part of the change and ferment and adaptation, then Christians will only be at home in a dead atmosphere around an altar." Our inclination to divorce worship from social action and human improvement seems to be further evidence of the "one great divorce" that followed humanity's original fall from God's grace.

Berrigan then offered a tangible example of this divorce by referencing a news story from a few years earlier that recounted how some Catholic youths had gathered on the steps of their church following mass and there decided to throw stones at the home of a black couple who had moved into their neighborhood. An accompanying photo showed them in action and with their Catholic medals dangling from their necks as they threw. "That's the dead end of this thing," Berrigan concluded. Perhaps our biggest challenge, he added, was to inspire simple actions in support of a single neighbor. Experiences at the Montreal hospitality house of his friend Tony Walsh—also present at Gethsemani that week in 1962—revealed how people needed to be coaxed like children to gain confidence and empowerment that they

33. Berrigan, recording 18:1, 13 Aug. 1962, TMC.

can actually "do one thing for one Negro." He paraphrased Catholic Worker cofounder Peter Maurin speaking of the need for such places where "fearful people of good will" could transform their introspection and fear into steps forward into action. Walsh's house of hospitality therefore becomes a source of "therapy for the affluent, middle class, suburban people [to] come and be cured in the process of serving and helping others."[34] At this juncture in his career, Berrigan may not have been predisposed to embrace the critique of technology that Ferry and Merton offered, but he would have sympathized with Merton's identification with the abandoned.

The outline from which Berrigan spoke at the 1964 Gethsemani retreat, if he prepared one, has not survived. This brief sketch of Berrigan's perspectives in the early sixties, however, greatly illuminates the fragmentary notes of his presentation that Yoder and Forest captured as they listened.[35] In reviewing these fragments, it quickly becomes apparent that Berrigan's presentation indeed drew upon his maturing synthesis of Teilhardian ideas about humanity's evolving divinity on the one hand with his respect for tangible action to manifest that divinity within human relationships on the other. He portrayed human development as an expression of Christ in the world and emphasized how the church needed to seek out the risen Christ, who lived in the world beyond the church's self-contained and self-protective structures. What these available fragments also suggest is that Berrigan led a vigorous discussion that alternated between his prepared material and open conversation.

Berrigan's opening remarks returned to the story of Franz Jägerstätter as a man acting on his own conscience against official church instruction. He served as an example of how the "Church of Protest"[36] can manifest as an individual whose model reveals that bound hands are better than a bound will when confronted with adversity. Catholic sociologist and pacifist Gordon Zahn had published a biography of Jägerstätter[37] that summer, and Berrigan offered a quote from the book that drove home the uncritical passivity of the church during that reign of evil: "Virtually anything the Nazi's want or demand, the Christians will yield."[38] Berrigan offered that perhaps martyrs

34. Berrigan, recording 18:1, TMC.

35. Content from Berrigan's session originates from two sources: Forest, "Gethsemani Retreat"; Yoder, "Transcription of Original Notes by JHYoder." See "Archival and Manuscript Sources" section of bibliography.

36. Both sets of notes captured Berrigan's phrase, "the Church of Protest."

37. Zahn, *In Solitary Witness*.

38. The full quote of Jägerstätter is: "It simply means that there is no longer any likelihood that there will be a bloody persecution of Christians here, for virtually anything the Nazis want or demand Christians will yield" (Zahn, *In Solitary Witness*, 113).

and closed churches would be better than such complicity, suggesting that human free will is of little value if our free choice fails to properly discern in times of war.

FIGURE 16. Ping Ferry, A. J. Muste, Philip Berrigan, and Tom Cornell during Thursday morning's session in the monastery gatehouse. A copy of Merton's book, *Seeds of Destruction*, lies on the table. The first copies from the publisher arrived that morning, and Merton distributed autographed copies to each participant.
Photograph by Jim Forest, courtesy of Boston College, John J. Burns Library.

From there, Berrigan began to lay out his Teilhardian understandings of our need to embrace the emerging universal presence of Christ in creation. Perhaps connecting that week's lectionary readings from the Gospel of John, he began to share with his listeners what Yoder characterized as a Johannine view of the world and church. It seems likely, in fact, that Berrigan had chosen the Mass scripture reading to help frame this presentation. He portrayed the world as that which "God so loved that he gave . . ." as recorded in John 3:16, and lamented that at this point, the world's conscience has moved ahead of the church's. In our current state, the church needed its own conversion *to* the conscience of the world rather than a conversion *from* the world. Current processes of socialization and humanization that emerge around us in fact express that the world itself is an "Epiphany of Christ's presence."

Berrigan next asserted that St. Paul's conversion to the church can serve as a model for us. His turn from the world, sparked by his Damascus road experience, ironically prompted a conversion of the church itself to embrace an expanded mission that now included Gentiles. Christ as our doorway therefore swings both ways between church and world. He also pointed toward Paul's sermon to pagans in Athens as recorded in Acts 17, drawing on where those people already were by acknowledging their inherent religious devotion. To Berrigan, the converted Paul could take such expansive steps in relating to those outside of Judaism because Paul encountered Christ not in his human form, but in his universal, risen form. As the notes of both Yoder and Forest captured it, Berrigan summarized the implications of this encounter as, "The tomb is empty and the universe is filled."

But Roman Catholicism of today, Berrigan proposed, is pre-Pauline and focuses instead on Christ as human and on legal observance, and it struggles to move beyond that. The church may have recently experienced a "Pentecostal" occasion in the emergence of Pope John XXIII, convener of the Second Vatican Council and author of *Pacem in Terris*, but conversion of the church nonetheless remains gradual. The council itself struggled to cast off its own blindness. Berrigan sensed that it feared "filling the world with the Logos of Christ" in contrast to the church in other parts of the world he had recently visited, such as the parishes of South America that forged onward though "in the midst of a ring of fire," and the antiapartheid movement of South Africa where activist John Harris had recently been condemned to death.

At this point Berrigan ended his introductory comments and a season of discussion bubbled forth from his listeners. Merton launched the conversation, suggesting the need for a *conversio ad mundum*, or turning to the world, and drawing attention to other traditions that nurture loving, moral insight. "There is idolatry in saying 'our God is good" and theirs is not, he shared. "Our vocation is to find in them the God they didn't know." As a case in point he cited Zen master D. T. Suzuki, referring to him as a holy man. Merton had met Suzuki in New York only four months earlier. On that rare excursion beyond his normally enclosed life, he revisited various sights and scenes of his youth and enjoyed a meaningful exchange with the master of another faith, and it undoubtedly remained fresh. Ferry promptly followed Merton's lead, asserting the shallowness of Catholicism when compared to Buddhism. Merton did not correct him but responded with observations about their inherent differences. "Our Western logic uses contradiction," he commented, "but Zen is a process of excluding contradiction, and therefore is *conversio ad mundum*. In Mahayana the Bodhivista turns his back on Nirvana and goes back to the world to save everyone."[39]

Perhaps trying to return to his original theme, Berrigan steered the conversation again toward the current shortcomings of Catholicism. The

39. Mahayana Buddhism is one of two major schools of the religion; it emphasizes a form of universal salvation.

recent inability of the Second Vatican Council to gain consensus on how it relates to the modern world and bring closure to its meetings as originally planned, a failure that required scheduling a fourth session for the following year, proved symptomatic. "It represents the Church's confession of unreadiness to receive the world," Berrigan chafed, "and its fearfulness is our confession of unconvertedness. We need a rediscovery of the riches of poverty through the developing countries, [because on its own] the Church has never been able to summon conscience. What is learned cannot be unlearned [and] penitence is required." Again returning to Paul's conversion—in contrast to that of Peter—as our modern model, Berrigan observed that, "Christ is larger and deeper than Peter dared to think," and offered a comment he attributed to St. Augustine: "There are so many who think themselves within and are really without, and there are so many really within who think they are without."

FIGURE 17. Bob Cunnane, John Howard Yoder, and Thomas Merton during Daniel Berrigan's Thursday morning session in the monastery gatehouse.
Photograph by Jim Forest, courtesy of Boston College, John J. Burns Library.

Ferry followed this string of comments about receiving wisdom from the world with skepticism. The critique he heard did not respect the destructive, institutional interests embedded within the very world from which this new consciousness would emerge. "Now that an awareness of the bomb is in our knowledge and consciousness, what force will suppress it? These arguments we are making are contemporary, as if one could turn cultural knowledge on or off. It shows a lack of depth in respect for the power of culture." Merton added an analogy of the pervasive cultural power of Charlemagne's influence, which had "judaized" the Middle Ages such that it essentially functioned as an "Old Testament" civilization. In doing so, he perhaps alluded once more to the monastic protest as a potentially countervailing pull against imperial control during the Middle Ages. At that, Berrigan sought to refine and clarify his views on culture and *conversio ad mundum*. He did not speak so narrowly, but rather of "conversion as to our sense of the issues, conversion to a universal conscience rather than to a superficial focus on 'in' issues."

Muste, however, chose to follow up on Merton's allusion to the culture of the Middle Ages. "The rise of Just War theory in its medieval origins was ridiculous and utopian, and the emergence of the 'Truce of God' was an irrational demand." Here Muste referred to a movement that emerged following the disintegration of Charlemagne's empire and the rise of feudalism, which in turn proliferated localized warring and violence. Clergy first sought acceptance of a "Peace of God," or *Pax Dei*, that prohibited violence toward noncombatants—a fundamental tenet of classic Just War theory. They followed *Pax Dei* with promotion of the Truce of God, which called for a halt to warring among Christian knights on certain feast days. Yoder's annotation indicates that Muste's comments were supportive of those efforts. He intended them as examples of how seemingly unrealistic efforts to counter pragmatic violence actually signal hope in something greater, and of how pragmatic "realism" is actually a form of unbelief. "Such measures were perhaps past examples of *conversio*," Muste elaborated, "a tactic of accepting the world, then telling it in its own terms to limit its violence"—perhaps a different slant on the concept than it would seem Berrigan intended. Muste added that in the world of 1964 (and beyond), "The nuclear dimension of society we now face was in the cards from the start. It is the judgment of God, since in practice the original just war rationale had slipped from limiting war to mandating it." At that Merton tacked on another example of medieval idealism. "The Irish penitentials of the tenth and eleventh centuries," he noted, "also sought to reduce sins of violence by excommunication of those who transgressed."

As their morning time together neared its end, Daniel Berrigan once more assumed his role as discussion leader to share his concluding thoughts. "Change is a blessing, change in our conscience," Berrigan began, echoing that emphasis on change from his 1962 lecture to the Gethsemani novices. His intrinsic poeticism then rose with his return to the idea of an emerging divine consciousness. "The world conscience is a delicate fabric that resounds when touched perceptively at any point." Issues that face us such as the pill, poverty, hunger, race, peace are all issues which touch this fabric. We as the church are a certain light within a larger vision or worldview, and we must enter into the world's conscience instead of dictating to it our own. In Christ, God leaves aside sectarian dictates, the outer shell, and reenters the world as its conscience rather than merely replacing it. We look to the universal God serving history, not our localized gods serving to protect us from the world.[40] We must choose whether to be a servant of history or slave of religion. Berrigan next brought his comments closer to practical implementation by the church. We must turn to the world with "a new identification in valid worship," again echoing a theme he had shared with Gethsemani's novices two years earlier. "Worship is not magic but mystery, a word to us turning us around. Which one it is, magic or mystery, shows in the church's being changed either from or toward relevance, and it can be tested by judging the relevance of the parish's life. We need more consideration," he concluded, "for the social implications of a true liturgy."

As discussion reopened, Berrigan's words regarding relevance of the church apparently sparked thought and emotion—and perhaps a certain resonance—in Elbert Jean, who offered an extended commentary worth recounting. He spoke from his own Methodist experience, however, and his comments betray his own personal frustration with the institutional church, fostered by his hands-on racial reconciliation work in the South. As captured by Yoder, Jean shared that:

> Desegregation is a human possibility; integration is only possible to God. Most appeals to reason in racial rights matters are irrelevant, we should not assume the world is reasonable. Martyrdom is silent—you only go to Jerusalem once. Pastors go into seclusion silently; that is our hope. Why stay in the "Church"? Why stay in it if it is phony? That the church speaks in the name of Christ is serious to God even if it is not to us . . . No hope rests in a perfect visible church. Still, treat it as a vessel, a real gift, but do not worship it. But if you tell brothers that to worship the church is idolatry, then you get thrown out. God's judgment is not in barging in to set things right. It works in our patience.

To Jean's reflection, Muste responded that the racial revolution they witnessed around them should have arisen from within the life of the church. It should not have needed to rely on secular education and legal action, as with the course that the civil rights movement had been forced to take due to the ingrained segregation that permeated American church life.

---

40. Yoder originally worded it, "not our *penates* protecting us from the world," a reference to Roman household gods.

FIGURE 18. Elbert Jean during Daniel Berrigan's Thursday
morning session in the monastery gatehouse.
Photograph by Jim Forest, courtesy of Boston College, John J. Burns Library.

Yoder's notes on Berrigan's session ended following Muste's comments. Jim Forest, however, captured a few disconnected yet pithy quotes that appear to have been voiced during this exchange but cannot otherwise be linked with specific questions or otherwise placed within the flow of dialogue. Their gist, however, exudes a rather jaded perspective of the integrity of the church, and therefore fits as likely additional responses to the discussion on its contemporary shortcomings. Forest's snippets of commentary include the isolated phrase, "theological Tammany halls," and someone's assertion that, "I don't trust history because the winners write history."[41] "The final decision—race or peace—is whether it will up the collection," someone else inserted, followed by, "The surest way not to find peace is to go out and look for it." Forest ended this section with a comment attributed to Merton: "The institution itself just does not commit."

Following these comments, Yoder placed a notation in his own record that suggests they broke from their session at that point. It may have been the break to prepare for their noon meal, or perhaps it was simply to bid farewell to John Nelson as he departed for his 12:20 p.m. flight from Louisville. When they reassembled, however, Yoder recorded that open

41. This quote also appears in D. Berrigan, "Notes on mimeograph," following Merton's presentation on monastic protest the day before. He attributes it to Elbert Jean.

discussion resumed for a time, but the content seems further removed from Berrigan's opening comments. The Jesuit's contribution had tended toward the ethereal, with little direct reference to nuts and bolts "protest." But this was a search for "spiritual roots," and his comments certainly offered that. In framing our protest, he implied, we must draw not simply and solely from the rigid and narrow boundaries of established dogma. Christ is present throughout creation, and is active within it. We must see him there, as well, and draw from his expanding influence in a world consciousness that can inform our protest and render it relevant even as it is faithful. The church itself is being outpaced as many outside the boundaries of the church encounter this Christ-created consciousness and respond to it. We must serve the church by embracing this consciousness, opening to it the church and the church's worship practices, and engaging in actions that respond faithfully to it.

As for the discussion that Yoder captured following the break, it seems to have occurred during a slot for responses to questions that had accumulated from the prior sessions. Merton opened these conversations by elaborating on monastic withdrawal: "Was it really a protest?" In support that it indeed was, he noted that the earliest monastic documents were in part a social manifesto. Accounts of St. Anthony's fourth-century conversion, for example, emphasize that in fleeing from bishops and women, he ultimately sought creation of an alternative society. His contemporary monastic, Pachomius, commented that they "went out" into the wilderness as Abraham had. "Their protest," Merton summarized, "was that you can't follow Christ when the Church is tied to the court."

Someone, perhaps Merton, facetiously paraphrased religious historian and theologian Reinhold Niebuhr as suggesting that "because I am a sinner I let national policy in the hands of the National Security Council."[42] Muste followed with a caution that, "Our only rightness is our humility," and exhorted, "we must begin with the conclusion: 'There is no way to peace, peace is the way.'"[43] Merton further extended the theme, "Humility is vital in dealing with dissent. Who is the 'I' who can say 'no' to something? Don't think it's a matter of me versus society. In the broader world, the principalities have a corner on reality, and I must overcome the identity they project on me. Inadequate counter-efficacy is not the problem." "No, don't

42. When typing his notes in 1994, Yoder speculated Merton had referenced Niebuhr; his original notes had simply referenced "RN."

43. This phrase was a favorite of Muste. Most sources attribute it as original to him, though it is sometimes attributed to Gandhi. Jim Forest believes that Muste encountered the phrase in a sermon by André Trocmé, a French pacifist resister to Nazi occupation and an international secretary for the FOR.

assume control," Muste affirmed. "Those who advocate war claim to be able to calculate, so we are tempted to counter-calculate. If we got the point, we would not play the game on their terms. But we still have a job to do," Muste urged, "so we undermine by non-cooperation." Perhaps thinking from his role with the Center for the Study of Democratic Institutions, Ferry, next asked, "Then what do we tell Secretary of Defense McNamara?" "Caesar will collapse," Muste assured. "We must say they will be overcome, but adhere to the belief that it is wrong to use their tools and wrong to assume that the fact they gained access to power legitimizes them."

John Howard Yoder—The Incarnate Christ as Our Warrant for Protest

The rain continued as the party gathered again in their gatehouse room for the Thursday afternoon session. This segment would commence with a presentation from the Mennonite ethicist and theologian John Howard Yoder. Merton had assigned him the topic, "Restatement of the protestant stance in conversation with the progress of the retreat thus far."[44] Yoder indicates he began drafting his notes following Wednesday afternoon's session at the hermitage. In typing up and annotating his notes from the event some thirty years later, Yoder commented that he could no longer determine whether his actual presentation differed significantly from these notes, except for a few annotations he had inserted at the time. Daniel Berrigan's and Jim Forest's independent notes suggest, though, that Yoder apparently followed rather closely the outline he had prepared. Though Yoder recorded some interjections that occurred at points during his presentation, he did not keep notes of any discussion that followed his formal comments.

As with Daniel Berrigan, Yoder had by 1964 accumulated his own body of writing and thought on which he could readily draw for a topic such as this. His overseas service with Mennonite Central Committee, acquisition of a doctorate in theology at the University of Basel, and experience from institutional positions with Mennonite Board of Missions and Mennonite Biblical Seminary together offered numerous occasions to write and speak about matters of church, peace, and nonviolence. His prior examinations of views on pacifism held by contemporary theologians Reinhold Niebuhr[45] and Karl Barth[46] would soon be republished as pamphlets by the

---

44. Yoder, "Notes prepared by J H Yoder for presentation by JHY."
45. Yoder, "Reinhold Niebuhr" [1955].
46. Yoder, "Karl Barth and Christian Pacifism."

Church Peace Mission.[47] Yoder by then had published material in French and German, as well as English, and he had translated the works of others to English. In 1962, for example, he published a German-language historical study of Swiss Anabaptism and an English translation of *Christ and the Powers* by Dutch theologian Hendrik Berkhof.[48] More recently, he had in 1964 just published his first book on peace ethics titled *The Christian Witness to the State*.[49] Yoder spoke publically of peace theology during the early sixties, as well. For example in August of 1964 he served as the key resource for an Episcopal Pacifist Fellowship conference on "The Outreach of Nonviolence" in Greenwich, Connecticut, offering three talks on "The Wider Theological Implications of Pacifism" with titles of, "The Pressure of our Common Calling," "Jesus Christ the Light of the World," and "Let the Church be the Church." At the same gathering, a panel discussing the potential power of nonviolence in interracial and international conflict featured Bayard Rustin and A. J. Muste.[50]

By Yoder's own admission, Berkhof would influence his thinking,[51] and he openly drew from it on this particular occasion. *Christ and the Powers*, originally written in 1953, contributed to a revived focus on St. Paul's reference to principalities, powers, dominions, and similar terms that emerged in biblical scholarship following World War II. That cataclysmic event made evident to many the presence of powerful systemic evil at play within human experience, prompting some to reconsider whether more might lie behind Paul's words than simply fanciful notions of goblins and ghosts. For Berkhof, Paul's "powers" in fact allude to the largely invisible substratum of structures and scaffolding that hold together human experience in the material world. Though created for good, in a fallen creation they ceased to serve as "linkages between God's love . . . and the visible world of creation." They instead had become gods unto themselves, "behaving as though they were an ultimate ground of being, and demanding from men an appropriate worship,"[52] thus serving to "unify men, yet separate

47. Yoder, "The Pacifism of Karl Barth"; Yoder, "Reinhold Niebuhr" [1968].

48. Berkhof, *Christ and the Powers*; Yoder, *Täufertum und Reformation*.

49. Yoder, *Christian Witness*.

50. "The Episcopal Pacifist Fellowship," flyer, Supp. #3/3, microfilm reel 89:38, Muste Papers.

51. Yoder acknowledged in his 1977 epilogue to the second edition of *Christ and the Powers* that Yoder's own summary of Paul's view of Christ in *The Politics of Jesus* was "little more than an expansion of Berkhof's analysis" (Berkhof, *Christ and the Powers* (1977), 70).

52. Berkhof, *Christ and the Powers* (1962), 23.

them from God."[53] Examples of powers cited by Berkhof include political, economic, technical, educational, legal, and other realms of human activity and experience. Christ in his crucifixion and resurrection broke the hold of these fallen powers, dethroned them, and now through his church renders them relative and modest in Christ's victorious presence. Christ's work has restored them to the place of mere instruments rather than deities unto themselves. This continues today because Christ's church consists of people "who will no longer let themselves be enslaved, led astray, and intimidated," thereby becoming figures "against whom the program of the Powers . . . suffers shipwreck." These people "see through the deception of the Powers, refusing to run after isms," such that while "standing within the community of a people or a culture, their presence is an interrogation, the questioning of the legitimacy of the Powers."[54] Such imagery could easily provide considerable substance for discussion of spirituality and protest and would help place the church's role front and center when considering human opposition to social ills.

Without a doubt, Yoder had come to conceive of the church/world relationship quite differently than Daniel Berrigan did when they met at Gethsemani. This could be easily seen in Yoder's 1960 essay, "The Otherness of the Church," published in an issue of the progressive Mennonite series, *Concern*.[55] Here he asserted that in the twentieth century's increasingly secular and warring West, "we can no longer so simply identify the course of history with Providence. We have learned that history reveals as much of Antichrist as of Christ."[56] Such sentiments seem quite dissonant with Berrigan's confidence in humanity's maturing partnership with God. The biblical concept of "world" for Yoder signifies "not creation or nature or the universe, but rather the fallen form of the same, no longer conformed to the divine creative intent."[57] Yoder also lamented the "Constantinian" transition of the early church from the distinct and faithful margins to the center of imperial power. This label refers to the Roman era when Christianity became formally tolerated in the empire under Emperor Constantine and eventually served as its official religion. It alludes to the conflation of state power with church authority, whereby the state—wielding its military and bureaucratic authority—becomes a vehicle for advancing Christianity. Constantinianism was a theme Yoder would draw on throughout his career.

53. Ibid., 25.
54. Ibid., 35–36.
55. Yoder, "Otherness."
56. Ibid., 19.
57. Ibid., 20.

But in this essay Yoder saw the magisterial reformations (Lutheran, Reformed, Anglican) as perhaps an even more flawed development in church history. At least through its monastic orders Catholicism had retained "a residual awareness of the visible otherness of the church." But the Reformation abandoned such expressions of otherness and, he felt, severed the link of creation to Christ that Catholicism had imperfectly sustained.[58] Protestantism then fully lost the pre-Constantinian conviction that history found its meaning though the church's work, which medieval Catholicism had kept alive.[59] This meaning emerges not from preserving Western culture, ideals of freedom, and material comfort, "but in the calling together of 'men for God from every tribe and tongue and people and nation,'[60] a 'people of his own who are zealous for good deeds.'"[61] In the end, Yoder asserted that those sharing in Christ's triumph will be the ones who follow him in abandoning both physical weapons and society's criteria for effectiveness and intelligence, seeking instead "the foolish weakness of the cross in which are the wisdom and the power of God."[62]

Though "The Otherness of the Church" anticipates some differences between the worldviews of Yoder and Berrigan at Gethsemani, a more recent engagement of Yoder's undoubtedly played greater significance in his preparation for Thursday afternoon's assignment. In December 1963, Yoder participated in a Church Peace Mission conference, "Revolution, Nonviolence, and the Church," convened in an Episcopalian center at Black Mountain near Asheville, North Carolina. The event, which had been conceived and coordinated by CPM Executive Secretary, Paul Peachey, gathered leaders from the Southern Christian Leadership Conference and the Student Nonviolent Coordinating Committee in conversation with historic peace church figures. Andrew Young and CPM President John Oliver Nelson cochaired the conference. Over thirty years later Yoder recalled the presence of African American leaders James Bevel, Vincent Harding (who at the time was also affiliated with the Mennonite Church), James Lawson, C. T. Vivian, Charles Sherrod, and Andrew Young. The only "supportive whites from the same movement" that he recalled was Will Campbell, the controversial leader of the Committee of Southern Churchmen who had nurtured Elbert Jean into the civil rights movement.[63] Notwithstanding Yo-

---

58. Ibid., 23.

59. Ibid., 24.

60. Yoder is quoting from Rev 5:9.

61. Yoder, "Otherness," 26. The second quote is of Titus 2:14.

62. Ibid., 28.

63. Yoder, "Racial Revolution," 98.

der's memory, however, the names of both Elbert Jean (then on staff with the NCC "Southern Project" that Will Campbell had recently abandoned) and Philip Berrigan also appeared on the program. Jean served as preacher for daily worship services and Berrigan provided comments on one of the formal presentations. Yoder apparently either failed to recall their presence or perhaps due to their institutional ties considered them to be outside the "movement" per se.[64] A. J. Muste had planned to attend but needed to alter his plans the week before the event.[65]

As for his own role, Yoder provided a major paper for discussion at Black Mountain on "the theological basis of nonviolence; and criteria for testing the movement,"[66] which focused on how Christians might relate to the civil rights movement. As such, it provided an incredibly appropriate occasion for Yoder to consider nuances and issues surrounding "spiritual roots of protest" nearly a year before Gethsemani. It may easily be that Yoder's exposition of such a directly relevant topic at Black Mountain inspired the conference coordinator, Peachey, to also invite him to the Gethsemani retreat. Peachey and Yoder had been working toward separately publishing the paper as a CPM pamphlet in 1964, so its content would still be fresh in Yoder's mind.

When reading Yoder's Black Mountain paper, many of its concepts and themes strongly echo ideas that would later appear in Yoder's impromptu outline for his Gethsemani presentation. For one, at the CPM conference Yoder again thoroughly addressed the problem of "Constantinianism," as he had in "The Otherness of the Church." On this occasion he articulated its implications for the Christian community's loss of a visible contrasting identity. That loss required Christian ethics to apply equally to everyone, and consequently "the heroic dimensions of Christian obedience, the self-abandon and the witness of nonconformity are necessarily gone." Those standards no longer provided the mark that uniquely identified a Christian; they became relegated to the "honorific irrelevance" of monks, the "'vocational' prophets and gadflies" who even then are not "evaluated by the rightness of their own position but by how they contribute to the whole." This

---

64. The program and the list of thirty-four participants were included in a post-conference report prepared by Peachey for the CPM Administrative Committee. The list did not provide an affiliation for Rev. Will Campbell, but associated Rev. Elbert Jean with the National Council of Churches (Peachey, "The Church Peace Mission. Report," 16 Dec. 1963, Supp. #3/2, microfilm reel 89:37, Muste Papers).

65. Muste to Peachey, 6 Dec. 1963, Supp. #3/2, microfilm reel 89:37, Muste Papers.

66. Peachey, "The Church Peace Mission. Report," Supp. #3/2, microfilm reel 89:37, Muste Papers. Peachey anticipated publishing this paper as a CPM pamphlet, but that never occurred. It was eventually published as Yoder, "Racial Revolution."

loss of distinction also elevates social effectiveness as the ultimate motive for action, and shifts focus from the value of persons and human relationships to the control of institutions. It in fact transforms the church into merely one of several social units with a vested, conservative interest in maintaining the existing order, such that "social creativity is left to the rebels who . . . [by necessity] are often also rebelling against religion." Yoder's conclusion: "*the vision* of creating . . . a *truly human* and therefore truly Christian *total* society *needs to be abandoned*" and we must now "seek for a more careful vision of the function of the church in a world which has come out from under her guardianship."[67]

Yoder's 1963 paper also elevated Christ's incarnation—rather than his resurrection—as central to social engagement. Christians derive their ethical norms and principles from Christ's full humanity. Further, Christians are called not simply to identify unjust structures, they are also called to help change them. But they remain "committed to changing them *in the way of Christ*," even though this prevents their ability to "sight down the line" and justify actions in terms of assuring good results. This approach to action is more costly than simply sympathizing with those who suffer injustice. It embodies a minority position whose goal is not to grasp control of power, because in doing so we lose the very substance of our message to the world of power.[68]

Yoder's paper echoed aspects of Daniel Berrigan's frustration with how ineffective the modern church had become in advancing the message of a new humanity in Christ. But rather than offer Berrigan's call for it to turn toward the world and learn from the world's conscience, Yoder cautioned against a tendency for resignation toward inadequacies of the church, and he encouraged listeners to creatively seek new structures of faithful Christian life. He warned against linking new rationales for secular involvement with skepticism of the institutional church to justify viewing modern culture as the primary vehicle of our hope for a transformed world. Such a response simply reconfigures the Constantinian model. The church is called instead to reject both sanctification of secular structures and glorification of Christian individualism, and choose a third way, that of establishing a new kind of alternative community. Such a community would necessarily accept the suffering that accompanied "confessing the name of Jesus as Lord in the midst of a society rebelling against him."[69]

67. Yoder, "Racial Revolution," 104–8; emphasis original.

68. Ibid., 108–12; emphasis original.

69. Ibid., 114–16.

In closing his paper Yoder encouraged listeners to serve as the conscience of the broader civil rights movement, not its chaplain. Rather than blessing particular causes, the churches should prod the conscience of a movement it neither controls nor directly energizes. Our hope must rest in Christ, not in democracy, Marxist vision, nor even freedom. Neither does our hope cling to pragmatic calculations of what constitutes relevant strategies. Rather, it favors expressions of relevance that repudiate claims we must force history to come out right. One of these hopeful expressions rests in the confidence that our dogged persistence in embodying principles Christ taught—in this case nonviolence—will ultimately provide the best path to realizing God's kingdom. A second manifestation of hope comes through offering "signs" to those around us, actions important not for what they tangibly accomplish but for what they signify—steps that need to be taken in confidence that Christ (rather than we) will ultimately use them to communicate some sort of message. Yoder advocated for listeners to view protest demonstrations in this light, as an opportunity to "demonstrate" something rather than to apply "tools of social coercion." Yoder also assured we may place relevant hope in "wonders," the unexpected outcomes that seem to appear miraculously at crucial turning points, a "'wonder to our eyes' . . . which would not have happened if the planners had had their way."[70]

When seen against this backdrop of Yoder's Black Mountain paper, it becomes apparent that many of his comments at Gethsemani had been well rehearsed; they were not simply a contemporaneous response to the occasion. Seated in the gatehouse room that fall afternoon in 1964, Yoder adapted a small wooden plant stand as an informal podium of sorts to hold the notes from which he spoke. In his presentation—reconstructed here primarily from his preparatory outline and the notes taken by Jim Forest and Daniel Berrigan[71]—Yoder offered five main areas of "restatement of the protestant position" in response to discussion from their prior sessions. Two of these provided virtual replays of concepts expressed at Black Mountain. He opened by offering potential responses to Merton's framing question, "By what right do we protest?" "The best answer if it worked," Yoder asserted, "would be to invoke the phrase which best defines catholicity: *quod semper ubique omnibusque*," which roughly translates as, "what (has been held) always, everywhere, by everybody." "This would mean that to be Christian is by its very nature always to protest institutional evil." But since

70. Ibid, 119–23.

71. Content from Yoder's session originates primarily from Yoder, "Transcription of Original Notes by JHYoder," which provides a well-developed summary, supplemented by Forest, "Gethsemani Retreat"; and D. Berrigan, "Notes on mimeograph." See "Archival and Manuscript Sources" section of bibliography.

that does not reflect actual practice, we might alternatively appeal based on our stature as standing in continuity with the many saints of the past who protested evil, as Merton had expressed in comments on the monastic tradition. Another approach, which Yoder linked with one of Ferry's previous comments (rather than Merton's), is that emergency situations such as evacuating a burning house do not require justification. Yoder's outline then offers his own particular view:

> My own response, and that of the tradition(s) I have been assigned to interpret . . . is "why not by right of the Incarnation?" . . . Is Jesus not the best warrant? In the view of "the peace churches," an antiwar protest is not the specialty of a vowed elite with special disciplines, nor an emigrant elite in the desert, nor an exceptional ad hoc response to a sense of unique urgency, but rather it is what is expected . . . of all people committed to simply "following" after the words and work of Jesus. We do not take this path out of considerations of social hygiene with a view to where it will get us, but because to do otherwise would be wrong.

For listener Daniel Berrigan, the essence Yoder's comments consisted of asking, "Do we have the spiritual weight to stand as prophets and saints against the consensus? The incarnation forces us to speak even though alone. This is not supererogation but simple obedience, not to get the world somewhere, but to [otherwise] go away is sin."

At this point Yoder inserted an interjection by Elbert Jean, who challenged, "It is Puritan to say it would be wrong to do otherwise. We should instead say that it is a gift to take this path."[72] Yoder failed to record his direct response, if any, but his outline suggests that he conceded that the position he expressed was not universally Protestant. He then brought closure to his opening point by voicing disagreement with those who might consider nonviolence unreasonable because it was an ethic "revealed" by Jesus. Or in Berrigan's paraphrase, "This [standard] gives us a scriptural norm in contrast to mere common sense."

Yoder next turned to matters regarding Jacques Ellul on technology, explicitly crediting both Merton and Ferry with raising them. Rather than consider their wrestling with that force as a uniquely modern dilemma, Yoder instead characterized it as an ancient concern that merely appeared in new form, one that fit within Paul's conception of "principalities and

---

72. Yoder later inserted a notation that to this point in his note taking he had spelled the name of Elbert Jean as "Jeans," adding that, "Maybe we were not adequately introduced." This suggests he retained no memory of Jean from Black Mountain.

powers." Here he recommended his translation of Berkhof's *Christ and the Powers* to gain a sense of how the concept applied in modern society. "The Powers, the structures of our culture," and by implication Ellul's technique, "are not morally neutral, nor good as they claim to be, but oppressive. They bear great creative potential, as they were intended in the original divine purpose to build the Holy City. But they have become warped by their rebellion, oppressive, and incapable of curing themselves." As Berrigan reported, this implies that "its claim *is* its idolatry, [and] it claims infinite creative power." Then perhaps in response to Berrigan's framing of an emerging world conscience that morning, Yoder suggested, "That is why it is deceptive to think about the contemporary social scene simply, affirmatively, in terms of Divine Image or the sovereignty of the one God." He next highlighted several points the New Testament makes about principalities and powers. "We cannot through our own wisdom or strength be freed from them, but because Christ is Lord, they cannot ultimately win. The total complex will trip over its own skirts," he assured, then echoed Muste's earlier comment, "Caesar . . . will collapse under the weight of his own pride. But in the meantime, we don't worship them, even if they kill you. Because of our allegiance to Christ, we are liberated and can make use of fragments of the system to reconquer portions of the turf and use it for good. But the way to do so is to tame it, make it modest, deny its idolatrous pretension, refuse to obey it."

FIGURE 19. Ping Ferry listens as John Howard Yoder presents during the
Thursday afternoon session in the monastery gatehouse.
Photograph by Jim Forest, courtesy of Boston College, John J. Burns Library.

Yoder's third main facet of response touched upon his ongoing critique of "the Constantinian heresy" of trying to establish "a Christian Society from the top." This was when the church began to use its power to compel people to join. We may be concerned for improving society but must not make it our primary imperative. This, Yoder felt, was the shortcoming of *Schema XIII*, the controversial statement on the church in the modern world that the Second Vatican Council was then grappling with. The council's inability to agree on this statement in fact played a role in calling a fourth session for 1965, which Berrigan had chastised earlier that day. The focus of *Schema XIII* on governmental duty—rather than primarily advising how followers of Jesus must respond to the world—weakened it. This priority adopts establishment logic, which tests an ethic by whether it can be generalized. "What if everybody loves their enemies? Who will stop the Russians? What if there was nobody to do society's necessary dirty work?" In his notes Forest condensed Yoder's rhetorical questions to, "How should the minority who care behave in society, no matter what the majority do?" and then summarized Yoder's response as, "The job of the soldier and hangman will get taken care of whether we do it or not, and it's not necessarily better to have the saints do it."

Yoder's own outline offered a fuller elaboration. For one, "nobody is listening." He asserted, "There are no pious sovereigns waiting attentively for their chaplains to tell them what to do, so diluting your moral demands in order to be taken more seriously by the powerful is not *really* the way to get a hearing." Second, it is self-defeating for several reasons. You cannot predict accurately. "Reinhold Niebuhr said this under the heading of irony. Jacques Ellul is full of how technological mystique makes promises it cannot keep. And to manipulate society for its own good, you must assume that everyone else will play by the rules." Further, as Forest paraphrased, "in using tools of the enemy to overcome the enemy, one is in fact overcome by them." Or according to Yoder, "it demoralizes the compromiser because you are morally defeated if you join the adversary in the use of his weapons. The mandate in Romans 12 to 'be not overcome with evil' does not mean 'be stronger than the bad guy in the use of his weapons' but 'do not use his weapons.'"

Yoder also offered a Gandhian anecdote, where the Mahatma allegedly responded to an innkeeper who justified his sale of alcohol because "I have to live" with the question, "Why do you have to live?" Gandhi's rather harsh implication: If what you do with life is something that should not be done, your life is not needed. Yoder shared still another basis for spurning the tools of power and control: "In numerous crucial (pun intended)[73] situations the way to overcome your enemy is to lose to him. The ultimate power is the Cross." In other words, "Christ did not come to deliver a history of effectiveness, but of martyrdom." Yoder closed this third area of response with what he termed a "whimsical" illustration that noted how the best British chocolates are made by Quakers (Cadbury and Rowntree) and the best Dutch chocolates by Mennonites (van Houten). While eighteenth-century state church members were running governments, militaries, universities, and other institutions that excluded sectarians, the sectarians were freed to focus on the real force for change of that era, world trade.

Yoder's fourth theme dealt with the futility of pragmatically seeking to control outcomes and maximize effectiveness to attain God's will through programmatic results, again echoing his Black Mountain paper. "The link between our fidelity and the achievement of God's purposes for the world are not causal but crucial. We cannot 'sight down the line' of our faithfulness to hit God's target, since our relinquishing sovereignty is part of the call." To Berrigan this meant that "martyrdom is never predictably effective, it is only victorious; the coming down of the holy city is not connected with Armageddon, but with the prayers of the Saints." Yoder went on to ask, "Does this mean there is no discernible connection between our obedience and God's purposes being achieved? Not at all. There are still modes of effecting change." Rather than rely on our calculations, though, we look in faith toward "signs" that point toward a greater underlying truth. These can include "portents": signs that actually participate in the reality or truth toward which they point, such as hospitals (originally created by the church but now passed to secular hands); "marvels" or "miracles" (the "wonders" of his Black Mountain address): occurrences that astound and provide unpredictable and unanticipated—yet real—signs, such as the first lunch counter demonstrations and the origin of the Student Nonviolent Coordinating Committee; and finally "springs in the desert": the surfacing of good things from pressures that had built up underground, unseen, over a long period of time. Such springs confound those who rely on clear logic of cause and effect—"People who saw water disappearing on the mountainside had no idea it would spring up in the desert." Using another civil rights movement example, the burst of tangible gains enjoyed in recent years might be considered the fruit of a century of pressure exerted through the "silent" but steady testimonies of George Washington Carver, Ralph Bunche, and Martin Luther King Jr.

73. The root of the word "crucial" is "crucis," or "cross"; an archaic usage of the term means "cruciform." Yoder alluded to a double meaning of both "important" and "persecution-inducing" situations.

In response to Yoder's appeal to relinquish human calculation and rethink matters of hope and relevance, A. J. Muste here injected his own clarification. "I should still do all I can," he assured, "but I am not justified by claiming greater efficacity through my nonviolent direct action. For an action to count as a sign it must signify clearly or be dictated by a moral imperative. No symbols for the sake of effect may be pursued at the cost of integrity."

Yoder's fifth and final response theme focused on how his own Radical Reformation tradition's access to peace differed from the monastic model described by Merton. He opened with an apparent restatement or para-phrase of comments offered by Merton the previous day: "Despair is our only hope, the cross the only victory, [and] our only reason to be hopeful is the fact we are against the wall." Perhaps intending to relate that perspective with his tradition, Yoder stated, "The radical reformers did not go volun-tarily into the desert. They were expelled." He elaborated that the basis of their expulsion rested with their refusal to accept sixteenth-century theo-logical rationales, which justified war and violent self-defense through the Just War tradition, as well as blessed the state's control over local churches and its persecution of religious dissent. In contrast, Anglican, Lutheran, and Reformed Protestantism each chose to adopt these features from medieval Roman Catholicism. These sentiments prompted Merton to interject, "Per-haps banishment and prison, when they are the cost of fidelity, are the only licit form of hermitage."

Continuing, Yoder suggested that the radical reformers' withdrawal focused mainly on removing themselves from circumstances that require violence, while they continued integration with other social institutions such as family (rather than celibacy) and commerce (rather than mendi-cancy). Instead of remaining entwined as compromised members of violent structures, "They migrated and colonized, creating nearly-autonomous commonwealth structures based on civil and religious liberty. They used it to build viable enclave cultures characterized by a high level of cultural creativity and social health and a minimum level of police violence." This relationship contrasted with a monastic symbiotic role within society where "some people have to stay wealthy so the Franciscans can beg, some people have to procreate so the religious can be celibate, and somebody has to buy cheese to support Gethsemani." No doubt his last comment played off of Merton's occasional laments regarding the increased role commercial pro-duction—particularly cheese-making—had come to play in his monastery's life.[74] Yoder recognized nuanced distinctions, therefore, between monastic

74. Merton had written an ironic poem titled "CHEE$E," using the pseudonym,

reasons for protest and those of his own tradition. Whereas monks opposed the "low average moral quality of run-of-the-mill Christians, which could be raised by the presence of a more virtuous elite," radical reformers opposed social, moral, and ecclesiastical abuses that "were just plain wrong," adding, "Their protest was not symbolic but moral." Their social rejection emerged from "a minority position in obedience," a natural consequence when "I try to be the kind of person Jesus was."

In closing, Yoder addressed the question, "Against whom do we protest?" We do not protest against a particular person in power in order to "remove him coercively from his driver's seat and put a better man on top." Rather, as Gandhi would advise, we instead "love him, and let him make us suffer. We are on his side. It's because of our love for him that we get in his way. *Protest* means affirmation. We stand against what we stand against because of what we must stand *for* as church—*for* the enemy, the poor, the truth. Protest is not simply the most manageable solution to some tactical problem."

Yoder did not take notes on any discussion that followed his own presentation, but Jim Forest indicates that at least one subsequent comment addressed questions of racial reconciliation work in Mississippi. Years later Tom Cornell would recall that Ferry and Merton had engaged in a memorable discussion on race, one that felt as though they spoke from within the African American experience.[75] This may have been the occasion he recalled. In a sense, the comments Forest captured might be seen to connect aspects of Merton's thoughts the previous day advocating "mystical substitution" for the rejected together with Yoder's description of "enclave cultures characterized by a high level of cultural creativity." Someone raised the question, "Are we going down there to help the Negros get rights or to help the Whites—who are the ones really going to hell with their present posture? Rather than see Mississippi as a place for whites to broaden their experiences and return, it would be better to stay there in the model of Charles Foucauld's orders of Little Brothers and Sisters, or better yet to raise their children there—care enough about it to give it their flesh." Daniel Berrigan captured another response, though unattributed, which asserted that, "the defeat of protest is to offer an alternative of the same order in place of the old structure." Replacing the old emperor with another wearing new clothes gains no victory.

"Joyce Killer-Diller." A parody of Joyce Kilmer's poem, "Trees," it refers to cheese as an asset with pleasing attributes, but which ultimately resides within the tower of Babel. See Merton, *Collected*, 799.

75. Cornell, 13 Apr. 2010, email to author.

Following Yoder's presentation, the men adjourned for the day. Though Tom Cornell would recall Yoder's delivery as dry and rather tedious, the ideas he shared impressed Cornell. Reflecting on the event years later he recalled that overall, "I wasn't excited by the content, except with John Howard Yoder. The theology of the cross was so clear, so beautifully put . . . He brought a cogency to it, a relevance, the theology of the cross that lives today. This is what salvation is about . . . It means we don't have to think about [the afterlife] very much, but think of it in terms of human life here on earth. How are we going to save ourselves from blowing ourselves up? Except by forgiveness? And being willing to accept suffering whether imposed or not."[76] Yoder had apparently impressed others, as well. For Cunnane, "I felt like he was profoundly simple—he said things in a very simple way that I followed, but they were very profound. He talked a little bit about the Jubilee Year, and the history of the counter presence of the whole Anabaptist tradition, which was really interesting."[77] For Merton, the day had yielded a "remarkably lively and fruitful" discussion, as he noted in his journal that night while recording an array of impressions:

> Yoder spoke well this afternoon on protest from the Mennonite viewpoint that is biblical. Revelation [sic] of technology to the "principalities and powers" of St. Paul (not at all akin to the mind of Ellul, whom he in fact quoted—a lecture of his). For personal intensity and sincerity I have also liked very much the remarks of Elbert Jean, a Methodist from the South—was a minister in Birmingham [sic] and was fired for his integregationist ideas ("Desegregation can be brought about by anyone, but integration only by the Holy Spirit"). A. J. Muste is impressive in real wisdom, modesty, gentleness. He is like Archbishop Floresh in a way, and yet much more mild and without cramps and compulsions.[78]

That Sunday, when reflecting to his novices on Thursday's two speakers, Merton's comments suggest that Yoder's points may have left the bigger impact. "Of course Dan Berrigan was lively," he shared, but then went on to offer that "there was one fellow, a Mennonite . . . a great guy, a really solid man . . . The one thing that struck me about him was that we were sort of discussing all kinds of questions on the future of civilization and all this sort of stuff, and he was down to the business of . . . your life has to be centered

76. Cornell, 29 May 2010, conversation with author.

77. Cunnane, 31 May 2010, conversation with author.

78. Merton, *DWL*, 19 Nov. 1964, 167. Floresh was Archbishop of the Louisville Archdiocese. Jean's ministry was in Little Rock, Arkansas, not Birmingham.

on one reality only, Christ . . . This is it. This is the thing. And from this everything else flows. We have no hope, there is no other hope, but Christ." Merton went on to contrast this with the material shared by Berrigan. "And of course Dan was talking Teilhard de Chardin sort of ideas, and they finally got pulled apart. I mean Teilhard does not cut enough ice with these people. They are Protestants, see. Teilhard does not cut ice with Protestants. Because all this business about . . . there's going to be a wonderful new civilization, and it's all going to be ducky, and it's going to be the new Jerusalem, and that sort of stuff—Protestants don't buy that at all," Merton claimed, drawing laughter from his charges. "What they buy is, the Lord died on the cross and we've got to hang onto the cross and fight our way through the thing . . . And I think," Merton added, chuckling, "it's a somewhat more realistic view of things."

Without doubt, Berrigan and Yoder—both drawing on years of thought and study—had presented contrasting views on the role of the church and her relation to Christ and to the surrounding society. There is also little doubt, though, that they found much in common. They affirmed the place of the church and remained loyally within structures of their respective traditions. But they also recognized significant inadequacies, and the priorities of each could strain the patience of those institutions. They could therefore individually affirm that their church might benefit from critique and wisdom originating beyond it. In addition, they both recognized that protest and confrontation of evil should ultimately offer a positive voice of affirmation for the good to be sought rather than issue calls to tear down enemies. And both could also assert that spiritual roots of protest must reach toward Christ. Their biggest contrast, though, lay in where they located Christ—where he could be tangibly found as a source from which to draw nourishment. For Berrigan, these roots spread outward toward creation and humanity, where the risen Christ dwelt and expressed himself through a progressively divine and "adult" human consciousness. For Yoder, they instead drilled toward the incarnate Christ, Jesus, the ultimate human who demonstrated perfect obedience to God's voice and called us to the same. Yoder's Christ dwelt primarily in a gathered body of committed believers who lived in contrast to a human society that rejected—rather than embodied—Christ's conscience.

Yoder had woven comments throughout his remarks that implicitly pointed toward some of these contrasts between his ideas and Berrigan's. But he more explicitly compared the perspectives of his own Radical Reformation tradition to that of Merton's monastic protest. Previously, in both his Black Mountain paper and "The Otherness of the Church," Yoder had offered a tepid nod toward a monastic role within medieval society that preserved the ideal of ethical obedience to Christ. At Gethsemani, however, Yoder seemed eager to plead for essential differences between monastic and Anabaptist protests against a church complicit and intertwined with a secular state. Those traditions had certainly experienced different realities. A voluntary journey to social margins through the accepted gates of a monastery contrasts sharply with joining a band of illegal outcasts. These traditions also related quite differently to liturgical expression, contemplative practice, and mystical experience, although broadly speaking the Radical Reformation included diverse spiritual forms.

But Yoder may have too hastily glossed over similarities. Early stages of the Radical Reformation sought a unified social order that reflected their vision for a voluntary church, and only after that failed did they withdraw. Radical Reformers could have, and sometimes did, opt to conform rather than face persecution. On some level, then, both traditions entail conscious choices to withdraw from the dominant order to pursue greater consistency with Christ's vision. Both traditions structured their lives around committed obedience to their community's rule. Modern expressions of these traditions also tend to blur distinctions. Although Anabaptist legal and cultural marginalization continued to limit social options in ways unfamiliar to monastics, the passage of time ultimately led both monks and Mennonites to peacefully nestle within the belly of the dominant order—a relationship tested (at least for Mennonites) mainly during state crises that demanded unbending loyalty. Drawing distinctions between their underlying social relationships in twentieth-century America seems strained, especially as monastic communities have increasingly turned toward commerce for their support. Yoder characterized monks as symbiotic with society while opposing the "low average moral quality of run-of-the-mill Christians, which could be raised by the presence of a more virtuous elite." This sounds hauntingly familiar to his characterization of ideal Christian interaction with twentieth-century American government. In *The Christian Witness to the State*, he advocated for Christians to reside in a parallel, agape-based sphere, but also interact with statesmen of the pagan sphere to encourage outcomes more closely aligned with agape-based priorities than if those statesmen had been left to themselves.[79] Both portrayals envision marginal lives that model nonviolent behavior, which nudge society toward a higher standard. From this view, the alternative ascetic lifestyles of monks and the alternative commonplace lifestyles of Anabaptists seem not so different.

At Thursday's close, several of the guests attended Compline, the last office of their hosts' daily monastic routine. Bob Cunnane especially

79. Yoder, *Christian Witness*, 71–73.

remembered a chant to Mary as the finale: "*Salve Regina*," or "Hail Holy Queen." "The Trappists had picked up a distinctive song," he recalled, "a Gregorian chant but of their own kind, a different slant. That was the part of Compline I remember most."[80] This memorable ending for their second day, however, signaled that the bulk of their time together had passed. Yoder would gain another opportunity for input through his homily at the next morning's Mass, and A. J. Muste had yet to lead the final discussion. But with John Nelson's departure that morning, Ping Ferry's that night, and only a half day remaining for the others, the retreat was winding down. Merton chose to spend that night in the solitude of his private cottage reflecting on events of the past two days. As he closed his journal entry that evening, Merton self-consciously alluded to his own ironic entanglement in the forces with which they had grappled: "Now—rainy night, I sit writing this in the green technological light of the Coleman lamp at the hermitage," adding, "They will leave tomorrow."

80. Bob Cunnane, 31 Mar. 2010, conversation with author.

6

Closing Day and Beyond—Unity and Friendship in a Movement for Peace

EARLY THE FOLLOWING MORNING the men began their final day together by gathering in seclusion once more for Mass. Merton's journal reflections on the first mass, recorded the previous evening, surmised, "I suppose it will be the same again tomorrow—in the old juniorate chapel, where the altar is better suited for standing around in a circle."[1] This chapel, an open space under the bell tower of the monastery church, had its altar positioned in the center of the apse at the front, rather than against a wall. Since the days of the retreat, this space has ceased to function as a chapel, and the former altar area is now enclosed to serve as a small music room. We know fewer details of how this morning's worship service unfolded than of Thursday's Mass. Other than Merton's passing journal reference, only notes left by Yoder and Bob Cunnane's memory provide any trace that it even occurred. Daniel Berrigan again led the Mass and celebrated the Eucharist, pushing interfaith boundaries even further by assigning Yoder to provide a homily.

Yoder's Homily on Unity

Yoder's preparation notes[2] for his message record that the lectionary pointed to John 17 as the day's Gospel text, which they read for the Mass. The

1. Merton, *DWL,* 19 Nov. 1964, 167.

2. Content regarding this Mass originates solely from Yoder, "Notes from J H Yoder 'Homily." See "Archives and Manuscript Sources" section of bibliography. An endnote to these notes indicates: "One account, which I cannot confirm, claims that this was canonically an offense against a ruling by the abbot that there should be no protestant dilution of the mass. Merton was the only person from Gethsemani who participated."

passage lies near the end of an extended teaching by Jesus that John placed between his account of the disciples' last Passover meal with Jesus and his betrayal and arrest. It contains a prayer Jesus offered for a blessing of his work, and he asks that his disciples may be united to carry that work forward into the world. Yoder relied on the New English Bible translation of this text, choosing to highlight six passages in this twenty-six-verse chapter.

Yoder opened by sharing that he would not reference other material in the book of John or themes from the retreat, but would only address the structure of the text itself. He built on the passage to discuss Christian unity as a means for mission and discipleship in a world that rejected the message Jesus embodied. Recent experience had provided him many opportunities to reflect on themes of both unity and mission. Following his studies at the University of Basel and European relief work, Yoder began to teach at Goshen College Biblical Seminary in 1958, and a year later he also served part-time on the staff with the Mennonite Board of Missions and Charities, taking the position of Administrative Assistant to the Secretary for Foreign Missions. In 1963 he had served as an invited advisor at a Montreal gathering of the "Faith and Order" effort established by the World Council of Churches to bridge confessional structures and doctrinal views.

Yoder had also recently written on such topics, mostly for popular Mennonite publications. In a two part series on "The Place of the Peace Witness in Missions," published in the denominational magazine *Gospel Herald*, he challenged Mennonites to consider their historic peace message as integral to their outreach efforts—to the point of suggesting it may form the very basis for justifying the existence of separate Mennonite mission organizations:

> We realize more today than we did 20 or 50 years ago the necessity for the Christian church to be a unity. This does not mean that we should have one great church organization, making everyone believe the same, speak the same, and worship the same. But it does mean that every time Christians and other Christians work at cross purposes, the cause of Christ Himself suffers. What is wrong with competition between churches is not that it is inefficient and wasteful, though it is. What is wrong with it is that it is a denial of what the Bible tells us about the body of Jesus Christ . . . The justification for continuing to work [independently of other churches] will depend on whether we have a message which is not being adequately received and borne further within the broader Christian context.[3]

3. Yoder, "Place of the Peace Witness," 15, 19.

Two years later, in the spring of 1962, Yoder wrote three installments for an ongoing series on "Studies in Church Unity" published by a different denominational magazine, *The Mennonite*. None of the three articles referred to John 17, but he did offer some sentiments loosely echoed in his Gethsemani homily, such as his claim, "The assumption that we must bring about unity by organizing agreement" is a "fruit of unbelief." Unity is offered us as "a gift of God—not by negotiation, lest any man should boast."[4] This series also may offer a glimpse into how Yoder viewed his presence at Gethsemani among these diverse churchmen. "The disunity which really rends the body of Christ has to do with the content of the Christian testimony . . . the meaning of discipleship . . . and the meaning of Christian fellowship. If these are the differences that really separate Christians, then our need is not merger but conversation; not to find ways to bridge over differences but to face them clearly." But he cautioned that seeking clearer definition of issues can become "itself a screen put up by our insecurity to guard us from the uncertain outcome of a real encounter with our brethren. If there is ever to be a breakthrough to new experiences of unity and a new working of the Spirit . . . it will have to involve someone's going more than halfway and getting into deeper water. The Spirit might just be speaking where we don't expect."[5]

At Gethsemani, as Yoder developed his homily from the Fourth Evangelist's discourse on unity, he began with comments on verse 7, "Now they know that all Thy gifts have come to me." He noted that here Jesus spoke to those who were—depending on the reader's perspective—"convinced" or "elect" as his followers. Therefore, when the prayer as a whole spoke of unity, it referred not to the unity all of humanity but to that of his followers. Furthermore, this unity was "not a given but a gift." From the start, then, Yoder continued his focus of the previous day on the church community as intentional and distinct from humankind as a whole. His note regarding verse 12—"I have kept them safe in the world which hates me"—does likewise, emphasizing the point that Jesus' followers neither exist outside of the world nor are removed from it, but instead remain here as aliens.

This role as aliens becomes clear in verse 14: "I have given them your word, and the world has hated them because they do not belong to the world, just as I do not belong to the world." From this passage, Yoder noted that their alien nature comes not from their intentional rejection of humanity itself, but simply because they have embraced the person that humanity—"the world"—rejected. Therefore, "the Unity of the Church is thus found not

---

4. Yoder, "Unity We Have," 166.
5. Ibid., 213–14.

in common interests, not in a common creed or shared sacraments, not that the disciples share a common perplexity or the diseases of civilization," but rather unity in a "common overagainstness" as carriers of Christ's message for humans. Despite his opening claim that he would not refer to retreat agenda, Yoder observed in a note inserted thirty years later that his comment about "diseases of civilization" in fact alluded to prior dialogue "that included references to Jacques Ellul's critique of technology, the Pauline vision of the rebel 'principalities and powers' I had spoken about in my talk."

Yoder went on to extract three insights into the character of this unity. From the text phrase, "They have believed my word," he concluded that their unity in their "common overagainstness" came not from nature but from the Word they had embraced. He based his second observation on verse 18—"As you have sent me into the world, so I have sent them into the world," concluding from this that "Unity is in mission." He then observed that their unity was "a share in glorification." Again he reneged on an opening promise, this time cross-referencing to John 12:23 where "Jesus answered them, 'The hour has come for the Son of Man to be glorified.'" This cross-reference, Yoder explained to the retreatants, indicates that the glory they share is actually their "participation in His suffering servanthood." Then correlating this to the chosen text, Yoder explained that John 17:22—"The glory that you have given me, I have given them, so that they may be one, as we are one"—and part of verse 24—"my glory before the world"—taken together offer its claim that the disciples' unity provides the basis for their glorification.

Yoder saved his lengthiest comments on this reading to address the idea that the unity for which Jesus prayed was ultimately, "That the world may believe," an idea found in both verses 20 and 23. Based on what preceded these verses, Yoder asserted that this unity of Jesus' disciples in the world ultimately is not to enable the world to believe "some truth or other about the nature of God or the world, but [to believe] the having-been-sent of Jesus." In other words, their unity around Christ in the midst of a broken and warring world would serve as proof that Jesus came from God. Yoder went on to suggest several more implications for our understanding of Christian unity as a vehicle for mission. For one—at least as expressed in John 17—it is not a value in and for itself, nor is it a preexisting reality the disciples already possessed, simply in need of acknowledgment by them. Rather, Christian unity is instead something that would only be realized through the "future fidelity of the disciples within the hostile world."

His final observations drew further on a church history that reveals patterns of failure to properly understand this unity. For one, it is wrong to view it as only spiritual, because Jesus expected it to be visible to the hostile world. For another, neither is it an institutional manifestation, as many sought in the modern era, such as the "Faith and Order" effort in which Yoder had recently participated.[6] Rather, again, Yoder viewed John 17 as a prayer "for a shared [Christian] stance over against the unbelieving world." For emphasis, Yoder again restated that the unity Jesus prayed for is not for our own sake, but "that the world may be enabled to believe" the legitimacy of Christ.

In the context of considering social protest, this homily strengthened a case that despite their different religious commitments, they shared a larger calling—that of proclaiming Christ as a power greater than the violent culture around them. Yoder suggested that heeding this call was in fact the very basis for realizing the unity that Christ demanded of his followers, and proposed that demonstrating this unity comprised the very heart of their earthly mission. Only in observing their unique oneness, which sharply contrasted with accepted social patterns, might others begin to take seriously the reality of Christ's alternative power. The contrasting priorities around which followers of Christ unite must be tangible and they must be visible. This unity that Christ prayed for was not an abstraction already present, as some claimed, playing invisibly behind the scenes for them to merely acknowledge. They could not attain this unity by engineering and crafting it, either. Rather, this unity was a gift that they would receive only as a response to their visible, shared commitment to bear Christ's word of peace and justice over against a culture that rejected this word. Their united witness would grant them "glory," but this glory would not resemble the glory coveted within the violent culture they witnessed against. Their glory would take the form of participation in Christ's suffering servanthood to humanity.

A. J. Muste—Shepherding a Movement in Transition

By Friday morning the previous evening's rain had ended, permitting the men to visit Merton's hillside retreat once more for their last session together. At about a quarter past 9:00 they gathered to retrace Wednesday afternoon's path up the hill and through the trees. Today their number was reduced to twelve in total. Prior commitments required Ping Ferry to be

---

6. Yoder's endnotes reflected on his ecumenical interactions, particularly regarding his World Council of Churches "Faith and Order" work. He noted that his reference to unity as ecumenical doctrinal agreement had been expressed at a 1963 WCC event in Montreal by Methodist Albert Outler, a who had written a book titled, *The Christian Tradition and the Unity We Seek*.

elsewhere on Friday,[7] and John Nelson remained absent since his departure the previous morning. They had settled on A. J. Muste as the event's
final presenter, and he had been assigned to speak on the "State of the Peace
Movement." Muste was ideal for this task. He had served the movement for
decades as a trusted, cohesive figure that helped to unite diverse egos and
priorities in collaborative action. Though his energy waned as he neared
his eightieth birthday, Muste's commitment to radical pacifism remained
undaunted and his productivity remained high—this despite having been
mugged and knocked unconscious on New York's streets the past August[8]
and having undergone cataract surgery a month later.[9]

Muste's depth of character and gentle yet unwavering spirit impressed
those in his company at Gethsemani. Bob Cunnane, early in his activist career and somewhat unfamiliar with the broader peace movement, had not
heard of Muste before the gathering, but "I knew by the way they treated
him who he was before I actually knew who he was. He was definitely looked
upon as the sage by all the people that were there."[10] Merton later would
share with his novices that while some "excellent people" had attended the
retreat: "one of the most excellent people was a very old guy who's been sort
of a peace movement type for years and years and years . . . He's eighty years
old, or something like that, and he's a really good man—a really simple, holy
man. He's been through the mill. He's been hit over the head, and put in jail,
and all that stuff, but he's very respected. I mean people have a very high
regard for him, even those who don't agree with him . . . He had some very
good things to say."[11]

On one of the previous evenings Merton had left a note for Muste,
encouraging him not to let prior advice about discussion topics or comments on the handout limit his presentation and to prepare as he felt led:
"Please feel free to ignore any of these suggestions. Particularly in the matter
of discussing 'programs.' In fact it would probably be very good if you did
bring up questions of policy, I think."[12] The notes of both Yoder and Daniel
Berrigan preserved a sense of the comments he offered in Merton's hermit-

7. Ferry to Merton, 20 Oct. 1964, TMC; Ferry to Merton, 14 November 1964, TMC.

8. *Liberation*, "Editor Mugged," 2. An unsigned paragraph notes: "A. J. Muste, who is
in his eightieth year, was mugged on a New York Street last month . . . A few hours later
A. J. was back a work—though confined to his room for a few days."

9. Muste to Mrs. Henry Richardson, 18 Sept. 1964, Supp. #1/ 4, microfilm reel
89:34, Muste Papers.

10. Cunnane, 1 May 2010, conversation with author.

11. Merton, recording 132:1, 22 Nov. 1964, TMC.

12. Merton to Muste, n.d., TMC. Merton added, "Tomorrow I will meet you all
about 9.15 a.m. Have a good rest."

age, and Muste's own planning outline survives to provide added insight into what he intended to share.[13] In addition, following the retreat Muste would respond to Jim Forest's request for a copy of his comments by saying that although he wished to "extend the influence" of "the Father Merton retreat," it would be awhile before he had time to write something down. But he added that he had written on the same themes in recent issues of *Liberation*, and suggested material found there might provide what Forest needed.[14] Therefore, material he published at the time in *Liberation* also provides insight into what A. J. Muste shared that morning.

In months leading up to the retreat Muste, as one of four *Liberation* editors, had indeed written prolifically, attempting to encourage, cajole, analyze, and generally revive a movement that had seemingly stalled out, while still supporting the civil rights movement that had absorbed much of the energy previously focused on peace. He strove in his writings to waken advocates lulled to sleep by the 1963 test ban treaty, urging readers to rally around the cause of unilateral nuclear disarmament. Muste demonstrated awareness of the growing U.S. presence in Vietnam as well. In July—even before the Gulf of Tonkin incident—he coauthored a "Memo on Vietnam" as a statement prepared on behalf of the War Resister's League,[15] and he published an October *Liberation* article on "Vietnam: The Political Reality."[16]

But most of his literary output in the latter half of 1964 advocated for renewed focus on nuclear disarmament. Following his September–October hiatus to recover from cataract surgery and preceding his November Gethsemani visit by just a few days, Muste drafted a *Liberation* contribution titled "The Primacy of Peace," which appeared in the December issue. In it he addresses the "aimlessness" and "loss of momentum" and "less popular appeal" felt among peace organizations, as well as "the idea that peace workers should be concerned about social problems other than war and should work in their own communities." In recapping the history of wars their century had endured, Muste cautioned against losing sight of the centrality of peace when pursuing a new society or "choosing the issue which has immediate and obvious 'drawing power'" to attract enthusiasm. His main closing point suggested that despite the atmospheric test ban treaty, "nothing basic has changed." Ongoing issues of racism and poverty remained important, but "[nuclear arms] proliferation goes on . . . the war in South Vietnam burns

13. Content from Muste's session originates from three original sources: D. Berrigan, "Notes on mimeograph"; Muste, "Gethsemani"; Yoder, "Transcription of Original Notes by JH Yoder." See "Archives and Manuscript Sources" section of bibliography.

14. Muste to Forest, 11 Jan. 1965, Supp. #1/4, microfilm reel 89:34, Muste Papers.

15. Muste, "Memo on Vietnam."

16. Muste, "Vietnam."

on . . . [and China has been] the first non-white, non-western, relatively underdeveloped country" to detonate nuclear weapons.[17]

"The Primacy of Peace" may have offered a good warm-up for preparing his discussion remarks in Merton's hermitage, but it would seem that Muste most likely intended to point Forest toward his follow-up article penned after the retreat and also perhaps to a pre-retreat editorial for the November issue. In "Unilateralism Reconsidered," published in the January 1965 *Liberation*, Muste laid out in more detail his assertion that there had been no basic change in the arms race, and current disarmament efforts served as little more than pretense to obscure a mad nationalistic scramble for military supremacy. Historical precedents demonstrated that calls to go slow and buy time with intermediary arms limitation efforts, as opposed to a radical end to arms buildup, would not prevent the inevitable. The "nonviolent revolutionary approach is the only available one—unless indeed we are prepared to associate ourselves with *violent* revolution."[18]

This particular article significantly parallels the first half of Muste's Gethsemani outline, to the point of repeating phrases verbatim and providing nearly identical sentiments. Its ideas are also closely echoed in both Yoder's and Berrigan's notes from the retreat. These parallels are so striking that they beg questions of whether Muste arrived at the retreat intent on developing the article in free moments and then adapted that effort to generate his Friday morning discussion or whether he later decided to construct an article from notes initially prepared for Friday morning. Perhaps elements of both are true. The rushed, abbreviated nature of his handwritten outline suggests hurried composition for reference in extemporaneous speaking, but his use of specific quotes (with citations) from October 1964 publications suggest he had brought material to work with. Either way, it seems likely the Gethsemani experience would have helped to shape his January 1965 article. His November editorial, "The Insecurity of Power," which he would have drafted before the retreat, likewise echoed reflections and references from the latter half of his outline, though more loosely than the January feature.[19]

Muste opened his comments that Friday morning, however, by citing others who had spoken earlier rather than with his prepared outline. He first referred to Merton's comment regarding Pope John XXIII and efforts to "[turn] world history in the right course," along with the monk's observations on the movement's need for inner, moral renewal and a mindset

17. Muste, "Primacy of Peace," 13, 15.

18. Muste, "Unilateralism Reconsidered," 22.

19. Muste, "Insecurity of Power."

that could place hope in peaceful solutions. He also addressed the Vatican Council's *Schema XIII*, as Yoder had, sharing his belief that it distanced itself from the recently deceased pontiff's "hope of *Pacem in Terris*." Christians and non-Christians alike now embraced a shift from pursuing peace to emphasizing equality of arms, he felt. Turning to his outlined comments, Muste noted that in recent years, nothing had really changed in the overall state of the nations, East or West. Even within the communist world, Russia and China were now pitted against each other in the race for national power that fed off of rivalry and conflict. Concerns that previously animated the peace movement such as "fallout fear, shelters, USSR tension, radical books," were now being replaced with misguided reassurance in the recent nuclear test ban treaty in which "nothing reassuringly happened. No reduction in arsenals, in R&D, in nationalism." The only reason testing stopped is because militaries no longer felt they needed it.

Muste then weighed in on the role of military technology in society, referencing a *New Yorker* article by Daniel Lang[20] that indicated this technology "has no relations to the world of people." Scientists devoted to weaponry, whose work produces results as horrific as any of the "great butchers of history," are as private individuals dedicated, disciplined, and decent. "That means they are insane." In his *Liberation* piece, Muste phrased this point a bit less bluntly. Although we wouldn't classify "the men at the top who operate the military system" with the monstrous "leaders of the barbarian hordes" or "totalitarian secret police," he wrote, the instruments devised by this "elite corps of the military services and the staffs of our scientific institutions [are] infinitely more devastating." The current "highly developed technological situation"—in which those who execute such destruction never see a victim they obliterate—would appear to block out the "sensitivity and humanity" that these specialists display in other areas of life. This can hardly be accepted as psychologically "normal."[21] Practically, it results in a proliferation of nuclear capability rather than a reduction of it.

Further questioning the sanity of cold war logic, Muste next critiqued the duplicity inherent in modern political agenda. The United States had given planes to France for nuclear transport. NATO in seeking to limit the number of nuclear nations, he suggested, was actually opening venues to extend nuclear potential to countries like India. "Why have we peace talk on the verbal rationalized level," he posed, "yet continue with arms and war preparation on the level of Realpolitik?" In response he offered three

20. Muste, "Unilateralism Reconsidered," 20, discusses the "vivid picture . . . given by Daniel Lang in a brilliant and comprehensive piece in the *New Yorker* of October 10th, entitled 'Inquiry Into Enoughness.'"

21. "Unilateralism Reconsidered," 20–21.

observations to explain this paradox. For one thing, the nations and states—those responsible for proliferation—are the same ones pursuing disarmament. In other words, "You can't ask the cat to bell itself; the negotiators are the armies." Similarly, militarization serves such an integral role in political and economic traditions, ethos, and value-systems that disarmament would ultimately mean the end of our modern nation-state systems as we know them. Therefore traditional "revolution is no longer possible." In this setting, "how then could there be basic change? The problem is no longer logically resolvable, [and] the necessary change cannot take place in the Pentagon." Our only realistic option for change is that "we must speak of a demilitarized world as a revolutionized world," and "the present order must revolutionize itself out of existence." To succeed at this transformation, mutual trust is "both the prerequisite and the goal."

But what happens in reality, Muste's third observation regarding the paradox, is that governments view military power as so indispensible that production and development of arms functions at maximum intensity even as they pursue disarmament. This behavior has become so ingrained in the logic of realpolitik that modern nations actually see their own expanding arsenals as *enhancing* peace. As evidence he cited Chinese Premier Chou En-lai, recently quoted in the *New York Times* as saying that "our new atom bomb is small, but from the very first day of its birth it joined the struggle for peace."[22] He qualified his use of this quote by cautioning that, "The point is not who is worse, but that they are all trapped." It was hard for Muste to see how disarmament and peace could "blossom out of this soil."

Moving on, Muste offered some assumptions that emerged from the political reality he had just described. For one, the idea that in arming themselves the superpowers served to pressure and impose disarmament on others had proven false. With its entry into the nuclear club, "China has settled it"—proliferation failed to discourage others from arming and "no nation can force disarmament." Because of this, secondly, a growing recognition of the futility in superpower negotiations for arms reduction and the inability of those powers to reduce their defense capacity was forcing rational people to increasingly recognize that a pivotal moment had arrived in "turning an ancient tide." Humanity approached a point when all must face a decision to agree on a track other than negotiated reductions. That other track, one which required nations to abandon the traditional houses of security they had constructed and begin building a new one, remained ambiguous. Pragmatic arguments to "buy time with small steps" toward that new house of

22. Muste, "The Primacy of Peace," also includes the quote and attributes it to the October 29th *New York Times*.

security is not enough. History, such as the 1938 Munich accord among European powers to permit Nazi annexation of Czech territory rather than openly confronting it, offered little evidence that postponing a war would prevent it. Such appeals offered only a "sleeping pill" to avoid facing needed action. What in the end does such avoidance ultimately buy but time?

As Muste approached his conclusion, he turned his spotlight directly on Americans and their ironies. If anyone should show greater responsibility in advancing radical alternatives, he felt it should be Americans, whose heritage tells us to believe we are not like others. We assumed "the Civil War had purged us to be the True Israel." This despite our role in two world wars, our introduction of atomic and hydrogen bombs over which the rest of the world must now agonize, and our complicity with Russia in detonating nearly 400 atmospheric atomic tests prior to the ban. Such smug self-righteousness and inability to face the implications of our actions presents a vast handicap. We need to confront our inadequate understanding of our own place in the world. He felt the rise of China's atomic capacity had radically diminished the role of the West in Asia.

Despite our own expansionist posture, we managed to view ourselves as the intrinsically virtuous ones "always being bothered by other sinners," who were the real troublemakers and aggressors. He cited as a case in point the hypocrisy oozing from a response to the Chinese detonation by Secretary of State Dean Rusk, who deplored it as a tragedy for the Chinese people that polluted the air and took food from their mouths. The fact that the United States currently occupied the Gulf of Tonkin, though China was absent from the Gulf of Mexico, apparently carried no irony for Rusk. To Muste's thinking, "we must be delivered from [such thinking] or we will be delivered to [nuclear disaster]." And rather than rely on our own virtue for delivery, we must "find this insight among others, where not expected," echoing Merton's points about encountering the other and receiving gifts from the stranger as a source of our own salvation.

Muste then closed with his own assertion of what must now occur. The global situation could not be resolved through continued pursuit of victory or conquest over communist competitors. No single nation could assume a solitary role as liberator of others. Each nation must first liberate itself from the falsehoods of realpolitik and posturing for power. Then all must seek ways of joining together for the liberation of all humanity. For either "all will be liberated and move into a new world of a new man, or all will be annihilated, or all will be delivered into the hands of a machine or a handful of 'scientists,' a slavery in which history as we have known it will be blotted out." For his final words, Muste chose to cite a favorite passage of his by poet Muriel Rukeyser:

Now again we see that all is unbegun. The only danger is in not going far enough. If we go deep enough we reach the common life, the shared experience of man, the world of possibility. If we do not go deep enough, if we live and write half-way, there are obscurity, vulgarity, the slang of fashion, and several kinds of death.[23]

FIGURE 20. Thomas Merton and Daniel Berrigan in the monastery gatehouse prior to the participants' departure on Friday.
Photograph by Jim Forest, courtesy of Boston College, John J. Burns Library.

After Muste ended his remarks, the voice of Thomas Merton entered Yoder's notes to begin their final session of open discussion together, though the clarity of the young theologian's recorded comments decreases as they wind down. Perhaps this reflects an element of fatigue from the notetaker's copious efforts throughout the event. What remains clear, though, is that Muste's reflections on the precarious state of the larger world had provided them considerable food for thought, and they grappled with the kinds of responses such a time as theirs warranted. Merton's initial suggestion ad-dressed the need for a healthy interior life in the midst of oppressing forces that surround us. He shared that "one of our jobs is conserving the 'lone zone' against the diabolical machine, [because the] fear of being alone drives [us] to Orwell's world." Merton felt "this was the job of Protestantism," to focus "back to the person." From this insight, "protest prophets have a secret [in order to be able] to go on alone." He lamented that perhaps the hope

23. As quoted in Muste, *Saints for this Age*, 22. Muste apparently jotted it from memory at Gethemani; it is not reproduced verbatim in his outline.

provided by the papal statement *Pacem in Terris* had in the end "pacified us into thinking it was done by a word from the top."[24]

Daniel Berrigan, no doubt drawing from his own work advocating for the impoverished, followed with the suggestion that perhaps there was "a way to anchor the peace movement in local service to the poor," rather than set sights on such a broad vision to "plan for the world" or look to "outer space city planners" for hope. Ultimately, "we find what most of life is about by serving the minority." When we do, "life gets more black and white, [exposing us to both] more freedom and more anguish." It may seem "inefficacious" but in truth it becomes "radiating." Such "ironic moments of concrete service are our illumination," he asserted, moments where humanity in the flesh, not ideas, is at stake. Berrigan then referred to comments by *Saturday Evening Post* columnist Stewart Alsop,[25] perhaps to offer a contrasting approach to address world problems. Using a "rodent metaphor," Alsop had apparently advocated for attacking the nerve center of what one opposes. We should "mop up the nest, take out their technical center." For all its shortcomings, *Pacem in Terris* had at least demonstrated that one can make a moral appeal for peace rather than a simply pragmatic one. Our modern tendency is to "boil it down to something to research." But the problem with pragmatic peace research is that in the end, it actually studies the phenomena of war rather than the art of living in peace.

Merton continued with his critique of *Pacem in Terris*, however, suggesting that its weakness is that it "is phrased so it can be put in a computer." But he added that simply "rebelling against the outfit is no way to rebel against the Principalities." Such rebellion against the institution falls short because the institution is itself no longer significant. In general, "schism is irrelevant," and in breaking away we on some level concede that the institution's own definition of itself is the final word. It grants the institution a control of life which is diabolical. "It makes others in the institution, those responsible for it, only sicker," and it "makes the schismatic even sicker," as well. Besides, Merton cautioned, as dissenters "we are not that strong such that our rebellion would matter." We must in fact "take care not to become sicker ourselves," for in truth, "loving at every point" is our real, ultimate

24. Yoder's notes read, "Protest prophets have a secret. . ."; it is unclear whether he means "prophets of protest" generically or "Protestant prophets" specifically. Later comments to novices about Protestant skepticism toward the advance of humanity and their view of our need to "hang on to the cross and fight our way through this thing" suggest he could be comparing Protestant and Catholic views here.

25. Alsop wrote a column titled "Affairs of State" that addressed various political issues. A review of his 1964 columns failed to locate his use of a "rodent metaphor" in this manner.

responsibility." Our obligation in facing a world bent toward war involves clinging to a "heroic Christian hope" and to "abandon all others." "Brethren," Merton asserted, "we are in a hell, but a hell of mercy."

This curious phrase originated from one of Merton's spiritual forebears, a twelfth-century Cistercian monk, Isaac of Stella.[26] It alludes to the phase of contemplative experience when one no longer feels God's presence and is filled with dread as one becomes purged of self and ego. It is the phase of contemplation St. John of the Cross referred to as the "dark night of the soul," when God seems absent. It reflects a point when one has lost all confidence and hope in one's own virtue as a vehicle to earn God's blessing and thus creates an emotional state of hell, but it was "merciful" in that such purging of self-based hope was required before a life of true hope in God might commence. Muste's reflections on the bleak state of their world's obsession with militarization and the scant likelihood that humans possessed the will or means to reverse those trends without divine intervention struck Merton as such a condition. The potential nuclear destruction spawned by their technological society hovered over them, creating a hell of uncertainty and anxiety. But it was a hell of mercy. It permitted only one path toward liberation, a path that placed no hope in human ingenuity and effectiveness, but squarely in God's unpredictable movement through obedient human actions. Merton contrasted this hell of mercy and heroic hope with that of Dante, which demanded, "abandon all hope ye who enter here."

Yoder next captured a reference to *Seeds in the Desert: The Legacy of Charles de Foucauld* by René Voillaume,[27] a book about the Petit Frere, or the Little Brothers of Jesus, which Louis Massignon had helped establish using Foucauld's *Directoire*. The order's story offered a model for those dedicated to pursuing peace. They felt it their "duty to stay in the country" where God had placed them among those they were called to serve. This duty, Merton explained, did not reflect a uniquely religious virtue, but represented "a natural value." Yoder then ends the written record of this gathering by crediting its final words to Tony Walsh, who advocated for all to return "back to the base, solitude to think, meditation."

---

26. Merton used this quote in *The Climate of Monastic Prayer*, 138. There he translates the original Latin, *In inferno sumus, sed misericordiae, non irae; in caelo erimus*, as "a hell of mercy and not of wrath."

27. The U.S. edition Yoder cited (Notre Dame, IN: Fides Publishers Association, 1960) followed an earlier British and the original French editions. Voillaume was one of the order's founders.

FIGURE 21. Charlie Ring, Philip Berrigan, and Tony Walsh in the monastery gatehouse
engage in informal discussion with several others prior to Friday's departure.
Photograph by Jim Forest, courtesy of Boston College, John J. Burns Library.

Their time of shared exploration had nearly drawn to a close. Though
Yoder focused on the church and Muste on a broad social movement, what
they heard from both that morning harmonized into a strong call to make
their presence felt in the world around them. They could not sit back and
blend in, making no waves; their strategy could not seek to gently humor a
sick culture in hopes that it might somehow reform itself. Nor could they
become seduced by assumptions that the world's future rested with maintaining the global superiority of a virtuous America. Yoder's unity as mission and Muste's mutual trust as prerequisite and goal both demanded more
than words of inspiration to motivate others. They required vulnerability
and risk to actually begin living out a better way, to live it together with
others, and to live it for all to see. The only danger, as Muste reminded, was
in not going far enough or deep enough to reach this common life, a failure
that invites "several kinds of death."

As they made their way back to gather their belongings and have some
lunch, Merton approached Bob Cunnane one last time, wanting to be sure
that the young priest had grasped the gist of his input. "I remember walking
down the hill with Merton. He really thought that he had done a bum job
of explaining, that he felt he didn't deliver his points well. It struck me that
he was very sincere about what he wanted to say, because I certainly wasn't
one of the big wheels at the conference, and he wanted to make sure that I
understood what he was trying to say. It was a sort of kindness to clarify, it
wasn't at all condescending. It was making sure I got it, somewhat. He was
very good with that."[28]

28. Cunnane, 31 May 2010, conversation with author.

Merton's guests could not linger long, however. A large group was arriving to fill the guesthouse that afternoon, and following lunch their rooms were needed for others. John Grady and Elbert Jean loaded their vehicles parked under the columns of trees that lined the gatehouse lane and headed in separate directions for their respective homes. The rest, joined by Merton, lingered in the gatehouse corner room dressed in their more formal traveling attire. As they waited for transport, they continued talking and processing their thoughts, savoring a few remaining moments together. Soon the vehicles arrived, and they bade farewell to Merton and Gethsemani Abbey, departing for the next leg of their journey. Daniel Berrigan, accompanied by Tony Walsh, needed only a few miles travel to reach the nearby Sisters of Loretto, where he would share from his past summer's experience in South Africa. The remainder began their sixty-mile car ride to the Louisville airport, where Yoder would catch his plane back to northern Indiana and the others would return to New York. As they rode, A. J. Muste offered Bob Cunnane one final gift by sharing about several colorful experiences from his decades-long pilgrimage as a peacemaker. "I was kind of overwhelmed by it," Cunnane remembered. "In some ways, the ride home probably left a bigger impression than the actual conference."[29] Following their departure, Thomas Merton returned once more to his monastic routine.

Into the World

Not long after they parted company that November, these men would encounter various occasions for putting to concrete practice the abstractions and ideas they had exchanged within Gethsemani's enclosure. Four weeks later, on December 19, what some consider the first substantive demonstration against Vietnam occurred, drawing over 2,000 people to the streets in nine cities. In San Francisco, Joan Baez led six hundred protesters in song, while Phil Ochs did likewise in New York to accompany speeches by A. J. Muste and others denouncing U.S. Vietnam policy. Then just two days before year's end, swayed by journalist I. F. Stone's impassioned pleas, the SDS national council agreed to coordinate a major antiwar rally for the upcoming Easter weekend, a time traditionally reserved for coordinated antinuclear protest.[30]

Soon after the new year began, A. J. Muste helped draft and recruit signatures on a "Declaration of Conscience" opposing U.S. involvement in Vietnam. The names of both Berrigans, Tom Cornell, Ping Ferry, and A. J.

29. Ibid.

30. DeBenedetti and Chatfield, *American Ordeal*, 100.

Muste appeared among the thirty or so initial signers. Muste had approached Paul Peachey, as well, but he declined. Despite strong personal support for the sentiments expressed by the declaration, Peachey cited concern that it might interfere with his vocational efforts, perhaps alluding to the ecumenical nature of his Church Peace Mission dialogues. He also expressed lack of clarity as to how his Christian-based pacifism might impose its vision when contradictory "dynamics of brokenness are operative and still have to be reckoned with." His response to Muste's invitation added: "I regard my suspense at this point to be unacceptable in the long run, but cannot with integrity overleap it. I am sorry I could not participate in the Merton retreat, because I had hoped that this issue could be tackled. Hopefully there will be another opportunity."[31]

FIGURE 22. Bob Cunnane, Philip Berrigan, Charlie Ring, and Tom Cornell pause for a photograph before boarding their flight home.

Photograph by Jim Forest, courtesy of Boston College, John J. Burns Library.

During these same weeks in December and January, several of Merton's guests also collaborated in planning a convocation that could perhaps be viewed as a reprise of at least some issues they engaged at Gethsemani. "Peace on Earth: Moral and Technological Implications—A Consultation of Leaders of Religion," co-sponsored by the Fellowship of Reconciliation and Ferry's Center for the Study of Democratic Institutions, convened during the first three days of March 1965. Five of the event's six-man administrative committee had played a role at Gethsemani—Phil Berrigan, Ping Ferry, and committee chair John Oliver Nelson had participated in the retreat, while John Heidbrink and secretary Paul Peachey played key roles in arranging it.[32]

31. Peachey to Muste, 8 Feb. 1965, D/4, CPM Records, SCPC.

32. The sixth member was Rabbi Michael Robinson. Glenn E. Smiley to Peachey et

As Peachey explained in letters of invitation to participants, the convocation had emerged from questions raised by Ferry's Center about "what Protestant–Catholic–Jewish doctrine and insight offer in regard to violence and injustice in the world today," and it sought "a real engagement of mind and spirit. Essentially dealing with 'The Triple Revolution,' the Consultation is to inform and explore rather than legislate or exhort."[33] The planners named primary background reading of *Pacem in Terris* and *The Triple Revolution*, to be supplemented by essays "Toward a Moral Economy" by Ping Ferry, "The Roots of War" by Thomas Merton, "The Future of the Civil Rights Movement" by Bayard Rustin, and Ellul's book, *The Technological Society*, among other literature. The program also showed John Heidbrink opening the gathering, Daniel Berrigan leading a working session, and both Ping Ferry and John Yoder responding to primary addresses given by others.

Earlier program drafts included a slot for reflections to be written by Thomas Merton and read by Daniel Berrigan.[34] Merton declined the opportunity, however, citing other deadlines and commitments already in place. He expressed appreciation for the event, though, sharing his concern that without careful discernment "the Church will end up as a religious Madison Avenue for the computer boys." Even so, he felt his own lack of technological competence rendered him a poor candidate to address the matter. Although his sense of hope assured that a true renewal of the church was certain, that outlook was not confirmed by modern technology because it could not be "programmed into a computer." But ultimately, together "with all the 'powers,'" computers would only elicit "divine laughter." Our task was therefore one of "raising our sights a bit and having a truer and more lasting hope."[35]

After Merton indicated he could not provide material for the conference, John Heidbrink filled the slot with Daniel Berrigan, suggesting the opportunity would have the Jesuit "whirling away with people who need to know you."[36] Following the event, A. J. Muste forwarded a note to Berrigan expressing his appreciation for the Jesuit's input and reflecting the growing interfaith bond these peace workers enjoyed: "I feel that I must put down in

al., 19 Dec. 1964, E/10, CPM Records, SCPC.

33. Peachey to Peachey, 27 Jan. 1965, E/10, CPM Records, SCPC. Invitation letter template from Peachey as Secretary prepared with himself inserted as addressee.

34. Heidbrink to "All Consultation Registrants," memo with "Peace on Earth" consultation program, E/10, CPM Records, SCPC. Martin Luther King Jr. also appeared on the program to provide a major address.

35. Merton to Heidbrink, 22 Jan. 1965, *HGL*, 418–19.

36. Heidbrink to Berrigan, Feb. 1965, 130, Berrigan Collection, CUL. Berrigan's comments and those of others from this event (including W. H. Ferry and John Yoder) were printed in the May 1965 *Fellowship* issue, comprised almost exclusively of material from the March convocation.

black and white my gratitude for your words. Your words and your presence sustain me and give me a new experience of the meaning of communion. I am sure this is true also for others."[37]

As the conflict in Vietnam expanded, the radical left's interest in *The Triple Revolution* per se would fade, but the fourteen retreatants continued in their commitment to radical priorities. Two, however, would not live to see the closure to the Vietnam saga. A. J. Muste continued to help unite the burgeoning antiwar movement up until his death in February 1967,[38] and Thomas Merton continued his quest for greater solitude and contemplative understanding until his own accidental death in December 1968 while on an Asian tour to engage his Eastern monastic counterparts. For his part, Ping Ferry also continued to advocate for social change and U.S. removal from Vietnam, but only months after Merton's death he was essentially fired from his position at the Center for the Study of Democratic Institutions. He then affiliated with a different foundation from which he continued to advocate for peace and distribute considerable sums for liberal causes until his own death in September 1995.[39]

Canadian Tony Walsh returned to Montreal, serving the poor at Benedict Labré House for two more years, after which he retired from that work and spent his remaining years leading retreats and discussions in religious communities. Walsh died in May 1994.[40] Elbert Jean remained with the Committee of Southern Churchmen for an additional year and for the next ten years helped administer various federally and state funded poverty reduction and community organizing programs in Tennessee. From 1975 through 1980 Jean ran the district office for Arkansas congressman Bill Alexander, and then returned to Tennessee, where he finished his active years self-employed in private business ventures. In 1990 he retired to a farm near Bowling Green, Kentucky, where he still lives with his wife Joy.[41] John Oliver Nelson continued his commitment to pacifism and hectic involvement on various boards and committees, while continuing as director of Kirkridge Retreat and Study Center until his formal retirement in 1974. He remained active long after retirement, however, in such organizations as the War-Nation-Church study group (successor to the Church Peace Mission),

37. Muste to Berrigan, 4 Mar. 1965, A/137, Berrigan Collection, CUL.
38. Robinson, *Abraham Went Out*, 220.
39. Ward, *Ferrytale*, 143, 152–90, 194.
40. Buell, *Traveling Light*, 78–87.
41. Jean, 18 Apr. 2010, conversation with author.

Fellowship of Reconciliation, Earlham College board, and numerous others, as well as maintaining a rigorous speaking schedule. Nelson died in 1990.[42]

The theological career of John Howard Yoder continued to flower and earned him increasing recognition as a seminal spokesperson of Christian pacifist thought. He became a full-time professor of theology at Goshen College Biblical Seminary in 1965, and in 1977 he began service in the same capacity at the University of Notre Dame, where he helped found the Joan B. Kroc Institute for International Peace. Yoder remained active as a Notre Dame faculty member until his unexpected death in December 1997.[43] Charles Ring continued his work as director of retreats at the Stigmatine retreat house near Boston and also served as superior of the order's U.S. province. Though supportive of Bob Cunnane's activism, he never joined the antiwar movement or engaged in protest. Ring contracted Lou Gehrig's Disease just a few years after the retreat, which led to slow decline and eventual death in 1986. He was remembered fondly as one who faced this challenge with courage and good humor.[44]

Although subsequent paths taken by most retreat participants expressed their strong commitment to peace and justice, choices by the remaining six most explicitly embraced the retreat's theme of "protest." As the Catholic Peace Fellowship took root, it helped to spawn and nurture a so-called "Catholic Resistance" element of Vietnam War opposition.[45] Each of these six men played visible, key roles in this resistance, engaging in acts of radical, nonviolent antiwar protest that resulted in court appearances and prison sentences. Mostly their efforts sought to challenge and ultimately impede the draft of young men. The first to chart such a course was Tom Cornell, who was arrested for publically burning his draft card in November 1965, just weeks after new legislation had dramatically escalated penalties for doing so.[46] In 1960 Cornell had also destroyed several draft cards he had been issued, but this later public action led to his imprisonment for five months. After his release Cornell continued his activist ways, offering draft counseling and speaking out on diverse issues. He continued to work as CPF and FOR staff until his position was terminated in 1979. He then

42. Yeasted, *JON*, 89–163.

43. "John H. Yoder, Theologian At Notre Dame, Is Dead at 70." *New York Times*, January 7, 1998; see also Mennonite Church USA Archives, "Inventory."

44. Cunnane, 27 Oct. 2012, conversation with author.

45. Patricia McNeal emphasizes that the terms "Catholic Left" and "New Catholic Left" are misleading in that the activism it references reflects a religiously motivated coalition focused on social and Church transformation; it did not emerge from a Marxist political context (McNeal, *Harder Than War*, 173–74).

46. Ibid., 147.

taught school for a couple of years until he accepted an invitation to operate a soup kitchen in Waterbury, Connecticut, where he remained for several years. From there he moved to Peter Maurin Catholic Worker Farm near Marlboro, New York, where he still lives with his wife, Monica.[47]

As priests, the Berrigans were not themselves subject to the draft, but they soon found radically creative approaches to confront it. They had publically opposed the war even before their Gethsemani retreat, and both would continue to do so during the months that followed—Daniel for example, helped found Clergy and Laity Concerned about Vietnam in 1965. But the Berrigans escalated the stakes in 1967. On October 22 of that year, Daniel was arrested and jailed for five days due to his role in a march on the Pentagon. When released on October 27, he was greeted with news that his brother Philip and three others had been arrested for a liturgically symbolic act of protest—breaking into a Baltimore draft board office, removing records, and pouring blood on them, followed by prayer as they awaited arrest. Less than a year later, on May 17, 1968, the brothers were again arrested along with seven others for removing draft records from a Catonsville, Maryland, draft board and this time burning them with homemade napalm. Then in early 1972, Philip again stood trial (with six others) on charges of conspiring to kidnap Secretary of State Henry Kissinger and bomb Washington, D.C., infrastructure tunnels—acts not seriously pursued but charged mainly based on idle conversations coupled with betrayal by a paid informant and other intrusive federal measures. The trial ended in a hung jury. As with Cornell, both Berrigans would continue their activism long after the war ended. After Philip married co-activist Elizabeth McAlister in 1973 they together formed a Baltimore "community of resistance" named Jonah House and established the Plowshares Movement that embarked on like-natured direct actions to challenge the nuclear arms race. Philip died in 2002, and Daniel, retired, lives in New York City.[48]

Though they collaborated closely and offered each other strong mutual support during their antiwar efforts, each brother carved a unique leadership niche within Catholic Resistance activity. Whereas Daniel's writing skills and speaking visibility positioned him as a major spokesperson and theologian for the movement, Philip provided relational mentorship, bringing together and encouraging many who would embark on their own

47. Cornell, 29 May 2010, conversation with author.

48. McNeal, *Harder Than War*, 190–218; Polner and O'Grady, *Disarmed and Dangerous*, 196–98; "Philip Berrigan, Former Priest and Peace Advocate in the Vietnam War Era, Dies at 79." *New York Times*, December 8, 2002. Online: http://www.nytimes.com/2002/12/08/us/philip-berrigan-former-priest-peace-advocate-vietnam-war-era-dies-79.html?pagewanted=all&src=pm.

draft board actions.[49] In the years that followed Catonsville, an estimate of anywhere from 50 to 250 draft boards raids occurred—most with some degree of Catholic Resistance ties.[50] During this time, Philip's longtime friend John Peter Grady would become a key supporter and coworker. As groups formed to enact raids, Grady on several occasions served prominently in their execution. His adeptness at planning and concealing these actions earned him the nickname "Quicksilver." During the war years Grady also ran unsuccessfully for congress as a Eugene McCarthy Peace Candidate and founded a Harlem interracial Montessori school. Then during an August 22, 1971, raid on the Camden, New Jersey, draft office that involved twenty-eight people, Grady was arrested and tried for his role. In this case, also involving an informant, all twenty-eight were found not guilty. Grady moved with his family to Ithaca, New York, where he taught at Ithaca College for three years. His death occurred in 2002.[51]

For their parts, the two remaining retreatants—Jim Forest and Robert Cunnane—also participated in a draft board action, this one occurring in Milwaukee on September 24, 1968. Fr. Cunnane had begun to speak out against Vietnam even before the Gethsemani retreat, and by 1967 he had gained a reputation as the Boston area's Catholic antiwar spokesperson. On October 16 of that year he served as one of five religious/moral leaders who accepted draft cards handed over by 280 men to be forwarded to the Justice Department. At this public act of civil disobedience sixty others instead spontaneously chose to burn their cards rather than "return" them in this manner. The event led to charges against five prominent figures, including William Sloan Coffin and Dr. Benjamin Spock. Cunnane's testimony at Spock's trial discredited charges of conspiracy and played a key role in gaining acquittal.[52]

Cunnane had intended to participate at Catonsville, attending a meeting in Baltimore with the Berrigans and others to plan for the event. He eventually chose not to join them, however, at least partly in response to recent political events such as President Johnson's withdrawal from the presidential race and Martin Luther King Jr.'s assassination. His choice received a cool response from the Berrigan circle, but participation at Milwaukee five months later went far toward regaining their favor. The Milwaukee action

49. Cunnane, 31 May 2010, conversation with author; Polner and O'Grady, *Disarmed and Dangerous*, 255–66.

50. McNeal, *Harder Than War*, 197.

51. Ibid., 287; Polner and O'Grady, *Disarmed and Dangerous*, 240, 248–49; Flores, "Obituary."

52. Cunnane, 31 May 2010, conversation with author; Mendelsohn, "The Church and Draft Resisters."

followed the pattern of Catonsville, with Cunnane, Forest, and twelve others removing and burning over 10,000 draft records. Most of the fourteen served more than a year in jail or prison as a result. After his release, Cunnane soon left the priesthood and married another resister, a former nun, Anne Walsh. Following the war, Bob and Anne continued working with ecumenical and integration issues at Packard Manse, speaking out on various social issues, and supplementing their income through teaching and various other ventures. Now retired, they continue to live in eastern Massachusetts.[53]

As with his longtime friend and collaborator, Tom Cornell, Jim Forest continued working with the FOR and CPF and advocating for peace in a variety of efforts. This included serving in press secretary roles for both the Catonsville and Milwaukee actions, actively participating in the latter. He served a prison term for his involvement in the Milwaukee 14. Forest especially demonstrated his nonpartisan commitment to peace and justice following the Vietnam War's end in 1975. As evidence grew that the united Hanoi government would prove as eager to jail dissidents as had the Saigon regime, and that it disdained religious expression as harshly as did most other Communist nations, Americans who had labored in the peace movement divided over how best to respond. Though some refused to accept the evidence or rationalized such actions as justified, Forest considered them as equally unacceptable to similar acts by other regimes that had been less favored within peace movement circles. He circulated a letter calling on Hanoi to permit Red Cross prison visits, an act that prompted accusations of CIA complicity and warnings that he jeopardized his "career in the peace movement."[54] It did no such thing, of course, and his commitment to peace continued. In 1977 he took a position with the International FOR in Holland where he served as its general secretary for twelve years. Forest also continued to develop his considerable literary talents and became a prolific writer; to date he has published nearly thirty books on various topics. Together with his wife Nancy, Forest still lives in Holland, where he continues to publish books—including *Living with Wisdom*, his biography of Thomas Merton—and edit a journal for the Orthodox Peace Fellowship.[55]

These and other experiences continued to shape the lives of those who had gathered at Gethsemani, merging and intertwining with memories of their brief but intense interlude in the fall of 1964. The impact of this encounter no doubt affected each in different ways—Daniel Berrigan, for one, has named Thomas Merton as a crucial influence in his actions, with the

53. Cunnane, 31 May 2010, conversation with author.
54. Forest, "Lessons in Peacemaking."
55. Forest, 26 May 2010, conversation with author.

retreat providing a memorable occasion in their ongoing relationship. It is difficult to attribute choices individuals make to the direct impact of one event. The retreat alone did not determine actions taken in the Catholic Resistance or elsewhere. But as Bob Cunnane shared, at the least it provided one of many helpful and encouraging reference points along the individual paths of many who attended. With the passage of time, their encounter has loomed large in the imaginations of many religious peace advocates. Its intent of gathering in mutual respect to consult one another regarding the spiritual implications of protesting the powers of domination supplies us with a profound, iconic image. It reminds us of a fundamental call to dig deeply and tap into spiritual roots that will set our priorities, sustain our vision, and navigate our pilgrimage as we give voice to hopes and aspirations that coax humanity closer to its created intent.

7

Impressions That Remained

ALTHOUGH THIS GATHERING AT Gethsemani might not be viewed as pivotal for many of these men, it nonetheless impressed its mark upon the memories of most. Traces of those impressions remain scattered along the trail of the correspondence, conversations, reports, and other communication they shared. The comments that survive—whether following on the heels of the event or recalled in later years—offer added color to the picture that we can still sketch of the retreat fifty years later.

Immediate Impressions

In the wake of this gathering, as one would expect, several of the men shared with friends and acquaintances their impressions of the retreat. Judging from comments that survive, it had impressed host and guests alike. That very Sunday, in addition to Merton's enthusiastic report to his novices of the contributions by Muste, Yoder, and Dan Berrigan, he also shared his overall delight with the event as a whole:

> We had a real bang-up week with this bunch. It was really an amazing group, it was lively. I mean each day two four-hour sessions. You know you don't fool around with a half hour conference and then go meditate. You really work . . . The purpose of this retreat was more or less a kind of organization, of getting the leaders of the peace movement . . . organized in view of a new phase. See we are coming around the corner. What's happened is that with the test ban and so forth, the peace movement sort of fell apart, and everybody sort of said, "What's there to do? Let's go into the civil rights," see. Now, with the Chinese

187

bomb, there is going to be all this ruckus and so forth again . . .
The idea was to get down to some spiritual roots . . . It was very
well worth doing. Very great.[1]

Just four days later Merton touched base with John Heidbrink, lamenting the absence of his hospital-bound friend and sharing his appreciation for the event. "I think we all felt it was a great experience," he reported:

I will not use the word "meaningful," as I have heard this so
much lately that the only bell it rings is the one for nausea. But
certainly I think we were in contact with reality and truth in a
way that is not met with every day. Thanks be to God for it. I
would sum it up in two words: (a) a sense of the awful depth
and seriousness of the situation; (b) a sense of deeper and purer
hope, a hope purified of trust in technological machinery and
the "principalities and powers" at work therein.

Merton then expressed pleasure at having met Nelson, Yoder, "and above all
A. J., who impressed me as much greater than anything that is said about
him, and much simpler. I suppose this is true of all who are really great in
some way or other." He voiced confidence that "we will always have light to
follow the truth and insights that are given us," despite a shaken "certainty
in institutions." Merton considered the week as "something of a 'last fling,'"
however, since his superiors were "not too favorable of this sort of thing and
developments seem to point to an end of retreats and a cutback in writing,
contacts and so on."[2]

Heidbrink responded a month-and-a-half later, thanking Merton for
his "life-giving" letter that brightened his hospital confinement. By then he
had received feedback from others, as well:

Both Ferry and A. J. have indicated that the geography of
thought and experience shared was breath-taking not to mention the living areas of underground water and wells so often
kept shut but which occasionally spurt and rock the boat. And
old John Yoder, solemn in his way but so sharp in vision and
judgment he easily could be one of the first rate creative theologs for Protestantism, was so shook and tried by the arrows and
water spurting he will never be the same again.[3] . . . Thanks for

1. Merton, recording 132:1, 22 Nov. 1964, TMC.
2. Merton to Heidbrink, 26 Nov. 1964, *HGL*, 417.
3. This reference may have referred to comments that interrupted Yoder's presentation. Heidbrink apparently regretted missing the chance to interact in a more informal setting. His 1998 interview commented on the retreat: "I missed getting better acquainted with some of them. Always I had respect for John Howard Yoder, but he

doing it, for meeting with Forest and Tom Cornell so their lines
of work can be at least focused by having been with you once,
and for keeping John Nelson climbing and roving.[4]

About a week after writing to Heidbrink, Merton also reported to Jean
and Hildegard Goss-Mayr, European peace advocates who had struck up an
exchange with Merton a few years earlier: "The FOR retreat was good, very
moving, and I think we all came away convinced that there is no hope to be
placed in human or technological or political expedients, but that our hope
is first and last in God and in the mystery of His will to save man, and his
promise of a reign of peace."[5]

Three days later Merton provided Ferry with some "long over-
due . . . scribbles" that included reference to the retreat: "It took time to
get back on the rails after our wonderful meeting, which everyone really
liked. You contributed very much and I appreciate it. I think the whole thing
worked out exceptionally well, and it was all real from beginning to end.
Retreats do not always achieve this unusual distinction."[6] In his reply, Ferry
closed his several paragraphs on recent happenings and readings by adding
that "Yoder on *Niebuhr and Pacifism* is splendid," most likely referring to
Yoder's "Reinhold Neihbur and Christian Pacifism," first presented in 1953
as a conference paper and published in 1961 as a pamphlet. Ferry had "met
many marvelous people at Gethsemani," he continued, "& [would] never
forget those two stunning days. How can a man do his duty these days?
Is there a spot short of the Jagerstatter [sic], Chaney [sic], Schwerner, and
Goodman spot where one can stand with his conscience at ease? I don't
believe so."[7] Then near the year's end Merton also shared with the French
Franciscan Père Hervé Chaigne, editor of a periodical *Frères du Monde*, that,
"In November a group of peace workers, including A. J. Muste, who is the
dean of American pacifists, and some from *The Catholic Worker* and Jim
Forest of the movement, came here for a retreat and discussion which was
very successful and full of good lights. There was much discussion about

---

was such a formidable character in our Church Peace Mission meetings and things
like that, that you never really caught him off guard being an academic, you know. But
I wanted to get better acquainted, because he did a perfectly wonderful reply to Karl
Barth" ("Interview of John Heidbrink," conducted by Richard Deats," 11 Sept. 1998,
D/37, FOR Records, SCPC).

4. Heidbrink to Merton, 15 Jan. 1965, TMC.

5. Merton to Jean and Hildegard Goss-Mayr, 2 Dec. 1964, *HGL*, 335.

6. Merton to Ferry, 5 Dec. 1964, *HGL*, 219.

7. Ferry to Merton, 14 Dec. 1964, TMC.

a book which I had at the time just read, Jacques Ellul's great work on technology."[8]

The experiences that converged that week may have affected Merton even more subtly and profoundly than he knew at the time. After he had finished recording the second day's events in his journal (November 19), he recorded a dream of the night before that "haunted" him all that day. It featured a Chinese "princess"—referred to as "Proverb," an occasional visitor to his dreams—who brought with her a sense of unattainable reality that knew and loved him in his deepest essence.[9] In his biography of Merton, Jim Forest suggests that this dream, coupled with the "Noah-like downpour" enveloping his hermitage as he filled his journal that night, may have prompted one of his most inspiring essays, "Rain and the Rhinoceros," which Merton would craft the following month. Perhaps a third stimulus that inspired this piece of masterful writing consisted of the probing dialogue simultaneously woven into his being during these few days in the company of fellow prophets.[10]

The correspondence of others also acknowledged the impact felt by their sojourn to Gethsemani. Tony Walsh had joined the group mainly for a much-needed break as the guest of Daniel Berrigan, and that objective seems to have been met. Prior to his departure, Walsh had written of his weariness and fatigue. "I feel washed out with no views or ideas, so will be like a Trappist of the old school, but one with not even knowledge of sign language."[11] Indeed, within the surviving record, Walsh broke his vow of silence on only two occasions, both during sessions at Merton's hermitage. His first comment affirmed the positive influence on others that one's own suffering can effect; his final comment closed the event's gathered discussion in affirmation for the benefits of solitude and meditation. Walsh undoubtedly accompanied Berrigan following the retreat to visit the Sisters of Loretto and probably joined him in Berrigan's New York apartment for a day or two after that before returning to Montreal the following Wednesday.

Two days after his return Walsh sent words of gratitude to his traveling companion. "A Jacob's ladder of thanks, extending to the heavens, for the number after number of kindnesses that you did for me during the week of change. It was certainly a *great week*," he wrote. Although he had "found the household in a mess" upon his return, he had "plunged right in, and within two days time, things cleared" and he was now "having an easy weekend."

---

8. Merton to Père Hervé Chaigne, O.F.M., 28 Dec. 1964, *WF*, 109.

9. Merton, *DWL*, 19 Nov. 1964, 167–68.

10. Forest, *Living with Wisdom*, 181.

11. Walsh to D. Berrigan, 11 Nov. 1964, A/145, Berrigan Collection, CUL.

Further, "I have wonderful news in that I have practically regained former energy, something that has not been the case for about two years. If this continues, then things should work out well. So the change was beneficial all the way around . . . Few people," he added, "have such healing hands of friendship as you do." Looking ahead he anticipated that "possibly by the end of next week, I'll be more down to earth (after jets and penthouses)."[12] Three weeks later he again wrote Berrigan to confirm that his renewed outlook continued: "I am writing to report that there has been a return of energy that I had not thought possible. Just shows you what Kentucky Bourbon and a New York penthouse can accomplish."[13] What emerges from the impressions Walsh left behind, then, is not so much an event that inspired protest and engagement, but one that offered a restorative and healing salve, kindly applied to an aging servant in works of mercy by his pastoral Jesuit friend.

On the day before Merton drafted his observations to Heidbrink in mid-December, Elbert Jean had prepared a letter to Merton. Ironically, as Merton was viewing the retreat as a "last fling" with such encounters, Jean was inquiring whether his close colleague, civil rights activist Will Campbell, might schedule a similar experience for his Committee of Southern Churchmen. Jean bracketed his request with words of thanks for the *Seeds of Destruction* copy and to,"say that the opportunity to be with you and the others last week was helpful. I have thought about your understanding of the Monk and the church. I have an internal struggle at this point which I am trying to force into verbalization but so far to no avail . . . Again I want to thank you for the hospitality and the meaningful encounter."[14]

On December 1, John Oliver Nelson wrote to John Heidbrink, expressing that "Nary another day must go by without my . . . thanking you for all that amazing Thomas Merton experience . . . [T]he Trappist deal—though too brief in my schedule—was right historic." In particular:

> What a hero Dan Berrigan! What heartiness in John Grady, and earnestness in Cornell and Forrester [sic] and the others! Merton was a candid, canny, concerned, and essentially saintly and reassuring one, and I appreciated him immensely. But the whole event—mass with partaking in both kinds, talk at the hermitage and elsewhere, some glimpse of the pale cloistered but rugged life, indignation among Roman Catholics about Vatican torpor

12. Walsh to D. Berrigan, 27 Nov. 1964, A/145, Berrigan Collection, CUL.
13. Walsh to D. Berrigan, 19 Dec. 1964, A/145, Berrigan Collection, CUL.
14. Jean to Merton, 25 Nov. 1964, TMC.

and footdragging about war—all this was great gain for me. I
want to keep up with those men.[15]

The enthusiastic response of Nelson was noteworthy, as his enthusiasm for
a Catholic FOR affiliate had seemed lukewarm to some, and nurturing the
inclusion of the CPF within the FOR family appears to have been a likely
motive for John Heidbrink's pursuit of this event.

Upon his return, A. J. Muste also peppered correspondence with
positive references to the retreat. Some of them, however, betray a typically
Protestant puzzlement over Merton's immersion in Catholic monasticism—
Tom Cornell later expressed personal disappointment that Muste had not
taken advantage of this opportunity to experience a taste of Gregorian chant
and Trappist observance of the Benedictine hours.[16] For example, four days
after his return, in acknowledging a financial contribution that had arrived
during his "visit with Father Thomas Merton," Muste had shared, "Thomas
Merton has really a very brilliant mind. It is something of a mystery to
me how he manages life in a Trappist Monastery. Of course, he has more
freedom than most monks. I gather that the Abbot may impose some restrictions upon him. At any rate, he has made a great contribution to the
thinking about peace and war."[17]

And then on December 1, he responded to another acquaintance, "As
you probably know, I was away for nearly a week attending a small conference led by Thomas Merton in the Monastery where he lives in Kentucky.
Though this is not a familiar environment for me, the experience of meeting
and hearing Merton was a very illuminating and encouraging one. One feels
no restraint in his presence."[18] On the same Friday that he had departed
from Gethsemani, Muste also dictated a letter to an acquaintance who had
visited his office that week, also using the occasion to express appreciation
for the gathering and its host:

> I am so sorry that I missed you when you were in the city. I
> understand that [personal secretary] Beverly [Sterner] told you
> that I was in Kentucky at the Trappist Monastery with Father
> Thomas Merton. It was an occasion arranged by John Heidbrink
> who has really done a remarkable job in this field. It was for me
> a very illuminating and encouraging experience.

15. Nelson to Heidbrink, 1 Dec. 1964, D/38, FOR Records, SCPC.

16. Cornell, "Merton on Peace," 23.

17. Muste to Harrison Butterworth, 1 Dec 1964 (dictated Nov. 24), Supp. #1/4, microfilm reel 89:33, Muste Papers.

18. Muste to Harold Fackert, 1 Dec. 1964, Supp. #1/4, microfilm reel 89:33, Muste
Papers.

> Incidentally, another book by Thomas Merton entitled,
> "Seeds of Destruction" has just been published by Farrar-Straus.
> Its middle section as to do with peace and war and is an excel-
> lent restatement of the radical pacifist position.[19]

Yet another appreciative reference by Muste crops up in minutes of the January 1965 FOR Executive Committee meeting. John Heidbrink had reported on the encouraging growth of the Catholic Peace Fellowship over the past year, reaching a formal membership level of one hundred and a contact list numbering 750. He attributed the growth to the effort of Jim Forest "outside his regular working hours" and noted that the CPF budget now permitted Forest's full time employment. The minutes indicate that Muste followed Heidbrink's report with comments that, "Attributed the mushrooming development of Catholic interest in FOR in large part to John's foresight and initiative. [Muste] reported on the sense of genuine communion that was found between the Roman Catholics and others who participated in the retreat with Thomas Merton at the Gethsemane [sic] Abbey in December [sic]."[20]

Lasting Impressions

Though the memory of Gethsemani may have faded with time, it did not disappear. From early on, some participants entertained thoughts of preserving the material and recounting it to a larger audience. Apparently Merton himself considered collecting for the record the thoughts he had presented. But already in February 1965 he shared with Daniel Berrigan that he was so busy he had "not even been able to type up the stuff from last November. Actually if it were just a matter of just sitting down and typing it would not be so bad, but I have forgotten what I said and the notes aren't much help, so I really will have to start all over again. Which I will, perhaps, in Lent. After I get another must job out of the way, in time for a deadline." Nothing emerged in print, however; it appears that by Lent, he had given up the idea.[21]

Perhaps none of the participants has sought more faithfully over the years to preserve and share the wisdom, insight, and urgency of these interactions than Jim Forest. He took substantive notes of retreat presentations and conversations, and even before that November ended he had embarked

19. Muste to Margaret von Seller, 1 Dec. 1964 (dictated Nov. 20), Supp. #1/4, microfilm reel 89:34. Muste Papers.

20. "FOR Executive Committee minutes," 26 Jan. 1965, A-2/6, FOR Records, SCPC.

21. Merton to Berrigan, 26 Feb. 1965, *HGL*, 86.

on an effort to collect the presentations in some form for the benefit of others. In his note asking A. J. Muste to write out his presentation for this purpose, preferably by December's end, he explained, "Several of the persons who were present at the conference, particularly Phil Berrigan, have urged me to mimeo up the talks which were delivered at Gethsemani—this would be particularly useful with Catholics. Perhaps, however, you could find a few persons among your own contacts who would be interested in such a booklet . . . In addition we have asked Ping Ferry to make an editorial contribution to this."[22] Muste failed to respond until January, however, explaining his recent preoccupation with visiting family and moving into new housing. "I want to cooperate to the utmost in extending the influence of that occasion," he assured. "However it is going to be some time before I can now tackle the job of getting some material down on paper," continuing with his suggestion to consult his recent *Liberation* publications. He concluded, "perhaps you can give me a ring on this."[23]

When Forest contacted Yoder a week into December for the same purpose, the Mennonite scholar demurred. He explained, "Having had considerable experience over the years with meetings the essence of which one wanted somehow to keep hold of, I have been impressed by the inadequacy of mimeographed materials circulated later as reflection and reporting either for those who participated or for others." Yoder went on to express skepticism that "the various contributions made . . . would create a helpfully unitary document for persons who were not present." He proposed instead that Forest pursue developing one presentation as a pamphlet or flier, or perhaps having one participant synthesize the material into a cohesive document. Though less than three weeks had passed, he felt that "much of what was contributed to the meeting by its immediate contemporaneousness is lost." Since his own contribution responded to comments others provided, it would "be the least appropriate for reconstruction in its own right." This reluctance did not manifest "lack of willingness to do my part" and was "especially not any indication of absence of gratitude for the Gethsemani experience." Rather, he doubted that "simply trying to reconstruct a past conversation is of any real help in keeping the concerns alive and visible which were then so self-evident." Still he would review his notes for anything "worthy of separate redaction" that could stand alone, "rather . . . than a playback of our earlier conversations."[24] Nothing transpired from this first attempt to capture the material shared at Gethsemani, however. Forest

22. Forest to Muste, 1 Dec. 1964, 44, microfilm reel 89:25, Muste Papers.
23. Muste to Forest, 11 Jan. 1965, Supp. #1/4, microfilm reel 89:34, Muste Papers.
24. Yoder to Forest, 8 Dec. 1964, 13, Yoder Papers, TMC.

revisited the possibility with Yoder again in 1974, indicating not only his personal interest, but usefulness for the Merton biography then in process by John Howard Griffin (a project ultimately taken over by Michael Mott). Once more, nothing ensued.

Forest's own prolific writing has contained references to the event, however. One of his earliest published writings that reflects back on these days appeared in a January 1969 issue of *WIN*, a magazine published by the War Resisters League. The article, titled "Some Thoughts on Resistance," provides an extended reflection on how to sustain the peace movement. Merton had died only one month before this issue's publication date, and Forest shared that "it has taken Merton's death for me to stop giving a vague *yes* to [concerns about peace activist burnout and flagging energy] and to begin thinking seriously about the kinds of things that must be done if the movement which hopes to humanize the future can become more humanized itself." He launched his observations using as a springboard Merton and his transition from a new monk who wrote in 1948 that "it would be outside the present scope of my vocation if I tried to make any political analysis of anything," to being in Forest's eyes "the world's most politically radical hermit." His opening discussion of Merton included several comments about the retreat, which he described as "a kind of talk and meditation gathering on the spiritual roots of protest." He continued:

> There was a general joy about the gathering. It was good to be together to talk about more worldly lives in a place that had been intended for those who had "left the world," as the term goes. The talk was meaningful to me in very personal terms. I had only recently (in helping to organize the Catholic Peace Fellowship) returned to full time involvement with the peace movement, having on several occasions left the movement in various stages of disgust and disillusionment . . .
>
> Merton's worried concern [with the sometimes intense and destructive pace of movement activity] was first expressed by letters (directly), and (more obliquely) in articles, then by the direct action of bringing people together in the flesh: our retreat for the purpose of digging into the life style in which protest is not only rooted but sustained and nourished. The Catholic term, spiritual life, would be relevant here; so would community. Merton was convinced that no movement toward nonviolent resistance could ever become powerful without an ongoing cultivation within the movement, occurring within a communal form of some kind (he was fascinated with Gandhi's ashrams), geared to develop an inner life which would

be continually deepening and energizing. He realized that this would be possible only if our attitude toward time and work was revolutionized . . .

Nothing of a programmatic nature came out of that gathering. But the impact of those discussions on the individuals involved was considerable. In a few instances, at least, he helped create a balance of community, meditation, and action which has pulled us through the subsequent years. Perhaps now, however, it is necessary to think in programmatic terms . . .[25]

Forest offered other, passing mentions of the event, such as in a 1996 tribute to Daniel Berrigan[26] and in his 2010 biography of Merton, *Living with Wisdom*. In the latter work he highlighted Merton's framing question of "By what right do we protest?" which he suggested was "an unsettling challenge to people who could be considered professional protesters." Forest also devoted a paragraph to the significance of Merton's references to Franz Jägerstätter, "a saint uniquely matched to a century of total war."[27]

Perhaps Forest's most extensive and insightful treatment of the event, however, appears in "Thomas Merton's Struggle with Peacemaking," his contribution to the anthology *Thomas Merton: Prophet in the Belly of a Paradox*. As recounted there, he recalled "laughter, but less of it" than at his only previous face to face encounter with Merton two-and-a-half years earlier:

> The times were deadly serious and so was much of the conversation. Merton spoke in earnest, listened with a quick and critical ear, and at times launched us into silence. I remember him best in those days not with us in his hermitage, though he was present with the group as much as anyone, but rather walking alone outside, pacing back and forth in a state of absorption in thought so complete and compelling that it brought home to me the gravity of what he was going to say in the conference that followed more than in the words themselves.
>
> Merton's contribution was to impress on us, often more with questions than answers, that protest wasn't simply an almost casual human right, but rather a terribly dangerous calling that, if it lacked sufficient spiritual maturity, could contribute to making things worse.

Forest again recounted Jägerstätter's experience as a catholic (in both senses) model for relating to the institutional church's complicity with political evil:

25. Forest, "Thoughts on Resistance," 4–5.
26. Forest, "Great Lake of Beer," 120.
27. Forest, *Living with Wisdom*, 181–82.

"We had every reason to expect the same from our own Church leadership as the Vietnam war worsened. But we had to hope for something better than that in our situation, and not waste a minute in working toward that end—toward a Church that would put its weight behind those who refused to wage war and who refused to see other humans simply as 'bio-chemical links.'"[28]

On occasion Forest's Catholic Peace Fellowship comrade, Tom Cornell, also weighed in with memories of Gethsemani. In early 1974, as the tenth anniversary of the gathering approached, he chose the medium of a book review to share his impressions. Gordon Zahn's *Thomas Merton on Peace*, an anthology of Merton's writings, had appeared in print and reproduced Merton's retreat handout, which triggered Cornell's reflections. He revealed that, "Frankly, though I remember the meetings for discussion as dull, with Merton looking like a cat who had swallowed a particularly feathery canary, the event itself was far from dull." Cornell shared several colorful images of A. J. Muste and mentioned Merton's "*quo warranto*" framing of the topic and Ferry's embrace of Ellul before recounting the infamous swilling of beer by the Catholic guests. In Cornell's memory, "The moment of highest interest" proved to have been Yoder's presentation that addressed the "hard Gospel" and "proclaimed the Cross, the unique element that Christianity brings to the mystery of the pursuit of peace and justice in a world ruled by perverse power." He assessed the retreat as memorable, but confessed that he doubted "it had much to do with the course of development the Catholic resistance was to take."[29] On a later occasion Cornell would also affirm Yoder's presentation as one of skilled biblical interpretation from a Mennonite perspective, but characterize his style as "dry as a dishrag." He also appended his 1974 assessment of the week by noting that it "probably deepened commitment of the more marginal."[30]

Though he did not address it in his autobiography, glimpses of the retreat have also emerged from Daniel Berrigan's pen (and tongue) over the years as well. In the 1970s he would portray the retreat as having "in retrospect, the charged aura of a myth: practically all who took part have by now either died or undergone prison."[31] Based on that track record, he would "suppose the retreat could be termed in some wild way a success."[32] In a 1971 letter to family members, Berrigan mentioned—implicitly affirm-

28. Forest, "Thomas Merton's Struggle with Peacemaking," 40–42.

29. Cornell, "Merton on Peace," 23.

30. Cornell, 13 Apr. 2010, email to author.

31. Berrigan, *Portraits*, 16.

32. Berrigan, "Berrigan on Merton," 6.

ing—the perspective of Catholic pacifist Gordon Zahn that the "infamous retreat in the early 60's started things off for most of us except of course vets like A. J. who were already aged in the golden harness."[33] In addition, Berrigan's fascinating account of Thursday's "way-out" mass has surfaced on at least three occasions over the decades as well.[34] In one account, he shared his sense that the interfaith Eucharist may have served as "a beginning of sorts, because Merton was listening to something that had gotten a little beyond control. And that was important for him also."[35]

When asked in his ninetieth year to reflect further, Berrigan offered that, "These days stand in my heart as precious and fruitful. I was heartened to go farther in '68," alluding to his acts of radical civil disobedience in protest of the Vietnam War and America's draft of young men to fight it.[36] He confirmed the strong impression Muste had left on him as a great person, and remembered Yoder as a shy man but a deep thinker. Regarding the influence of Teilhard de Chardin that resonated in his presentation at Gethsmani, Berrigan would note that after he read comments Teilhard had written that portrayed the development of nuclear weapons as an expression of humanity's emerging maturity, he became disillusioned with Teilhardian theories and would later rely on them less.

From this vantage of ninety years Berrigan could also see that one of the primary fruits harvested from the gathering was "friendship." He found it a new and edifying experience to engage so intimately with others who also bore an intense burden for peacemaking—until that point, perhaps only with his brother Philip had he felt such close affinity with others holding similar priorities. As with Forest, hearing these issues discussed in a contemplative setting would also provide helpful grounding. He also confirmed that the focus did not plan any "next steps" in peacemaking; they did not leave with some sense of "this is what we will do next." What they left with, though, was a framework of relationship and discussion they could later draw upon when needed. And, he felt, it provided that for Merton, as well. Even as Merton moved further into his life as a hermit, his need for this sort of spiritual friendship grew. For Berrigan, the image of Merton casually and unpretentiously sitting among his guests while signing and distributing freshly printed copies of Seeds of Destruction symbolizes the connection and bonding provided by those days together.[37]

33. Berrigan, America is Hard to Find, 168.

34. Berrigan, "Berrigan on Merton" (1973); Portraits (1982); Testimony (2004).

35. Berrigan, "Berrigan on Merton," 6.

36. Berrigan, 3 May 2010, letter to author.

37. Berrigan, 22 March 2011, conversation with author.

For his part, Robert Cunnane, was a thirty-two-year-old burgeoning activist priest when he made the trip to Gethsemani. Though never publishing any observations of the retreat, forty-eight years later Cunnane's private reflections support Berrigan's assessment. "What struck me most was that the people seemed like people you could trust almost immediately just by their attitude and their bearing. These people really had a view of life that I could partake of. It was kind of transformative, but in a slow way, almost by osmosis, picking up from them attitudes. The whole mood of the conferences was one of a lack of condescension. We had some heavy hitters in there but they all acted as part of the group."[38] At the retreat, "I was charging myself—meeting all these great people gave me strength . . . My friendship with Jim Forest began here, as well as with Tom Cornell. I read John Yoder's book on the Jubilee Year[39] shortly after. Meetings like this were serious play—enjoying one another's company yet talking about protests, our faith, effectiveness. It solidified my idea of the church to this day."[40]

This experience, and others like it, particularly impressed upon Cunnane the potential for a public and non-privatized faith.

> My growth was from the thought deep down that Christianity was something to be held in private. I think this is part of our secular culture—privatize, privatize. The more I listened to these people, I said, "My God, this stuff works!" You're told to sacrifice and do all these things, and you think it's an arduous task that you have to strain to do, but these people seem to do it so simply. I never would have done publically what I did if it weren't for that. They really showed that you've got to step up, not just in a missionary sense of running to Asia and trying to convert some other people, but in your own culture really standing up for the values you have. Instead of whispering to each other that you're against war or something, stating it in a way that makes people allied with you rather than furious with you.[41]

He remembered Merton's hermitage as "a small cottage, many books, and within walking distance of the monastery."

By 1985 John Howard Yoder had joined the faculty of the University of Notre Dame theology department, and he had grown more open to revisiting options for documenting the 1964 retreat. Early that year he contacted

38. Cunnane, 31 March 2010, conversation with author.

39. Probably referring to Yoder, *Politics of Jesus*. Chapter 3 is titled "The Implications of the Jubilee."

40. Cunnane, 15 Apr. 2010, email to author.

41. Cunnane, 31 March 2010, conversation with author.

Robert E. Daggy of the Merton Studies Center at Bellarmine University to propose gathering information about the event. Since "both for the Berrigans and for Merton himself it has been said of this conversation that that it made a difference in their becoming more clearer [sic] in their peace position," he, along with Sister Elena Malits, a colleague and Merton scholar, wondered if the event "might be worth some focused attention soon." He suggested a series of interviews with participants, perhaps by a student under Daggy's guidance, as Yoder and Malits could not personally pursue it for some time.[42] Daggy's response apparently suggested publication options, for Yoder responded by suggesting instead a priority of simply "getting the archives straight" through an oral record of those still alive. "I simply wanted to have the memories tied down before they are lost."[43] In April Yoder wrote once more indicating that perhaps his wishes had been fulfilled in the work of a New York friar who had been doing research on the topic, and had already talked to Ferry. Perhaps Daggy could coordinate with the friar "to round out the process of gathering all the memories there are"? As before, however, this thrust seemingly evaporated without tangible results, and no trace remains of that work.[44]

Then in late spring 1993, Yoder reported that once again "from several quarters, pressure is rising on me to write something retrospective on the meeting at Gethsemani."[45] One of those quarters involved his University of Notre Dame department chair, Lawrence Cunningham. In response Yoder contacted Ping Ferry, Jim Forest, and Paul Peachey that summer to see what resources they might have on hand. At "the meeting in which both you and I had the privilege of participating," he reminded Ferry, "One of the parts of that event which is clear in more than one record is the fact that you introduced most of us to the thinking of Jacques Ellul, whose understanding of the 'principalities' and 'powers' I was somewhat acquainted with,[46] and

42. Yoder to Daggy, 29 Jan. 1985, 13, Yoder Papers, TMC.

43. Yoder to Daggy, 7 Feb. 1985, 13, Yoder Papers, TMC.

44. Yoder to Daggy, 17 Apr. 1985, 13, Yoder papers, TMC. The Graymoor archivist indicates that nothing of Charles Murphy's effort on this topic remains in their archive; the Thomas Merton Center also has no trace of his work.

45. Yoder to Preachey, 17 May 1993, 13, Yoder Papers, TMC.

46. Dawn, "'Principalities and Powers' in Ellul," explains how Ellul wrote as both a lay theologian and also as a social critic, but kept those two frames of reference separate in his writings. I am grateful to Andy Alexis-Baker for pointing me to this document. Ellul addressed concepts similar to the "powers" in writings that predated the retreat, which Yoder may have accessed. According to Wylie-Kellerman, "Naming the Powers," Ellul's book, *The Meaning of the City* is considered Ellul's theological counterpart to *The Technological Society*.

which Daniel Berrigan made some later use of in his prophetic ministry."[47] Ferry responded that his notes on "this altogether remarkable meeting" had "disappeared long ago."[48]

By 1993 Peachey could no longer recall the event he once helped arrange but could not attend, nor could he provide any documentary material.[49] Yoder's inquiry to Forest that year, however, resulted in the exchange of their respective note collections, and Yoder set about processing what he had on hand and performing a literature review of what had been published on the topic. In late 1994 Yoder forwarded his transcriptions and background annotations, together with his collection of Merton-related files, to the Thomas Merton Center archives at Bellarmine University.[50] This material, however, betrays little of what Yoder himself actually thought of the retreat or how the experience may have touched him personally. But his willingness to maintain files on both the event and on Merton himself, collect and annotate his original notes, compile supplemental observations, and advocate for research to preserve related memories all suggest he considered it significant. On a couple of occasions, however, his own thoughts about Merton's presence at the retreat seep through. In response to a 1986 inquiry seeking insight on Merton as an educator, Yoder shared that he did not sense Merton's intent to function "as an instructor" at the retreat. Rather:

> My impression was that the originality of the event for Merton was that he was inviting persons from other spiritual and ecclesiastical traditions than his own, with some authentic thought that they might from their traditions have things to say that he had not heard. It was for instance news to him that protest could be based in the words and person of Jesus, which had seemed to me to be obvious but which struck him as a new idea.[51]

Then in August 1993, Yoder shared with Lawrence Cunningham some comments he had made on a student paper that investigated Merton's integration of contemplation and ethics. When sharing it with Cunningham, Yoder suggested that in retrospect some of those comments "were perhaps partly the result of my own going back to Merton" in 1964. As such, Yoder

47. Yoder to Ferry, 26 July 1993, 13, Yoder Papers, TMC.

48. Ferry to Yoder, 29 July 1993, 12 Yoder Papers.

49. In mid-1995, however, the long-dormant files of the Church Peace Mission surfaced in the basement of a Washington, D.C. Methodist building, finding their way to the Swarthmore College Peace Collection. J. H. Yoder to Anne Yoder, 9 May 1993, 3, Yoder Papers, TMC.

50. Yoder to Forest, 23 July 1993, 12, Yoder Papers, TMC.

51. Yoder to Tom Del Prete, 29 Sept. 1986, 13, Yoder Papers, TMC.

thought, they might help illuminate how he personally perceived the event. "I have the impression, which most of his interpreters support," he had noted to the student, "that [Merton] only came to antiwar protest slowly, after others were running with it, and that he did not anchor it deeply in what he had been thinking about before . . . It is not . . . that he had a normative position [on protest] and [activists] then misrepresented it, but that they were already rolling, in the power of the heritage of Dorothy Day (whom he honored . . .) and he felt left behind." His comments on the student paper also suggest that Yoder—a rigorous ethicist whose own work relied heavily on a paradigm of Christian obedience—seemed a bit disconcerted by Merton's embrace of solitude and monastic obedience on the one hand and his ambivalence about his own public face and imposed limits to interaction on the other. Yoder asks whether Merton may have been:

> Denying his thesis [on solitude] by investing as much as he did in writing, publishing, being such a public person, displaying his passing thoughts on all kinds of questions in collections like *Conjectures* [*of a Guilty Bystander*] . . . When I was his guest in 1964 he signaled rather an impatience with the monastic discipline, talked of having his friends sneak into his hermitage without telling the abbot; as if there were not a healthy complementarity but a difficult tension. He was expecting that his freedom to receive visitors would soon be cut off, and it was, and he accepted that discipline . . . but he kept writing.[52]

These snippets offer a glimpse of Yoder's snapshot impression of Merton and the monk's engagement with his guests during the retreat. Yoder accurately sensed that Merton failed to process ideas through the rigorous, sequential logic employed by his own discipline of religious ethics. Yet had Yoder known more of Merton's earlier exposure to Louis Massignon's model for dissent, he may have better understood how Merton's views on protest were in fact anchored to some extent in his previous exchanges with the French scholar. Such awareness might also have encouraged Yoder to view his host's work at the retreat more as seeking to integrate what he was hearing into his mentor's mystical framework than simply trying to catch up with the perspectives of his friends.

Herbert Mason, who knew not only Merton and Massignon, but Dorothy Day, as well, has contrasted the approaches to protest taken by Day and Massignon. Regarding the latter, Mason noted that "he believed it essential to recognize the humanity of both the victimizer and the victim," and goes on to quote Massignon himself as saying that, "without that recognition one

---

52. Yoder to Cunningham, 31 Aug. 1993, 13, Yoder Papers, TMC.

risks denying the existence of a conscience to one which only enflames him to greater violence."[53] Mason saw Massignon "rein himself in with anguish at times to witness both the humanity of violators and victims . . . [He understood] that arrogance is most lethal at the self-righteous level of individual spiritual violence . . . Massignon, a military man from a bourgeois family, who respected tradition, social norms, and orthodoxy, adhered above all— under the guidance of the radical reader of his heart, Hallaj—to the inescapable Truth, wherever He led."[54] Mason saw Dorothy Day, on the other hand, as more ideological, but one whose fervor was tempered by compassion. She approached activism by standing between victimizer and victim while "facing the victimizer without fear, and with an absolute refusal to meet violence with violence." However, "both radical activists were disciplined persons. Their spirits and teachings confronted fully but are not limited to their times."[55] Mason regarded Thomas Merton as a "lifelong learner of new and strange unexpected things" and a "social idealist" whose humor helped curtail his enthusiasms.[56] Perhaps he is best seen as in some way standing in the gap between these two radical activists, seeking to encourage Massignon's suffering and substitutional embrace of victim and victimizer, at the same time that he entertained Day's unflinching resistance to oppression on behalf of the oppressed.

Lingering Themes

The impressions that survive suggest a handful of themes as the event's strongest legacies. Some offer deeper insight into the challenges faced when protesting for peace, while others suggest stronger tools to face those challenges. Ideals of nonviolence and rejecting war certainly permeated the week and could be considered a theme. Some such as Bob Cunnane and perhaps others may have emerged from the week more open to nonviolence as a viable option than when they arrived. It mostly played out in conversation, though, as an underlying assumption that everyone brought with them, rather than as a newly developed insight. References to those who practiced nonviolence cropped up, but nonviolent theory and specific tactics did not receive extended focus.

Another possible theme might pertain to the value of a contemplative core as a personal resource for engaging in protest. Jim Forest addresses

53. Mason, "Unexpected Friendship," 12.

54. Mason, 28 Nov. 2012, email to author.

55. Mason, "Unexpected Friendship," 12.

56. Mason, 28 Nov. 2012, email to author.

this in connection with the retreat, and Daniel Berrigan mentioned it in passing. The monastic environment certainly lent itself to contemplative awareness by virtue of example, and Merton had included it in his handout as a possible topic. But this also failed to emerge as a strong or broad focus of extended conversation. The notes of Yoder, Forest, and Daniel Berrigan capture few direct references to it, and those that appear largely surfaced on the final day. Their interactions seemed intense though respectful, and much of their dialogue revolved around concepts and ideas rather than quiet reflection. As Merton shared to his novices, at such an event, "you don't fool around with a half hour conference and then go meditate. You really work." Certainly those who knew and interacted closely with Merton over time would absorb a sense of his contemplative priorities, but whether it provided a central theme for these three days in particular remains less apparent.

Much conversation revolved around the concept of marginality, however, and they wrestled with the role of marginalization experienced both by others and by themselves. Merton's comments about those pushed to the wall, abandoned, and derelict serving as bearers of the true spiritual roots of protest sparked considerable discussion. Across their sessions others offered comments that seem to support looking for grounding and inspiration to the poor, weak, primitive, and non-Western, rather than to those of privilege and power. At various points they engaged Massignon's critique of how Western technological society pushed those in its way to the side.

But they also addressed the significance of their own marginality, not only in relation to Western U.S. society, but within the church itself. Without fully abandoning the institutional church, most lived in varying degrees of tension with it. Merton expressed this in his discussion of the monastic protest. Yoder conveyed it in portraying their work as "over against" the world, and also in comparing distinctions between the relationships of monastic and Radical Reformation traditions to the society around them. Several had shared frustration with how the church as a whole lagged behind their prophetic vision for peace and justice. Though he continued to embrace his ordination, Elbert Jean felt that his pilgrimage had ultimately led him out of the church per se in order to fulfill his true ministry. A. J. Muste sustained a deep and profound spirituality while rarely participating in denominational or congregational structures. Daniel Berrigan faced an exile to Central America by his superiors. Philip Berrigan would leave the priesthood, endure considerable jail time, and resurrect cemetery grounds to establish Jonah House and its prophetic Plowshares ministry. Others with Catholic Peace Fellowship and Catholic Resistance ties often personally bore the brunt of their Church's inclination toward preserving status quo.

Rejection, repression, and perhaps even persecution for their service would come naturally and expectedly. Few others would understand or appreciate their commitments. But these men seemed to agree that their rightful place rested within the lonely margins, alongside the abandoned and rejected, where God's word and the powers that oppose it clash most intensely.

At the same time, though, their work together that week modeled, and in some cases created, a powerful salve for easing the burden of isolated marginality—what Daniel Berrigan would characterize as "friendship." Most of the comments that followed the event voiced appreciation for the camaraderie and mutual respect they enjoyed, the fellowship, the "sense of genuine communion" present among them. Significantly, the fibers of this bond originated more from their common commitment to Christ's spirit of resistance to domination and accompaniment of those dominated than it did with confessional structures and ties. Their communion that week bridged and transcended the faith traditions they represented, traditions that often embodied modern, acculturated, compliant structures heavily vested in their own internal stability, self-preservation, and social accept-ability. This sense of connection would not end with Friday's departure. Their days together had helped create a reservoir of affection from which they could later draw in times of discouragement. In ways both tangible and mystical, many barriers holding at bay Protestant and Catholic fellowship melted that week through the power of relationship, cultivating a model for those who would follow.

Another highly significant theme would be the nature of larger forces at play against them—that of "principalities and powers" in general and the "power" of technology in particular. Merton later referred to them more than once, and Yoder felt that his treatment of the concept had caught the attention of at least some. When collecting retreat material in the mid-nineties, he commented to Ferry that Daniel Berrigan had used the concept in his prophetic ministry. Yoder also added a notation to his transcriptions that during his next interaction with Berrigan, the Jesuit shared that he had read further on the "powers."[57] Most likely this next meeting occurred three months after the retreat, at the conference, "Peace on Earth: Moral and Technological Implications," where Berrigan's meditation and resulting *Fellowship* article had been titled, "Man's Spirit and Technology." Also most likely, Berrigan's further reading included the work of William Stringfellow, who had by then corresponded with Jacques Ellul and begun to publish his own ideas on the principalities and powers of St. Paul.[58] Berrigan first met

---

57. Yoder, "Notes from J H Yoder 'Homily.'"
58. Wylie-Kellerman, "Naming the Powers," 26. See for example Stringfellow, *Free*

Stringfellow about this time. They lived across Central Park from each other in New York City and shared a strong commitment to advocacy for the poor. Stringfellow's work on the powers, aimed squarely at American society, carried a more incisive and critical edge than Hendrik Berkhof had offered via Yoder's translation. A strong friendship would blossom between Berrigan and Stringfellow in the late sixties, influencing and further sharpening Berrigan's social critique and activism.[59] Within a few months of the "Peace on Earth" conference, Berrigan published a second piece in *Fellowship* billed as "The sequel to 'Man's Spirit and Technology' by the courageous Jesuit Editor, Daniel Berrigan, SJ." Titling it, "Act of Faith and the New Beast," he quoted Heinrich Schlier on the principalities and powers and applied imagery in the Book of Revelation to modern political and social expressions.[60]

In a 1970 letter to fellow Jesuits, Berrigan again invoked the concept when explaining why he and his brother Philip would "declare themselves fugitives from injustice" and refuse to report for imprisonment as sentenced following their destruction of draft records at Catonsville, Maryland, in 1968: "The property we destroyed was an abominable symbol of idolatrous claims in human life . . . Can Christians, therefore, unthinkingly submit before such powers? We judge not. The 'powers and dominations' remain subject to Christ; our consciences are in his keeping and no other. To act as though we were criminals before God or humanity . . . seems to Philip and me a betrayal of our ministry."[61] If Yoder's implication is correct that retreat conversation sparked (or at least stoked) Daniel Berrigan's reflection on modern manifestations of principalities and powers, it may serve as one of the event's most significant legacies. The Berrigan brothers' visibility and influence in subsequent faith-based protest has attained iconic stature.

This theme left its impression on others who attended, as well. Tom Cornell mentioned their awareness of "a world ruled by perverse power" in his 1974 recap.[62] Ping Ferry's focus on technology recurred in numerous memories—Merton, Forest, Cornell, Cunnane, Yoder all mention this

---

in Obedience.

59. Details of the relationships among Berrigan, Stringfellow, and Ellul were obtained in author's conversation with Bill Wylie-Kellerman (31 Oct. 2012), a former student and friend of Daniel Berrigan. Special thanks to Wylie-Kellerman for sharing these details.

60. Berrigan, "Act of Faith." Both *Fellowship* essays appeared in modified form later in 1966 as chapters in Berrigan, *They Call Us Dead Men*. In the book, the first essay carried the same title of "Man's Spirit and Technology"; the second was titled "New World, New Forms of Faith." William Stringfellow wrote the book's introduction.

61. Berrigan, *America is Hard to Find*, 35–36.

62. Cornell, "Merton on Peace," 23.

across the decades that followed. Those participating in the retreat could glimpse the influence of "principalities and powers" embedded in and interwoven throughout a culture saturated with technology and increasingly driven by technique's chilling logic. Those powers in fact helped to fossilize the institutions these men served, including the church itself—how might activists engage such forces without themselves soon growing fossilized, as well? This awareness could offer them a sense that they participated in an epic struggle, a cosmic story that had been playing out since the dawn of human civilization. Theirs was not merely a quest for particular political ends. They were players in the ongoing pilgrimage of humanity to assume its intended place of shalom and harmony within the universe. Their resistance to the seductive pull of technological efficiency and its stifling of human freedom, as well as their calls for peace, would represent an extension of the grand biblical narrative itself.

Finally and equally crucial, a key tool of empowerment that they took from the gathering would be greater reliance on "hope." Rather than place confidence in their own efforts and the effectiveness of their calculated strategies to neutralize those powers, some had gained a stronger sense that the outcome of their work rested in greater hands. They remained confident that their efforts were faithful to the intent of their Creator, but they left Gethsemani especially aware that in the end success would emerge through the work and timetable of that Creator rather than directly through exertion of their own will. Merton explicitly mentioned hope as one of the lessons to emerge from the retreat, and it was implicit in Cornell's allusion to the power of the cross as a memorable focus. Armed with such hope, they could endure frustration, continue beyond seemingly ineffective results, and know that what felt disappointingly apparent was ultimately not real. God's movement courses beneath the visible surface of public life. As both Merton and Yoder implied, in time it will seep through some crevice in the dominions' constraints and at some unpredictable moment emerge as a life-giving spring in our desert of apprehension. Merton's guests were therefore free to act, resist, and protest without regard for personal consequence or apparent effectiveness. But they could only sustain those actions, as Merton put it, when grounded in a hope offered by "the mystery of [God's] will to save man and his promise of a reign of peace."

Epilogue

Fifty Years Later: Continuing the Conversation
on Powers, Protest, and Hope

IN ITS FINAL ISSUE of 2011, *Time* magazine unveiled its perennial Person of the Year as "The Protester."[1] Widespread dissent had seemingly overflowed that year, which began with the unseating of Arabic rulers, segued into mid-year riots and rallies on five continents, and ended with international protest under the "Occupy" banner. The details of *Time*'s narrative perhaps failed to appreciate the continuity and scope of political resistance expressed throughout the decades before 2011, especially when viewed in a global context. But few can argue with the news weekly that in 2011 mass protest had gained renewed attention in the American public's awareness and seemed increasingly real and relevant to larger numbers of people.

In the year that followed 2011, however, these movements underwent varying degrees of either success or repression that helped dissipate some of their cohesiveness and quell their momentum. But given the enormous challenges and inequities that continue to roil within the United States and across the planet, it becomes hard to imagine that impulses toward protest and revolution will quietly recede into oblivion. Projects like "Idle No More," "Rolling Jubilee" debt relief, resistance to fossil fuel extraction, louder calls for gun control, and numerous other voices have sustained the rumblings of grassroots dissent. This mood mirrors that of the early sixties in important ways. The ongoing specter of nuclear weapons may not haunt our awareness as fully as in 1964, but a potentially greater threat of irreversible climate change increasingly looms. Then, it was Cold War politics that fed the Vietnam conflict and prompted the public's reactions to it. Now, a relentless drive for remote fossil fuels—coupled with increasingly erratic patterns of drought, wildfires, super storms, and other climate variation—feeds our

1. Anderson, "2011 Person of the Year."

expanding public unease about economic and food security. Then, African American frustration that was built on centuries of racial inequality prompted widespread civil rights protest. Now, random economic inequity, fiscal cliffs, hapless legislatures, elitist judiciaries, and unstable economies breed generic fear and frustration. The growing gulf between the powerful rich and everyone else continues to accelerate as the expanding human population competitively scrambles to sustain our unsustainable aspirations. Such trends as these seem destined to spur even more intense and frantic reaction than the 1964 retreat participants faced in the decade that followed their gathering.

Writing about that Gethsemani event on the dawn of such uncertainty and the heels of Arab Spring and Occupy Wall Street begs asking the question of how those retreat discussions intersect with protest fifty years later. The topic warrants a book in itself. But to help consider this question, four individuals with a vested interest in how the answer might play out agreed to share some thoughts on it. They were invited to this virtual dialogue based on the unique experiences and perspectives that each brings to contemporary, faith-based, public protest.

Ched Myers,[2] an activist theologian, was nurtured under the wings of the radical tradition that emerged from the "Catholic Resistance" of the sixties antiwar effort and enjoyed the mentorship of Philip Berrigan and Elizabeth McAlister's Jonah House community. He also drew from the biblical pacifism of John Howard Yoder, and now formally identifies with the Anabaptist Mennonite tradition. In addition to his ongoing activism for peace and justice in recent decades, Myers has written prolifically to share biblical studies that animate those ancient writings and illuminate their radical call for Christ's followers to confront evil in pursuit of lasting Shalom. His best known effort, *Binding the Strong Man*,[3] offers a political reading of the Gospel of Mark, portraying many of Jesus' encounters as calculated challenges to the entrenched powers of his day. Myers brings to this conversation many years of engagement with diverse faith traditions—Catholic Worker, mainline Protestant, Anabaptist, African American, to name some. In addition, he has directly participated in many protest projects, and he interacts with many protest activists while remaining conversant within academic circles of biblical theology. His current association with the Mennonite tradition injects an appreciation of its perspectives as well.

---

2. Ched Myers' comments were obtained from an interview with author on 10 Oct. 2012.

3. Myers, *Binding the Strong Man*.

Jake Olzen's[4] voice has been informed by the Catholic Worker tradition coupled with broad experience in acts of resistance. In addition, he studied theology at Chicago's Loyola University, helped found the White Rose Catholic Worker House in Chicago, and currently reports on global resistance movements. Olzen has also demonstrated on behalf of Guantanamo detainees, traveled to Afghanistan, and supported undocumented immigrants along the U.S.–Mexican border, among several other actions. His location within a younger generation of protesters brings to the table the priorities of one who is personally faced with living out the next six-or-so decades of human experience in this nation and on this planet.

Elizabeth McAlister[5] actively opposed the Vietnam War in the late 1960s, and in 1973 she married one of the Gethsemani retreat participants, Philip Berrigan. Together they partnered in a life of faith-based protest, founding the Catholic Worker Jonah House in Baltimore as a community of resistance and launching Plowshares acts of radical nonviolence to oppose nuclear proliferation. She continues her work today as part of that community. McAlister, formerly a Roman Catholic nun, brings the benefits of her early religious formation and decades of participation in the U.S. faith-based peace movement. She provides a direct link to the flurry of antiwar action that immediately followed the 1964 retreat. As the sole woman who agreed to share in this particular dialogue, her perspective adds critical value to the conversation.

Lastly, George Packard[6] is a retired Episcopal bishop from New York who participated in the swell of Occupy Wall Street activity in 2011. When the Zuccotti Park encampment was forcibly disbanded, Packard added his voice to calls for a nearby Episcopal church to open an adjacent vacant lot as a replacement. After the church refused, Packard became the first of several who scaled the surrounding fence to occupy the property, and was promptly arrested for his trouble. Packard continues to engage in various expressions of Occupy's legacy, including conversations known as "Occupy Faith." His unique contribution to this conversation includes his visible role within that notable expression of recent mass protest. But he also offers the voice of a traditional Protestant whose career has been deeply rooted within established church structures. His provides a contrast with careers of the other three representatives, who have mostly functioned on the margins of those

4. Jake Olzen's comments were obtained from an interview with author on 15 Oct. 2012.

5. Elizabeth McAlister's comments were obtained from an interview with author on 5 Nov. 2012.

6. George Packard's comments were obtained from an interview with author on 23 Oct. 2012.

structures and have chosen to self-identify with Catholic Worker/Catholic Resistance movements and similar traditions.

These activists did not have the advantage of direct dialogue with each other as did those at Gethsemani in 1964. Nor did they have the opportunity to study the details of that event before commenting, and their responses were influenced by the different tracks that each of our individual conversations took. But through their separate and individual venues, each has shared helpful thoughts on several of the questions that Merton and his guests discussed. Upon splicing together their responses into an imaginary round table of sorts, a brief snapshot emerges of how the agenda set fifty years ago remains relevant to those of faith who continue that nonviolent quest for meaningful change today.

Rights, Objectives, Powers

"By What Right Do We Protest?"

The question Merton used to open the retreat in 1964 may be fielded at multiple levels. Taken at face value, as a straightforward question of basic rights, the answers seem clearer now than they may have in 1964. As Myers observes, those times fostered greater anxiety about people of faith (particularly ordained leaders such as the Berrigans) publically opposing the pronouncements of established political authority. In the years that followed, as more became accustomed to such actions, protest gained greater recognition as an established right of democratic expression, though that right today seems increasingly under siege. In this context, as noted by both McAlister and Myers, protest begins to assume more the character of a responsibility than a right. But at other levels, the question may take on a more reflective aura that invites self-examination about motives. Along these lines, Jake Olzen recognizes merit in applying the question in specific contexts, such those that disrupt the lives of ordinary people going about their routines. In the end, he names commitment to following biblically informed, communally discerned acts of conscience as the grounding for his "right" to protest.

George Packard embeds protest within an innate right to exist as a human being. The act of standing up and proclaiming, "Enough!" becomes a step toward reclaiming human dignity. It asserts that, "This is not acceptable. It's keeping people from being fully alive and human. It's making them something other than what they were created to be. God created this dignity for you to live it and express it, not to have it commodified, clamped down, reshaped, rejiggered, and handed back to you." Packard's responses imply that if we have a right to exist as humans, we have a right to protest when anyone becomes threatened with an existence that is less than human.

What Are the Objectives of Protest?

When their conversations turned toward what they sought to accomplish through protest, the 1964 retreatants considered and rejected options like pragmatic effectiveness, defeating opponents to replace them with better people, and mere credibility with others. Objectives they affirmed, on the other hand, included giving voice to the oppressed and abandoned, redeeming and transforming one's opponent, and altering human awareness. The responses offered fifty years later did not contradict those views, but the respondents shaped their replies somewhat differently.

Ched Myers noted several aspects of what protest seeks to realize, aspects that are historically observable in particular traditions and movements. He names democratic renewal as one objective especially relevant to Western societies. Martin Luther King Jr. reflected this thrust in his relentless call for American society to re-envision and live up to its own principles and ideals—to complete the democratic experiment. Protest provides a venue to enter that process and further the debate on how those ideals should be lived out. For a second objective, Myers appeals to the Gandhian insight—one also grasped by King—that "in order to make the peace, you have to disturb the peace and disrupt business as usual." One does not pursue disruption for its own sake, but rather to expose into daylight the injustice, violence, and oppression masked within the circumstances protested.

Beyond mere exposure of these forces, protest also seeks to resist them, and here Myers notes two prongs of biblically based resistance represented at the Gethsemani event. What he termed "prophetic resistance" soon would become embodied in the antiwar, anti-draft actions of Catholic resistors such as the Berrigans, Forest, Cornell, Grady, and Cunnane. These he interprets as public offerings of a "prophetic sort of sign-act" to "embody the prophetic word in a kind of public liturgy where the symbols of the church go out onto the street—whether that's blood or ashes or crosses or bread—and those symbols confront evil in the public square and create a moral crisis." Myers observes a second prong of biblical resistance in the gist of John Howard Yoder's call for Christ-imitating obedience that will "let the church be the church." It reflects a call to form distinct, alternative identities that contrast with those grounded in aspirations toward domination, oppression, and socioeconomic power. But, Myers adds, such obedience is not ultimately about one's own purity. It is instead about "being faithful to a tradition that calls us to be otherwise, to be contrary, to non-cooperate, to militantly engage, to unmask." Solidarity with those oppressed reflects still another objective for Myers, one consistent with Merton's expression of monastic protest, which was grounded in participation with those who find themselves abandoned and pushed to the wall. And finally, he feels these acts provide an element of spiritual and political empowerment for those who perform them, "particularly minority or dissenting groups, who don't see themselves mirrored in the media and who otherwise are rendered invisible in a mass culture." Paraphrasing Philip Berrigan, Myers comments that "you don't know how domesticated you are by the powers of law and order until you actually break the law" of a state that rules through fear of it. Facing and dealing with that fear becomes not only a path toward empowerment, but also toward "spiritual and political maturity in a mass culture." Although protest may have tactical or short-term objectives to address a particular issue, challenge a particular law, or impede some particular force, Myers sees these five or six emphases as core longer-term, strategic objectives of sustained engagement.

Others echoed elements of Myers' framework for thinking about protest objectives. McAlister seeks to express in the public arena dissent from the priorities of those making harmful decisions. "It's a matter of saying there are voices against this—they are real, they are serious, they mean it." She sees her work directed not just toward political leadership, however, but also to "widen the circle of resistance" by communicating that "it isn't special people who do this. It's something we all ought to be about on some level." George Packard's comments about expressing and preserving human dignity also suggest objectives of both democratic participation and individual empowerment. And while he values activism as democratic participation and an expression of "good citizenship," he expands its implications into the realm of solidarity. Given our "paradoxical times," we need to acknowledge that "we're citizens of the world who bring natural identities to those roles— we are not solely nation-state residents anymore."

Jake Olzen also blends elements of Myers' framework when discussing protest objectives, naming obedience to the model and teaching of Christ while seeking to hold in tension both the prophetic and alternative identity aspects of resistance, "I think a life of faith may lead to the cross, and Jesus modeled the way to do that with grace." This includes "a community organizing model of just being with people" that offers interconnectedness and community while also reflecting Jesus' example of "how first we need to resist." Olzen recognizes a danger in focusing so narrowly to "build that new society in the shell of the old that we are not really resisting. We are not saying 'No!'" But he also senses that too much emphasis on a "Jesus of the way of the cross" can diminish "Jesus on the road to Emmaus. He was walking

with people and sharing the good news and building up this society of sharing. Those things need to be reconciled." Olzen places considerable weight
on what Myers referred to as "tactical" objectives, emphasizing a need for
more intentional reflection within protest circles on efficacy. He comments
how the long-standing adage that religious activists must focus on being
faithful rather than effective sometimes "rubs us young people the wrong
way." After all, "why are we engaged in social struggles if we don't want
to change anything?" He recognizes the wisdom in not seeking pragmatic
institutional power at the cost of one's integrity. But Olzen also wants to
find effective ways to "spread the radical message of this vision" nurtured
by many of those at the 1964 retreat, to "articulate it to the mainstream in a
way that doesn't put them off." While acknowledging much can be learned
from earlier movements, particularly skills to "weather the storms of prison
or violent conflict zones," he also feels that their specific tactics can fail to
"translate into the kind of movements we saw back then" and more context-
specific approaches are needed. In the end, he laments that we often seem
to "lack the language or tools or mediums with which to communicate that
spirit, experience, skill, and wisdom."

Is the Concept of "Principalities and Powers" Still Helpful?

In 1964, conversations that associate St. Paul's "principalities and powers"
with modern social structures played an important role in thinking about
protest objectives. They still do in conversations today. George Packard
notes that in the Occupy Faith affinity group, revisitation of this concept
has provided an important focus. Naming the work of Walter Wink in particular, he recounts how they started a reading list, sought "books on the
dusty back shelves down at the local bookstore, and then passed around
these dog-eared paperbacks among us and talked" about their ideas. "You
realize how timely they are," to the point of seeking ways to bring them into
broader awareness among Occupy circles. Packard describes our current
power configuration as a "demoralizing, dehumanizing, dark entity" that
"has us all under its thumb." It "hovers around us like a kind of dark energy
that other people control. It doesn't necessarily have to be the One Percent,
but a good amount of this occurs because the One Percent has a certain
insecurity or has learned how to manipulate the system."

McAlister names the concept of principalities and powers as "central
to my understanding of what we are doing in terms of resistance . . . It is
a part of the language of our leaflets, and it is part of the language of our
organizing." Myers sees the post-World War II revival of this concept, after

centuries of dormant obscurity during the rise of an Enlightenment emphasis on reason, as a necessary response to the unimaginable or (to use Merton's term) "unspeakable"[7] horrors World War II had spawned. In "fast forwarding fifty or more years, nobody then could have anticipated today's global warming or genetically modified everything or drone warfare. Only the theological language of principalities and powers is big enough to hold that conundrum, and it is more crucial than ever." Olzen agrees that the concept is helpful and important for understanding his work in the context of his faith tradition. But in seeking to connect with those outside that tradition, he finds the language of "principalities and powers" and "empire" may be less helpful—off-putting, even. Rather, Merton's language of the "Unspeakable," especially as applied in the writings of James Douglass,[8] and concepts like "military-industrial complex" may gain greater traction in wider circles. Still, Olzen affirms that "the powers exist, the Unspeakable exists, in interlocking systems of corporate wealth, military might, the national security state, racism, and hierarchy," and awareness of them remains integral to the work of protesters.

What Role Does or Should Technology Play in Protest Today?

At the 1964 retreat the discussion on powers and principalities revolved mainly around questions raised by Merton and Ferry about technology and the degree to which it compels humans to incorporate its intrinsic priorities and logic. At the time, those questions yielded mixed responses that reflected both appreciation of and concern toward the role technology played in their lives.

These twenty-first-century activists express similar ambiguity about our complicit reliance on technology's benefits despite its ability to define and direct our choices. They also agreed that questions about technology still need to be asked and wrestled with. As Myers notes, the 1964 retreatants' focus on technology was "prescient because those guys are naming things that other people didn't come to until the eighties and nineties." He finds it ironic that in practice they used technologies to organize such as dial telephones and mimeographs that were already dated for their time but were thinking deeply about technology. Yet "ironically, fifty years later, we've got all this technology, but we're not thinking very deeply about it, particularly in protest culture." McAlister recognizes that her adoption of certain technologies like computers and email binds her to them and observes how "they have

7. See Merton, *Raids on the Unspeakable.*
8. Douglass, *JFK and the Unspeakable.*

become so integral to our lives that we feel we can't live" without them. She also understands our "illusion that we use these tools and they serve us" when in fact "we're really serving them and becoming subservient to them." Still, McAlister acknowledges that like most of us, she fails to fully act on that awareness, "I am not enamored of this technology, even though I use it, and I think it's very, very dangerous," especially in its ability to dissipate flesh and blood community. For example, "community nights" for some younger folks she observes can devolve into "sitting in one common room, each one with his or her own computer doing his or her own thing."

Olzen added another dynamic to the question that was not fully on the radar of those who met in 1964—concerns over technology's reliance on fossil fuels and its impact on patterns of consumption. From that vantage, use of certain technologies enters the realm of social and ecological justice, beyond its broader impact on human agency and freedom. Still he doesn't reject it wholesale. He sees something "profoundly democratic" about the internet and its potential for organizing effective mass resistance, and he notes the benefits of certain technologies at work on the farm where he lives and works. Development of some cutting edge technologies, such as perma-culture and agroforestry, will become essential to meet human food needs. He feels we need to "keep thinking about these things and building resilient communities that are using appropriate technologies, both environmentally and socially, but I don't think that is anti-technology." At the same time, though, "this is a hard conversation to have because there are a lot of things we don't know. Can the tools that built the master's house be used to dis-mantle it? I don't know, but it's a good question and I think we should be talking about it more."

George Packard has noted trends among his younger Occupy friends that resonate with Olzen's, in some cases with perhaps an even sharper edge. "This is an age group that believes technology is really not the way to go, and they want to be away from fracking environments, on the land, and do-ing their own farming. These folks are dropping out of the technology that birthed them in a lot of ways. They have reached their own tipping point. They see technology as a great benefit, but a force that denudes them of the very human dignity that they are protesting to not lose. So there is an in-teresting duplicity going on here." Overall within the Occupy movement he senses "a level of cynicism about where we are as a culture, and I think that has a lot to do with the technological advances." One aspect of this skepti-cism has to do with unequal access to it. As a cancer survivor, Packard is grateful for the technology that he benefited from, but he laments that those benefits are typically limited to people in his age and income brackets. He expresses remorse that we have "somehow hit the bonanza jackpot in this technologically saturated economy" while the vast majority of "the rest of our family in the world" cannot access it. Packard also points toward Walter Wink's analysis that these forces are not inherently evil, they only become so when we give them power. The hyper-consumerism exhibited by many U.S. households, such as excessive accumulation of redundant gadgetry, ultimately morphs into not only a lost sense of "your own human dignity, but a lost sense of your day and your environment. You lose touch with the very world that surrounds you."

Myers acknowledged how modern electronic communications had served well movements such as Arab Spring and Occupy activity, and he is learning more from younger tech-savvy colleagues how to use some of this media. But he remains skeptical and feels that "the jury is still out." "Point-and-click" activism like online petitions and posting to Facebook in hopes it goes viral "does not necessarily translate into engagement with the powers." On the other hand, using social media to mobilize bodies represents a healthy application of technology. But he also asks, will such uses ultimately "offset the use of the same technology for surveillance and control? Will adoption of social media ultimately empower or neutralize?" Further, Myers asserts that "no intermediate technology can replace the fundamental spiritual and political vocation of engagement with the dominant culture." Turning to Jacques Ellul's broader understanding of "technique" as a social process—the concept that drove much of the 1964 discussion—he continues, "technique will never unlock democracy for us, and it will never unlock spiritual maturity within us. The temptation is to over-rely on the utopian promises of technique. That would be my fear."

Roots, Sustaining Practices, Hope

How Does Today's Institutional Church Relate to Protest?

The role of modern institutional churches cast a long shadow over the Gethsemani conversations as they turned from questions about the external dynamics of protest to ones that address the spiritual nurture of faith-based protest. Many of those who gathered had by 1964 already experienced the structures of Christendom as impediments rather than encouragement to actively resist to evil. Similar ambiguity and disappointment endure today. Myers' reflections on institutional church support for resistance and challenge express mixed feelings. On the positive side he recognizes that "peace theology and nonviolence are so much more a lingua franca" in the mainstream church than fifty years ago, even though they remain at the edges of public discourse. He also notes the declining social power churches now have in contrast to 1964, naming that as ultimately a good thing. The Anabaptist understanding carried by Yoder's Mennonite tradition of "what it means to be a disestablished church is the only future our churches have. That's slowly but surely dawning on other churches." However, even within the church, "institutions still cling to their shrinking power, and that sometimes makes them less inclined to take risks." They remain "on the fence in terms of the degree to which they are allied with protestors." For Myers, relating to institutional churches remains in keeping with a slogan coined in the seventies: you work with them "but you keep a foot in the streets, and you keep your weight on the foot that's in the street."

Episcopal bishop Packard, in his support of the Occupy Wall Street movement, has experienced rather harsh expressions of institutional church power, and consequently he tends to lean quite heavily on his street-based foot. Simply put, institutional church structure is for him "an expression of the powers. Nothing more, nothing less. It's irrelevant to this movement. It has just not showed up." Though individual congregations have supported Occupy Wall Street efforts and Packard gets emails from lay people across the church, he receives no substantial interaction from denominational leadership because "they're part of the system that needs to stay in place." To them, "I am the Lord Voldemort," he jokes. "They don't speak my name . . . it's sort of amusing."

Packard is careful to distinguish, however, between the institution and the tradition. He suspects that those at the 1964 event had "a clearer sense of the tradition and how it speaks to moments in history." Today, though, he senses that "the current caretakers of the tradition are out to lunch . . . They are just not tuned in to what can happen." Packard sees hope in expressions of the "emergent" church, where some denominations "tolerate versions of themselves, lower the doctrinal and liturgical bar, and let some people do some experimentation. That's the smartest thing anybody could do, because it allows people to begin to tentatively enter into the spirituality that's offered from a very venerable tradition we've inherited from the saints. They put down blood to become saints. It wasn't tidy. So I honor the saints and that history, but the current denominations are nothing more than museums and floorshows." Even in the fifties and sixties aspects of progressive social movements drew on certain established religious energies that he feels churches no longer supply. In contrast, citing writers like Marion Grau,[9] Packard sees today as a time of "polydoxy" that does not diminish individual traditions but recognizes the primacy of individual hu-

9. Most recently, Grau, *Rethinking Mission.*

man dignity within each. He finds this spirit coalescing not in institutions of the church but "in the streets where people meet each other and have a common discovery." Using an experience with the Occupy Faith affinity group, Packard shared an example of how these forces can intertwine according to the spirit of a particular occasion:

> Occupy Faith included 45 protestors who entered the protest perimeter. We came into this space opposite Zuccotti Park and were in prayer before blockading entry into the financial district. Because we knelt for prayer, we had this kind of cellular sense. Other affinity groups who were nomadic and not connected to anything, connected to us. So we went from 40 to 80 to 120 to over 500 people. We said little prayers, and I thought to myself, "Here is instant church, instant spirituality." In this moment in time they had this sense of being together, of being involved in a kind of energy. They felt a connection with each other. They had each other's back and a sense of liturgy, so to speak. They had a kind of respect for the Other of God. It was quite moving to be there. This is the kind of new thing we're discovering in the street, this kind of sense of the Last Supper or the shared meal, this kind of shared moment.

What Are the Spiritual Roots of Protest?

If the institutional church fails to consistently offer the soil that nurtures today's spiritual roots of protest, where can one find it? In his notes, Merton had summarized his understanding of this fundamental root as our "identification with the underprivileged; dedication to their 'universe' as 'epiphany' [and] as intercessory for us." For Merton this was not some ethereal exercise, for he called on us to manifest the "reality of this belief in suffering, in refusal of privilege and protest against the arrogance and stupidity of the privileged." He asked us to place "true hope in the spiritual privilege of the poor." For Merton, the poor in this sense referred not simply to economically disadvantaged Americans. Inspired by Louis Massignon's critique of how Western technology and economic force had disrupted Islamic respect for human persons and sacred hospitality, Merton also named other indigenous and "undeveloped" peoples among those who faced despair and possessed this spiritual privilege.

In their responses, all four activists offered comments that harmonized with Merton's summary. Rather than deploy Merton's phrasing of participation or identification with those who suffer, though, they tended to invoke the term "solidarity." Myers initially names the larger prophetic tradition—one that incorporated the likes of Amos and Isaiah in addition to Jesus—as a fundamental spiritual root for protest. This prophetic tradition has provided ongoing sustenance for those moving within the Berrigans' legacy, as has obedience to the incarnate Jesus for those standing within Yoder's Anabaptist tradition. But Myers also addresses the "imperative of solidarity with people who are suffering right now." Packard phrases it in terms of a core appreciation for and sensitivity to universal and innate human dignity, a "priceless commodity that must not be sacrificed or minimized." He further notes how his own personal involvement with the homeless during the eighties laid important groundwork for his later involvement in the Occupy movement. McAlister observes how "the people I know that are most consistent about direct action against wars and weapons and laws that subjugate the poor are the people who live in proximity to the poor. There's that sense of compassion, that the way these people are being treated is radically wrong."

Olzen offers perhaps the most extensive commentary along these lines, indicating that for him "that intersection of faith and protest is about solidarity." Often "I as Jake Olzen don't have the power to do anything" to stop foreclosures, abuse of migrants at the Mexican border, injury and death to the innocent in Afghanistan, "But if I have faith that I can just be with this person in their suffering and be an ally and accompany them, I think that creates space for something bigger to be born. I'm at my best when I'm just able to sit with somebody and not have to solve it or be effective, but trust that this relationship is what matters. Out of that spirit, usually if you are asking the right questions, tactics and strategies and a campaign can emerge that may change the circumstances that we find ourselves in." Olzen's comments in fact begin to approach a mystical sense of participation that seemingly dovetails with Louis Massignon's understanding of participation and substitution:

> I think my faith, my spirituality has brought me at times to a place of such deep compassion that I'm empathizing, feeling a pain that is very real to me. It's like I don't want to live in this world. That experience I have of pain, of heartbreak, of despair, of anger at times, of anxiety, it comes out of this belief that the Kingdom of God is at hand. It's already here. When I wear an orange jumpsuit in solidarity with Guantanamo Bay prisoners and hear people laughing at me and making comments like, "We should just torture and execute you," it's a heartbreaking experience. But I find a lot of God in that experience, too. That's the Beatitudes. Those are the blessed. The more I put myself into

these kinds of public experiences of resistance and calling for a
new world, the more clearly I come to understand the Gospel
and identify with Jesus. I think of the garden in Gethsemane
when Jesus was about to be handed over to his death. I can feel
his anxiety and fear, because I too felt it the nights before actions
where I didn't know what was going to happen. When we were
going to chain ourselves to doors or to trucks or block heavy
machinery to protest environmental destruction or any number
of things, it brought me to a more intimate knowledge of the
God who is incarnate in us all.

What Practices Sustain One in Protest?

The men at Gethsemani mentioned in passing the value of contemplation
and solitude in their work, but they generally did not focus in depth on what
sustains one in commitment to recurring protest. Such questions naturally
emerge when probing this topic, however. If today's practitioners of protest
name solidarity and participation as fundamental spiritual roots, it comes
as no surprise that they also view regular interaction with the poor and
suffering as pivotal in sustaining their resistance. Ideally, this means living
near, with, and similarly to them.

When reflecting on why she feels those most dedicated to peace and
justice advocacy live among the poor, McAlister, notes that,

you can't love those neighbors that surround you and not try to
address what's keeping them so subjugated. When they remain
out of sight you can just drift away from it and act like these
people don't exist. But when you live amid them and when you
work with them, then you're their sisters and brothers, and you
know it. They are the people that Jesus told us we ought to be
serving on a daily basis. You don't maintain that by living in
suburbia, where you don't have that connection with human
suffering. There may be great souls who can do that—I believe
there is a level on which Merton was one of them—but I think
it does require that greatness of spirit and imagination. I also
think he was somewhat tortured by his distance from some of
those realities.

McAlister also finds that traditional spiritual disciplines like reading Scripture, meditation, contemplation are essential, "The forces that militate
against us are just too powerful and we'd jolly well better nurture the spirit
if we want to stay with this or we aren't going to last." Participation in a

supportive community offers still another source of sustenance for McAlister's life of protest, including periodic retreats of like-minded people who function like an enlarged family. It provides the broader, sustained "friendship" suggested by Daniel Berrigan as one of the key benefits to emerge from the 1964 Gethsemani experience. If there are gender differences within protest circles, McAlister has found that openness to community support and mutual nurture may be the most apparent. "It's a lot easier for women to express reservations, disappointments, needs than it is for men to do that culturally. I think it is easier for women to have that mutuality, to have that depth of community sense. It's beautiful to see that in men, but I think it's harder for them," since they are often conditioned to "stand up and take it." Particularly when they find themselves imprisoned together for their actions, "there's an incredible thing that happens with women . . . just because of their ability to sit and weep with other women if that's what's called for. There's a sharing that goes very, very deep, and that changes the place. It doesn't change the oppressiveness, but it becomes a place where women can be together and nurture one another in ways that many of the women we meet in those circumstances have never been able to experience before."

Packard makes similar observations about the power of community and friendship. Sitting in a courtroom with fellow protestors he noted a sense that "you can't think of any place you'd rather be than in there with friends who you have been with before." It's reminiscent of the bonds he recalled from combat experience in Vietnam, where "you are in a fearsome place and you hold on tight to each other." He likewise notes the benefits of associating with those who do not hold traditional positions of power, including women. "One of the greatest criticisms I have of the Occupy movement is that it has to have more females and more people of color and more people who are poor and physically challenged. I have to say that when we bring those kinds of concepts into conversation we're met with smart-ass answers." Packard further agrees with McAlister that prayer and contemplation are fundamental. He references the work of Sister Pat Farrell, president of the Leadership Conference of Women Religious, who Packard commends for urging people not to just "blunder out into the streets" but to approach it with "a sense of prayer and reflection, a sense of energy, then witness, and finally resolve." From his experience, Packard notes that "the only way we can function as Occupy Faith and people of faith is if we have these moments of sentience and clarity in shared silence and meditation before we enter into the fray, because the street action is pretty chaotic. It's just plain scary. You need to have a sense of centeredness and a discovered sense of presence or divine covering, as the Quakers would say, before you enter into doing something like this. It's the real gift that Occupy Faith can convey to the Occupy movement, I think."

For Olzen, looking at Jesus' first-century community models not just an objective to seek for organizing resistance, but it presents a source of sustenance as well. It shows how "we are stronger together than we are alone. There are a lot of younger people who want a communal faith experience that believes in resistance. We look at the early disciples and that community and think, 'Wow, how awesome would it be to be a part of something like that?'" Regarding the interior life, Olzen mentions a needed awareness for "trauma stewardship," or addressing "the sort of trauma that one experiences by witnessing the trauma of someone else." Whereas many who attended the 1964 retreat were grounded in spiritual disciplines and benefited from mentorship and perhaps seminary training, "a lot of us right now don't know how to be silent. We're not comfortable with ourselves or maybe not in touch with our emotions, and I don't know if we recognize the pain that we carry from this work." Activists can "end up in pretty vulnerable states now and again, whether that's instances of physical abuse with law enforcement or private security—I think we saw it with the Occupy movement. The more prep work we can do for ourselves to give us the resolve to come out of that and not be totally damaged and debilitated and still support others, I think our movements will be stronger." He shares Packard's view that listening to feminism and addressing sexism are integral to nurturing sustainability. And like McAlister, he observes gender differences related to "spirituality and activism that are associated with identity and what people are comfortable doing in terms of protest."

Myers echoes many of these observations about sustaining practices. "I think any veteran activist would say, because this is a long, long intergenerational struggle, we can't be wooed by the power of spectacle. We need to pace ourselves and have the spiritual discipline to be in it in the long run. It seems to me the old question about spirituality versus politics is really a non-issue." Economic behavior provides another sustaining practice for Myers. "It's not just what we do in a public protest, it's about how we live, what we buy, how we treat money, our ecological footprint. If our lifestyles aren't trying to move toward a greater consistency with our objectives, our chance of development grows less sustainable." He also concurs with McAlister that "social location" and "concrete interface with marginalized people" are key, that "where we live and who we are in conversation with make a difference." He suspects that "people in academia don't get it. There remains too much insularity in a lot of peace theology, liberation studies, and so on. We've got to get beyond the idea of white men thinking about peace and justice into a much more diverse conversation." Within religious circles, this insularity often extends to religious traditions, and Myers appends to this a discipline of "spiritual cross-fertilization, which extends to interfaith work" as the 1964 retreat modeled for its own time. He also fleshes out something those at Gethsmani more or less took as a given: the discipline of nonviolence, which he considers "absolutely key." Myers believes it warrants revived emphasis today, given that "it has come under renewed attack from activists, particularly in certain environmental circles who think that only ever more dramatic actions like sabotage are going to turn this ship around." While he might concede that some forms of property destruction could be seen as "not necessarily not nonviolent," at the same time "we can't use the tools of power to dismantle the rule of power."

Finally, Myers sees historical awareness and knowledge of social movements as another key to sustaining one's ongoing involvement. "If you think you're the first person who has ever done this, you are going to give up because what you are up against is too big. If we were more disciplined about teaching and learning movement history—with particular concern to be literate about nineteenth and twentieth-century movements and indeed teaching and learning church history *as* movement history all the way back to deep roots in the prophets—I think we'd be better able to raise up mature activists." Which returns Myers to November 1964 at Gethsemani Abbey:

> One of the biggest aspects of that gathering, in my opinion, is how Yoderian Anabaptism, Catholic radicalism and Protestant political theology began to converge really for the first time. In many ways that synergism has been the greatest development for faith based activism since '64. Now *all* of us are in some sense "children" of the conversation that began at Gethsemeni. We are *profoundly* shaped by Berrigan direct action and Merton contemplation-as-resistance; by Anabaptist pacifist, disestab-lished ecclesiology; and by Muste's engagement-oriented Prot-estantism (which would have been echoed by King had he been at the retreat). Christian activism today (ironically, especially among the newly radicalized post-evangelicals) even takes this confluence for granted—which is perhaps a sign of success. But we need to remember that it was a historic project, and every time any of us get together in a retreat setting to figure out what the hell is going on and what we should do about it, we are walk-ing in their footsteps.

What Offers Hope for Attaining Lasting Change?

In the end, perhaps the greatest and most powerful force for sustaining engagement and protest becomes that which Merton identified following the retreat: "a sense of deeper and purer hope." As Yoder suggested, our ability to take note of the portents, marvels, and unexpected springs in the desert that materialize in the midst of human activity nurtures hope. When questioned about this idea of hope, today's protesters reveal that at a fundamental level, acts of protest are themselves expressions of hope even as hope sustains those acts of protest. They are inextricably intertwined. Journalist Chris Hedges has also suggested that, "You cannot use the word hope if you do not resist. If you resist, even if it appears futile, you keep hope alive."[10] Ultimately, the hope expressed in protest and resistance clings to the possibility that somehow and some way, through public demonstration of dissent from the status quo, our collective human consciousness may transform to embrace and realize new priorities.

For Packard, though, the realm of hope seeks both individual and collective expressions. For individuals, it becomes "a certain wonder about the possibility" inherent in one's own life—"a mystical connection with that possibility." He illustrates with a young adult he encountered who "wanted the possibility of living a life that was special and contributory, to have the freedom to embrace the possibility she could tease out of the future." He understands that view as "a way this generation senses it. You cannot extinguish the ignition of that sense of excitement when people have the freedom to engage the future." Regarding hope in the sense of collective possibilities, Packard concedes that "we wrestle with this all the time. There are no guarantees to this. None. Zero. The only guarantees are the people on the right and the left of you." But acting with those people is itself what manifests hope. "You bind intensely with the people around you who are like-minded in the belief that the other world that is possible is the one we are creating right now in this space. There's the possibility, or hope, that it will catch on. But here's the point—we don't have any other alternative. The current alternative is so deathlike. You have no power, no personal agency, no discretion. So connecting and bonding with like-minded others to claim a new world is the only way to proceed."

McAlister agrees, "I think hope comes in acts of hope, and I think that hope is combined to direct action and civil resistance. It not only nourishes hope, but it also creates it. I understand despair more where people don't have access to other like-minded individuals, that sense of community

10. Hedges, "Truthout Intervews Chris Hedges," para. 14.

we've been talking about—where they haven't an avenue to give voice to the hope that's in them." For Olzen, his work as a journalist is chronicling social change movements, "mostly of ordinary folks around the world who are organizing, resisting, engaging in the struggle, and in some cases actually winning—that gives me hope." He adds, "Hope is where your belief is. If I don't believe in anticapitalism, if I don't believe that nonviolence can always overthrow regimes of violence, then I have no hope. I don't think it's a naïve belief because data support it. The hope is in the struggle."

When focusing on issues of climate change in particular, though, the matter of hope raises some unsettling questions for Olzen. "It has profound theological implications for eschatology, because it asks, 'Are we creating our own end times?' Would God allow us to do that through our free will? That was the fear of nuclear weapons in the sixties, but with climate change it's a little different. For my generation the environment is involved in everything. Every protest I do needs to have its concern for ecology." He continues by elaborating on its interface with the church at large and names education as a crucial expression of hope. "I think this possibility of creating our end times should create a major crisis of faith within Christian peoples, but it's not. In my classes, seminarians from other denominations would talk about how hard it is to speak about climate change in congregations because of too heavy a reliance on hope in direct divine intervention."

In such a milieu, Olzen speculates that what may be required is "to get our boots on the ground and do more traditional door-to-door organizing, get in our churches and educate people. I think we need a radical popular education movement in the country because we don't have the consciousness to be able to recognize how screwed up we may really be." Olzen's comments resonate in significant ways with writer James Howard Kunstler's reflection that, "I certainly believe in facing the future with hope, but I have learned that this feeling of confidence does not come from outside you. It's not something that Santa Claus or a candidate for president is going to furnish you with. The way to become hopeful is to demonstrate to yourself that you are a competent person who can understand the signals that reality is sending to you (even from its current remove offstage) and act intelligently in response."[11]

Seeking cracks in the edifice of modern culture's hold on human endeavors also offer hope for Myers. Since the fall of the Iron Curtain,

> We are in a sort of one-horse town where Capitalism and technocracy hold all the cards. That holds some opportunities for our work as Christians, because I think we ultimately have a

11. Kunstler, *Too Much Magic*, 245.

historical narrative that is every bit as radical as Marxism-Le-
ninism in its critique, but not nearly as fatalistic in its prescrip-
tion. The ultimate objective of protest culture, particularly when
faith-based, is to spill the seeds of political imagination. That has
always been the case in human history. At their best, movements
have thought outside the boxes and opened up the possibility
for people to imagine the world differently. Look at the amazing
things that have happened among sisters and brothers of faith
and social change movements. People in 1964 could not have
imagined the world without an Iron Curtain. Today we can't
picture the world without global warming. It took four or five
hundred years for that Anabaptist insight of a free church to
prevail. It took a hundred years for us to figure out chattel slavery, child labor. I think I agree with Yoder. Miracles happen in a
lot of small ways as well as big ways, and we may not yet be able
to predict how people are going to rise up and resist.

At the same time, Myers emphasizes a distinction between "radical hope"
and "managerial optimism." In looking to past human responses with "historical humility," Myers concedes that:

We may not be able to save this thing. Sometimes things have
to die in order for things to get better, and who knows how and
why that dying needs to be in our case. I'm not talking about
people, I'm talking about institutions and structures. But we can
be incarnational in the midst of it all, always holding out hope.
The work of organizing is to keep experimenting with gatherings and actions and conferences and retreats and practices
and demonstration projects in hopes that some of them will be
strategic and yield incredible imaginative work in the way that
the '64 conference did. Fifty years later I come down exactly
where they came down, and I think it's a good place to be in
our case. It's neither resignation nor despair, nor is it unwar-
ranted optimism. It's just the determination to do what Merton
called for repeatedly in the 1960s, which is to refuse to abandon
our humanity in the light of all these terrible forces with us and
around us.

Continuing the Conversation

These comments confirm that the questions considered at Gethsemani in
1964 remain relevant, even vital. They continue to address how our lives
and actions intersect with forces around us today. The social, political, and

religious terrain of our own times may require other questions and different answers than those voiced by Merton and his guests. But we still do well to revisit their work when responding to the powers of the Unspeakable that sustain our culture today. Responses by their twenty-first-century counterparts, whose experiences span decades, reveal the limitations of parsing their ideas into categories like "objectives" and "roots" and "sustaining practices." Allusions to solidarity, hope, and nonviolence recur with shifting nuance and weave throughout these conversations, past and present. Their insights touch upon both the means and ends to challenge what diminishes individual persons or distorts humanity's role within creation. Perhaps protest, dissent, resistance—whatever word most aptly describes this call—is best seen as a fluid and adaptive outlook on how we might face those distortions. Comments from both eras suggest that spiritually rooted protest might even take on the aura of a spiritual discipline, one to be encouraged and practiced among those of faith when confronted with the Unspeakable. As an expression of hope, protest stands at a juncture between the fallen realities of our material lives and a transcendent call offered by religions of many shades. That call beckons us on a pilgrimage toward *shalom*, balance, mindfulness, wholeness—toward life in harmony with creation and Creator.

A pivotal question for us all asks to whom these Gethsemani conversations apply—to the "professional protestor" only? If protest does reflect a spiritual outlook, a form of devotional practice, the answer must be, "No." As Elizabeth McAlister noted, it is not just for "special people" to consider, "it's something we all ought to be about on some level." We are all called to serve as one of Louis Massignon's messengers who reveal our Creator's presence to others, one of Abraham's "ten just men" whose presence stays the hand of destruction. The foundation that enables Christ's followers to live into this call is the work of Christ himself; our own task is to remain receptive and positioned to mature in that role. Exposure to Trappist asceticism provided Louis Massignon essential schooling for this. The emphasis of voices from Gethsemani fifty years ago and activists today, however, suggest that we look for this schooling to those abandoned at social margins. Those who Merton believed embody the "real spiritual root" of protest. Those Jesus called "Blessed."

In his book, *Daily Demonstrators: The Civil Rights Movement in Mennonite Homes and Sanctuaries*, Tobin Miller Shearer asserts that during the mid-twentieth century, "racial change unfolded as co-believers [of different races] took communion, sat down to dinner, and discussed marriages. Rather than sites of escape from the civil rights movement, living rooms and sanctuaries become arenas of racial agitation. Those who ventured across racial lines in intimate settings displayed courage equal to that of demonstrators who faced fire hoses and attack dogs."[12] His work supports the significance of resistance and protest as a continuum of personal and public expressions that defy the logic of the powers and lead us closer to those abandoned by the powerful. Once we learn to defy that logic, new possibilities for protest open. We can choose modest homes in modest neighborhoods, and invite the abandoned into those homes for conversation and hospitality. We can invest surplus funds in communities of the marginalized at modest financial gain rather than gaze with tunnel vision down Wall Street solely to maximize our return. We can minimize energy-intensive and superfluous possessions rather than maintain an armada of redundant gadgets and trinkets. We can also publicly and visibly call for dramatic social change. But only taking to the streets for flashes of protest and then retreating behind gated walls of fossilized privilege will not fulfill Abraham's first prayer. Choices that seem small, private, and personal can begin to nurture spiritual roots of protest that tap into the same energy and public vision reflected among those who met at Gethsemani.

As Ched Myers noted, those conversations fifty years ago anticipated a convergence of Yoderian Anabaptist, radical and contemplative Catholic, and engaged Protestant voices, a convergence taken for granted among to-day's faith-based activists. It crossed boundaries and charted new territory. Continuing those conversations in our own settings requires the same. At the time, John Heidbrink asked how those of faith relate to secular movements, proposing that retreat discussions should probe the basis for inter-acting with others who mainly rely on human reason. Merton felt the best approach was to "stop emphasizing we are different" because "we are all concerned with man[kind] living and surviving." In the end, he assured, "the word of God reaches us somewhere in the middle of all that." But Merton also cautioned against protest that drifted into the realm of "mere human griping." Our inclinations to guard ideology and personal agenda run deep. Protest culture and practice, even when faith-based, can become messy and very human. Alternatively, as George Packard experienced, a milieu of protest that arises outside of faith-based activism can sometimes embody a spirituality that profoundly expresses God's incarnate voice. Our call to keep talking and experimenting and acting, then, includes doing so with all, re-gardless of faith, who seek to nonviolently resist the Unspeakable and build a world of *shalom*. The task also requires conversation across generations as modeled at Gethsemani Abbey, where ages ranged from twenty-three to seventy-nine. Bridging the aspirations of youth and insights of experience nurtures adaptable wisdom.

12. Shearer, *Daily Demonstrators*, ix.

In 1964, overflowing nuclear arsenals helped foster the urgency behind faith-based acts of protest. Today, not only do those arsenals remain, but the advance of climate change has emerged as a second global threat to life that we have conjured. The logic of technique and the scope of technology continue to spread and nurture a society increasingly rooted in economic imbalance, militarized surveillance, and perpetual war. These forces weave throughout our daily routines and gain strength through our mundane activities. Only widespread and radically changed human behavior can alter their momentum. In other words, our ability to address these powers rests in responses that Merton's "voice in the wilderness" would name as repentance.

Rather than repentance that scurries toward social ideals of purity and piety, however, this voice in the wilderness names a repentance demanded in Luke 3—repentance that raises marginalized valleys and levels privileged mountains. This voice calls us to reject false gods that promise limitless growth and to share our surplus with those who have none. It invites us to abandon our quest for human domination, recognize the roots of profound wisdom planted deeply within creation, and embrace a Creative Force who bids reverence for mysteries that sustain all of life, not just ours.

Knowing this, it remains for those of us who embrace this ancient faith tradition and its call for repentance to persistently engage and challenge those false gods. We can do no better to prepare for this task than by joining with others to extend the conversations shared in these pages and pursue the deepening of our own spiritual roots of protest.

Afterword

"THE GOD OF PEACE is never glorified by human violence," Thomas Merton once wrote. I think the opposite is also true: "The God of Peace is always glorified by loving, truthful, human nonviolence."

When Merton gathered peacemakers together for a retreat at Gethsemani in 1964, he was sowing seeds of peace and nonviolence that glorified God and strengthened the growing global peace and nonviolence movement. I know because his retreat touched me and my friends profoundly.

I began to read Thomas Merton and Daniel Berrigan when I was in college in the 1970s. Their Christian conviction and bold witness electrified me. By the early 1980s, I determined to read all their writings in an effort to catch some of that conviction. They showed me, along with Dorothy Day and Martin Luther King Jr., how to be a Christian in our postmodern, nuclear world.

The Nonviolent Alternative, a collection of Merton's peace writings edited by my friend Gordon Zahn, captured my particular attention. It was there that I first read of this famous retreat. The thought of those holy days with some of the most creative peacemakers of our time electrified me all over again. Merton's rough outline from the retreat handout that Zahn had published pushed me to connect my own emerging peace activism with my spiritual journey. With his guidance and then Daniel Berrigan's friendship, I tried to balance contemplative peace with public activism and prophetic protest.

Later, I asked Daniel Berrigan about that retreat. What I remember most is his sudden solemn demeanor and his quiet reflection about how powerful those days were. Dan rarely spoke of Merton, but once he told me that he thought most biographers and critics misunderstood him. Merton was a committed antiwar, anti-nuclear, pro-peace activist, a brilliant Christian who anguished over the world and labored to change it, even as a monk and a hermit. Merton can only be understood, Dan believed, in the context of Gospel peacemaking and Gandhian nonviolence. As I became more involved in the global peace movement, I saw that Dan was right. Gospel peacemakers see the world through the lens of peace and nonviolence, and Merton's vision encompassed the whole world.

Over the years, I came to know and befriend many of the retreat participants—Dan and Phil Berrigan, Jim Forest and Tom Cornell, John Grady and Ping Ferry, and John Howard Yoder. Then, in the 1990s, when I became executive director of the Fellowship of Reconciliation, the peace group that proposed and sponsored Merton's peace retreat, I came to know the great John Heidbrink.

John was one of the many unsung heroes of the U.S. peace movement. In the early 1960s, he realized, as Director of Interfaith Activities for a mainly Protestant peace organization, that Roman Catholics were sorely needed to round out their ecumenical effort. Aside from the legendary Dorothy Day of the Catholic Worker, there were no Catholic figures publicly on the side of peace and nonviolence. What to do? He contacted the three most famous progressive priests in the United States—Thomas Merton, and Daniel and Philip Berrigan—and helped their transformation into peace activists. That is my understanding of what happened, from what Dan and Phil confided to me over the decades.

The retreat was John's vision, prompted by his first visit with Merton. He encouraged Merton to host it, and helped with the logistics and funding for some of the participants. Bayard Rustin and Martin Luther King Jr. would certainly have attended had Dr. King not just won the Nobel Peace Prize. One wonders how different the retreat would have been if women peacemakers, such as Dorothy Day, Mary Luke Tobin, and Joan Baez, had been included. Later, in 1967, Merton wrote to Dan proposing another retreat, this time including Dorothy, Joan, Rosemary Radford Ruether, and other women. Before his untimely death, Merton did host two retreats for women religious. The last one, he wrote, was the greatest retreat of his life. He intended to host Dr. King, Vincent Harding, and Thich Nhat Hanh for a week-long retreat in mid-April, 1968, but Dr. King was assassinated.

John Heidbrink and I corresponded and spoke periodically on the phone. Shortly before he died, he sent me an extraordinary gift: a copy of A Thomas Merton Reader, signed by everyone at this famous Gethsemani peace retreat. The week before the FOR retreat, in November 1964, John fell ill and was admitted to the Nyack, New York hospital, near FOR headquarters. As the gathering concluded, Merton asked every one to sign the book as a gift. "To John—from Tom Merton." "To John with love—from Dan Berrigan." "To John—from A. J. Muste." And so forth.

John Heidbrink wanted me to have it, and sent it on as a gift. I always felt that the good seeds sown by Merton, the Berrigans, and these other peacemakers took root in my own life. In particular, this peacemaking re-treat inspired me to connect with other like-minded friends in the work for peace. The retreat lives on in my own life and among my friends, with that signed book as a living reminder.

And now—we have this powerful book to remind us of those holy peacemakers and their days of retreat. It invites us to carry on their work of protest, prayer, and peacemaking, to sow our own seeds of peace for a harvest of peace that we also will not live to see. It is hard to grasp how groundbreaking this retreat was. Christian leaders simply did not get to-gether like this, much less share over such serious topics. It may be that only Merton, with the backing of the Fellowship of Reconciliation, could have brought such visionaries together.

Perhaps no other retreat has ever been so thoroughly dissected and studied—and rightly so. Gordon Oyer has done an extraordinary job tell-ing us the story of the retreat and its participants, and digging out the details of their conversation.

"The encounter has loomed large in the imaginations of many reli-gious peace advocates," Gordon writes. "Its intent of gathering in mutual respect to consult one another regarding the spiritual implications of pro-testing the powers of domination supplies us with a profound, iconic image. It reminds us of a fundamental call to dig deeply and tap into spiritual roots that will set our priorities, sustain our vision, and navigate our pilgrimage as we give voice to hopes and aspirations that coax humanity closer to its created intent."

Since then, of course, retreats on peace and nonviolence have been held around the country and the world. Over time, the Berrigans made such retreats a critical part of their public actions. Phil Berrigan conducted hundreds of them to mobilize people against the Vietnam War and nuclear weapons. Daniel Berrigan led hundreds as well, focused on Scripture pas-sages calling us to resist war and make peace. I made dozens of weekend retreats with Dan, many of them at Kirkridge, in Eastern Pennsylvania, the most progressive Christian retreat center in the United States, which was founded and directed for years by retreat participant John Oliver Nelson. I often pondered how Dan carried on Merton's gift of hosting peacemakers to share their spiritual roots and build community.

Gordon Oyer's research and reflections offer many lessons for today. Let me reflect briefly on three.

First of all, there's the visionary leadership of Thomas Merton. Through his prolific writing, contemplative prayer, and peace witness, he showed the world how Christians can stand with the peacemaking Christ and resist the culture of war. Merton dug deep roots into the spiritual life of peace, steadfastly sought the God of peace, denounced the lies of war and shared his discoveries with the world. He taught that every one of us is called to be a peacemaker.

Deep down, Merton possessed a fierce commitment to peace. Gordon Oyer cites one of many compelling passages from the mid-1960s to demonstrate Merton's peace position:

> It is my intention to make my entire life a rejection of, a protest against the crimes and injustices of war and political tyranny which threaten to destroy the whole race of humanity and the world. By my monastic life and vows I am saying NO to all the concentration camps, the aerial bombardments, the economic tyrannies, and the whole socio-economic apparatus which seems geared for nothing but global destruction in spite of all its fair words in favor of peace. I make monastic silence a protest against the lies of politicians, propagandists and agitators, and when I speak it is to deny that my faith and my Church can ever seriously be aligned with these forces of injustice and destruction. But it is true, nevertheless, that the faith in which I believe is also invoked by many who believe in war, believe in racial injustices, believe in self-righteous and lying forms of tyranny. My life must then be a protest against these also, and perhaps against these most of all.

With this solemn declaration, Merton takes a stand against war, injustice and tyranny. We all need to do the same today. In today's world with its thirty wars, twenty thousand nuclear weapons, corporate greed, a billion people starving, and impending catastrophic climate change, we need spiritual and religious leaders who speak out and protest against systemic injustice and war. Merton the hermit shows that every one of us can make a difference. Every one of us is needed. Every one of us can make our life a protest against violence, war and nuclear weapons.

Merton's leadership for peace helped change the church and strengthen the peace movement. By linking his contemplative prayer, monastic life and peace activism, he uncovered the spiritual roots of protest. By bringing together other like-minded visionaries, he strengthened the emerging peace movement. In doing so, he called us all to root our protest in prayer before the God of peace, and thus to see it as God's work. His example, teachings and leadership still shine much needed light as we struggle today with "the Unspeakable."

Second, Merton's Zen koan remains equally timely: "By what right do we protest?" Everyone who dares to speak out and protest the world's wars needs to sit with that question. In the last few decades, some scholars claim nearly two-thirds of the human race has been personally involved in grassroots movements for peace and justice. Over eighty-five nonviolent revolutions have occurred. The Arab Spring and the Occupy movements show the power of public protest to bring about change. They were most powerful when they were nonviolent.

The ongoing violence in the world's protests reveals the need to examine our motivations. Why do we protest? Are we helping to disarm the world, or bringing about more harm? Merton and his Christian friends grappled with these questions and invite us to do the same.

Gordon Oyer shows how Merton looked to monasticism for answers, while Daniel Berrigan sought clues in Teilhard de Chardin's vision of human progress. But it was John Howard Yoder who answered the question for them and the rest of us. We protest, he said quietly, because we are followers of the nonviolent Jesus who protested war and empire. Our hope is in Christ. Our protest comes from our discipleship. We practice a theology and spirituality of the cross, and so, we stand up, speak out, protest and resist. We do so, like Jesus, in a spirit of peace, love, and nonviolence, come what may.

We protest, in other words, because of the nonviolent Jesus. Because the God of peace would have us abolish war, nuclear weapons, extreme poverty, and corporate greed. Because creation is on the brink of destruction. Because we are created to be nonviolent, called to be peacemakers, not warmakers. Merton's koan helps us keep the focus where it belongs: on the nonviolent Jesus, the God of peace, and the coming of God's reign of peace and nonviolence.

Third, the Merton retreat teaches us the importance of coming together to pray and share with other Christians about the world of war and our responsibility to make peace. As we reflect on their time together, it is important to note what they did *not* talk about: they did not argue about the papacy, denominational differences, salvation, or our individual relationships with God. They discussed the world and our responsibility as Christians. Perhaps most remarkable of all, they looked to twentieth-century martyr Franz Jägerstätter for guidance.

Such peacemaking retreats are needed now more than ever. We need to connect with one another, with all those who struggle for disarmament, justice, and peace. We need to share our concerns, our despair, our hopes and our lives, and discover together the spiritual roots underlying our work. Together, we can seek the God of peace, renew our discipleship to the nonviolent Jesus, build lasting friendships, and discover new depths of faith, hope, and love. Perhaps then, we will be better prepared to welcome peace as a gift from God.

The world is stuck in permanent warfare and hovers on the brink of destruction. When Merton called other Christian peacemakers to reflect and pray together, he strengthened the growing movement of Gospel nonviolence. That's what happens whenever we gather to reflect, pray and share our concerns over the predicament of the world: we are reenergized to follow the nonviolent Jesus and go forth as protesters and peacemakers to build up the growing global grassroots movements of nonviolence.

Thank you, Gordon Oyer, for this great contribution to Merton studies and resistance literature, but most of all, for inspiring us to join Merton and his friends on retreat and go forth to do the work of disarmament, justice, and peace.

With Thomas Merton and his friends, we pledge to deepen the spiritual roots of protest, build community together, turn again to the risen Christ and welcome his resurrection gift of peace. With Merton and his friends, we go forward to proclaim God's reign of nonviolence.

Together, we will help abolish war, poverty, nuclear weapons, and every kind of violence, and in the process, glorify the God of peace. Nothing could be more beautiful.

John Dear

Santa Fe, New Mexico

March 12, 2013

Appendix A

Thomas Merton's "Peace Meeting" Outline[1]

Notes for Peace Meeting

1) Technology & its spirit (ascendency of device)

2) Technology makes war almost inevitable (the basic principle—what is possible becomes necessary)

   —t. changes whole attitude toward killing

   —makes it all the more intense in that it is efficient

   —depersonalizes—alienates

3) Attitude of peace movement to technology will determine its spiritual base. *Is the very membrane of technological society self-destructive?*

4) The Christian challenge of a "break with the world"—society basically corrupt.

5) "Thus the development of economic techniques does not formally destroy the spiritual but rather subordinates it to the realization of the Great Design—the whole of man's life has become a function of economic technique." 226[2]

6) The reason why peace is "moved-on." There is no technology of peace comparable to that of war. *Can there be any?* We should still ask for it. (Not only alternatives to war but an alternative *technical complex . . .*) *Importance of Peace*—impact on world events.

7) Ideological disarmament? Chuang Tzu?

---

1. Recorded in Reading Notebook 3 (1964–1965) held in the Thomas Merton Papers, Special Collection Research Center, Syracuse University Library.

2. Page reference to Ellul, *Technological Society*.

8) Idea of war more acceptable than idea of peace, even nuclear war, because it "rings a bell"—is "definite," familiar. Peace is unfamiliar, "new." Does not accord with the orientation of tech. society.

9) The *grace to protest* is a special gift of God, requiring fidelity and purity of heart, & distinguished from mere human griping (by discernment of spirits)

10) The *grace to love & to wish for opponent a better situation* in which oppression no longer exists (not merely regarding him as obstacle)

Appendix B

Thomas Merton's "Further Notes on Spiritual Roots of Protest"[1]

Further notes—on Spiritual roots of protest. *Deposuit potentes de sede.*[2]

1) The question of *judgment & privilege* in the prophets.

   Sense of the responsibility of the "privileged nation," and the danger of privilege.

   To have privilege is to be under judgment.

   To protect privilege as an absolute by belief in legalism and technology.

2) That one can use one's privileged means to heal the ills of others? To meet their needs? One can certainly *try* to. But the important thing is a detachment from privilege which enables one to recognize the higher value of sharing the suffering and struggle of others *to heal the visible nihilism of which it is a symbol.*

3) Dialectic of the Bible: the stranger, the underprivileged, the "younger son," the one who "has not" comes with the message and the love of God. The Jew, the gentile, the Negro, the Greek philosopher (the Buddhist).

4) Readiness to abandon theory before the unjust demands of experience (& meeting "the other" who has an "answer").

5) *The end*: "Recapitulation." Conveyance of all in Xt [Christ].

6) But the *privileged collectivity and privileged institution* stands in the way, not by warfare but by abuse of privilege.

1. Recorded in Reading Notebook 3 (1964–1965) held in the Thomas Merton Papers, Special Collection Research Center, Syracuse University Library
2. "[He] put down the mighty from their thrones" (Luke 1:52).

> "*Certes, il serait désirable, en ces jours d'action sociale, depouvoir s'appuyer sur le témoignage public des collectivités constituées et bénies à cette fin; mais c'est précisément l'abus de leurs privilèges qui les fossilise et nous prive de leur aide.*"
>
> —LM OM III 805[3]

7) The privilege of Abraham and his intercession for Sodom—his belief that there are just men in Sodom.

8) The *real root*—

  a) identification with the underprivileged.

  b) dedication to their "universe" as "epiphany"?

  c) as intercessory for us?

  d) reality of this belief. in suffering, in refusal of privilege & protest agst. arrogance & stupidity of the privileged—true *hope* in spiritual privilege of the poor.

Inadequate roots
—The "official policy" of any church or party.
The problem—we think that our protest will be meaningless unless we are clearly identified with this or that group—servility to "orthodoxy"—as in liberal ideas etc.
Compare this. Massignon—re Monchanin.

> "*Entre tant de théologiens indifférents et de missiologues trop in-téressés, M. s'était placé dans une sorte de 'no man's land' exposé aux projectiles des deux camps.*"[4]

3. "Certainly, it would be desirable in these days of social action to be able to rely upon the public testimonies of communities constituted and consecrated for this purpose. But it is precisely the abuse of their privileges which fossilizes them and deprives us of their help." From Louis Massignon's 1949 essay "Les Trois Prières D'Abraham," which Merton read in Massignon, *Opera Minora*, 3:804–16. English translation from Massignon, *Testimonies and Reflections*, 5.

4. "Among so many theologians who are indifferent and so many missiologues who seek personal, material gain, Monchanin had assumed his place in a sort of 'no man's land,' exposed to attacks [missiles] from both sides." From Louis Massingon's 1957 eulogy, "l'Abbé Jules Monchanin," which Merton read in Massignon, *Opera Minora*, 3:770–71. English translation by Dr. Hollie Markland Harder, Brandies University.

Appendix C

"Spiritual Roots of Protest" Handout[1]

jhs

RETREAT November 1964:
"Spiritual Roots of Protest"

We are hoping to reflect together during these days on our common grounds for *religious dissent and commitment* in the face of the injustice and disorder of a world in which total war seems at times inevitable, in which few seek any but violent solutions to economic and social problems more critical and more vast than man has ever known before.

What we are seeking is not the formulation of a program, but a deepening of roots.
Roots in the "ground" of all being, in God, through his word.
Standing in the presence of His word knowing that we are judged by it.
Bringing our inner motives into line with this judgement.

Protest: Against whom or what?
      For what? *By what right?*
      How?
      Why?

---

1. Originally published in Thomas Merton, *The Nonviolent Alternative*, revised edition of *Thomas Merton on Peace*, Gordon C. Zahn, editor (New York: Farrar, Straus, Giroux, 1971/1980). Reprinted with permission.

It would help if in our meetings we could show our various ways of answering these questions, thus helping one another to attain new perspectives. We can help one another to a new *openness*. We will not necessarily cling to sectarian programs and interpretations. We will think, speak and act as brothers, conscious that one same Spirit works in us, according to the gifts of each, for the manifestation of the justice and truth of God in the world, through Christ. But what do we mean by this? Does it mean only meditation on familiar themes or the awakening of a new (eschatological?) conscience?

Emphasis has been placed on the question: "*By what right* do we assume that we are called to protest, to judge, and to witness?" If we once (in the past) had a clear right, have we now forfeited it? And are we simply assuming such a "right" or "mandate" by virtue of our insertion in a collective program of one sort or another? An institution? A "movement"?

It is suggested that at each of our meetings, someone might act as leader of the discussion after himself starting off with a talk on any aspect of the question that seems relevant to him. For example:

Wednesday Afternoon: T. Merton, "The Monastic Protest. The voice in the wilderness."
Thursday Morning: A. J. Muste
Thursday Afternoon: John H. Yoder
Friday Morning: Fr. Daniel Berrigan, S.J.

Further Points:
Among the special problems that might be kept in mind, we might consider the *nature of technological society*, whether such a society is by its very nature oriented to self-destruction, or whether it can on the contrary be regarded as a source of hope for a new "sacral" order, a millennial "city" in which God will be manifested and praised in the freedom and enlightenment of man . . .

In any case, technology is not at present in a state that is morally or religiously promising. Does this call for reaction and protest, if so what kind? What can we really do about it?

The question of accurate information and the formation of a lucid and moral public opinion: or even the possibility of forming a really straight personal conscience? (Problem of mass-media and our own means of *communication*).

The relevance of our preaching and our worship in the present social context?
The relevance of traditional forms of social and political action?

The relevance and validity of the interior life? The question of "asceticism," "contemplation" or the "prophetic witness," intercessory prayer?

The meaning of *metanoia*, total personal renewal, as a prerequisite for valid non-violent action? The role of sacrifice and suffering in (redemptive) non-violent protest.
The question of reparatory sacrifice for the sins of racism, war, etc.

Appendix D

Thomas Merton's "Notes for F. O. R. Retreat"[1]

[*Cover Sheet—Front*]

Notes for F.O.R retreat
November 1964

[*Cover Sheet—Back*]

Technology—

1) "What can be done *must be done.*"

2) It will (& must) be done before people are able to understand what it means and what its consequences must be, 50/50 chances it will be opposite to desired effect.

   Proliferation of means—end vanishes p. 430[2]

3) How in such a situation can we possibly speak of control?

4) If this is out of control can cooperation be "moral"?

5) How can one not cooperate?

6) If one cannot help cooperating, how can ones cooperation be immoral?

7) Mystique & technology 422–423[3]

---

1. Held in the archives of the Thomas Merton Center at Bellarmine University, Louisville, Kentucky.

2. Page reference for Ellul, *Technological Society*.

3. Page reference for Ellul, *Technological Society*.

[Speaking Outline Sheet]

SPIRITUAL ROOTS OF PROTEST

Introduction—   Where *not* to start: The familiar litanies (Catholic protest agst. dress etc.)

> Greene on torture
>
> *Domine ut videam*[4]

[Note on Mon. vocation. St. John Gaulbert 'cloistered' by his forgiveness]
[exemption of relig. from mil. service—Canon Law (Can 121). Forbidden to. Number 141]

1) The Technological fact, the establishment
   The Church and "adjustment" to the situation.
   (return to technology later)

2) *Privilege.* The privileged collectivity.
   (must be seen agst. background of *choice* and *exclusion.*
   acceptance and *refusal*)

CHOICE

    a) Idea of the privileged collectivity and their
   'avaricium'[5] in Bible.

      Deposuit potentes de sede[6]

> Jews & gentiles—Pharisees and Sinners
> Gentiles & Jews
> Jews & Moslems—(Gen. 21:8–21)
> White & black
> The 6% & 50+% of income (US)
> "CARGO" the white and the "undeveloped"

    b) Hope and the deformation of hope (John of +)

> *Seeking an opening*—after the manner of power or of "water"?
>
> on being a "Christian" in Kierkegaard's sense—
> *losing right* to protest (& the capacity)
>
> "*le point vierge*" (China, Islam, etc.)
>
> The five privations.
> Humanity—poverty—sickness—sleep—death.

---

4. "Lord that I might see" (Mark 10: 51).
5. Greed, avarice.
6. "[He] put down the mighty from their thrones" (Luke 1:52).

RECIPROCITY

Reciprocity in the spirit (participation in personal life)—not evaded by paternalism.[7]

Reciprocity and liberty. (as opp. to doctrinaire attitudes on liberty)

Not trusting in legalism and mechanism but in the unplanned encounter, risk, & breakthrough given by God.

Mark of the "spiritual encounter." [*illegible*]. L.M.

c) *Judgment* of the privileged.

To have privilege is to be under judgment.

Can one use one's privilege to heal others?

* Not if one's privilege blinds one to relationship with other (only *giving*)

Privilege *fossilizes*. (this is its judgment)

We cannot rely on the witness of a privileged collectivity.

d) The Privilege of Abraham

—That he was visited by the 3 Angels?

—*That he could believe there were 10 just men in Sodom*

e) The idea of substitution. *Badaliya*.

SUBSTITUTION

1) for innocent victim

2) for oppressor-enemy

—the ram for Isaac—the paschal lamb—Christ

—substitution for captives

—prayer centered on graces necessary for rival

—spiritual good of the "opposition"?—the nice rightists

"No one is truly a believer until he prefers for his brother what he prefers for himself."[8]

Yet in Islam—idea of substitution is played down

('no one will save me but God' Cor 72:22)

('No one will bear another's burden' Cor 6:164)

(*alter alterins onera portate*)[9]

---

7. In Merton's handwritten outline, he drew a line that connected this comment to the asterisked line below ending with "(only *giving*)."

8. See, chapter 4, footnote 55.

9. "One of another's burdens."

Presenting oneself in the place of others before the judgment of God by taking upon oneself consequences of their sin = *their anger & hate.*

(yet the comedy of this is Catholics & (Chinese) communists)

Appendix E

Abbey of Gethsemani Grounds ca. 1964

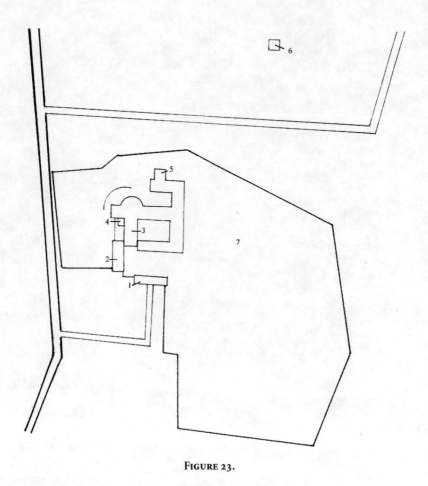

FIGURE 23.

(1) Gatehouse—Site of Wednesday morning, Thursday morning, and Thursday afternoon sessions

(2) Retreat house—Where retreatants slept and ate

(3) Church

(4) Juniorate chapel, beneath bell tower—Site of Friday morning Mass

(5) Novitiate chapel—Site of Thursday morning Mass

(6) Hermitage—Site of Wednesday afternoon and Friday morning sessions

(7) Farm buildings and workshops

Bibliography

Archives and Manuscript Sources

THIS BOOK RELIES HEAVILY on original archival sources from multiple depositories and includes numerous quotations from them. For the sake of readability, footnotes have been minimized to the degree possible in the following ways. Full archival collection citations are noted in the "Manuscript Collections" subsection below, and abbreviations for these collections are included in the "Abbreviations" pages at the front of the book. Footnote structure for citing specific documents follows the format: item, date, series/box numbers, collection/depository abbreviation. When the collection does not have both series and box number, only the box or series number is cited. All series/box references for FOR records pertain to section II of the collection.

Because no transcripts of the five formal retreat sessions exist, narratives of these sessions were constructed using extensive quotation and paraphrasing from original notes taken and speaking outlines used by retreat participants. Quotations in these sections therefore reflect written words of outline originators or note takers, not necessarily words actually spoken. The source of quotes and paraphrasing are frequently identified in the text, but for the sake of readability, their origin from a specific set of notes is not individually footnoted. The particular documents used to create the narratives that reconstruct session content are listed in the "Session Notes and Speaking Outlines" subsection below. A footnote at the beginning of each session narrative identifies which of these sources were used to create the narrative for that session.

Manuscript Collections

Berrigan, Daniel and Philip Collection, #4602. Division of Rare and Manuscript Collections, Cornell University Library, Ithaca, New York.

Church Peace Mission Records, #DG177. Swarthmore College Peace Collection, Swarthmore, Pennsylvania.

Fellowship of Reconciliation Records, #DG013. Swarthmore College Peace Collection, Swarthmore, Pennsylvania.

Ferry, Wilbur Hugh Papers, #ML–21. Rauner Special Collections Library, Dartmouth College, Hanover, New Hampshire.

Forest, James—Thomas Merton Collection, #MS 1989–02. John J. Burns Library, Boston College, Boston Massachusetts.

Merton, Thomas Collection. Archives of the Thomas Merton Center, Bellarmine University, Louisville, Kentucky.

Merton, Thomas Papers. Special Collections Research Center, Syracuse University Library, Syracuse, New York.

Muste, Abraham John. A. J. Muste Papers, microfilm. Wilmington, DE: Scholarly Resources, 1991. Originals in #DG050, Swarthmore College Peace Collection, Swarthmore, Pennsylvania.

Yoder, John Howard Papers, #H.12. Archives of the Thomas Merton Center, Bellarmine University, Louisville, Kentucky.

Session Notes and Speaking Outlines

Berrigan, Daniel. Retreat notes written on margins of "Identity Crisis and Monastic Vocation" mimeograph, n.d., B/98. In Daniel and Philip Berrigan Collection, #4602. Division of Rare and Manuscript Collections, Cornell University Library.

———. Retreat notes written on margins of "Spiritual Roots of Protest" handout, .n.d., A/23. In Daniel and Philip Berrigan Collection, #4602. Division of Rare and Manuscript Collections, Cornell University Library.

Forest, James. "Gethsemani Retreat (The Spiritual Roots of Protest): Nov. 1964," 13. In John Howard Yoder Papers, #H.12, Archives of the Thomas Merton Center, Bellarmine University, Louisville, Kentucky.

Merton, Thomas. Notebook, 1964–65, 3. In Thomas Merton Papers, Special Collections Research Center, Syracuse University Library.

———. "Notes for F.O.R retreat. Nov. 1964," E.1. In Archives of the Thomas Merton Center, Bellarmine University, Louisville, Kentucky.

Muste, A. J. "Gethsemani," n.d., 2, microfilm reel 89:1. In Muste Papers. Originals in #DG050, SCPC.

Yoder, John Howard. "Notes from J H Yoder 'Homily' at Gethsemani. Separate Mass for the retreat guests, early morning 20 Nov 1964," transcript printout late 1994, 2. In John Howard Yoder Papers, #H.12, Archives of the Thomas Merton Center, Bellarmine University, Louisville, Kentucky. Yoder's original homily notes are found in series 13 of this collection. His transcript provides emended and edited versions of the original notes, which are not separately identified in quotations.

———. "Notes prepared by J H Yoder for presentation by JHY Thursday PM," printout fall 1994," 1. In John Howard Yoder Papers, #H.12, Archives of the Thomas Merton Center, Bellarmine University, Louisville, Kentucky. Original handwritten notes are in 13, Yoder Papers, TMC. Yoder's original presentation notes are found in series 13 of this collection. His transcript provides emended and edited versions of the original notes, which are not separately identified in quotations.

———. "Transcription of Original Notes by JHYoder, Gethsemani c/o T. Merton 18–20 November 1964," transcribed June 1993, 1. In John Howard Yoder Papers, #H.12, Archives of the Thomas Merton Center, Bellarmine University, Louisville, Kentucky. Yoder's original notes of discussion and presentations by others are found in series 13 of this collection. His transcript provides emended and edited versions of the original notes, which are not separately identified in quotations.

Published Sources

Anderson, Kurt. "2011 Person of the Year: The Protester." *Time* 178/25 (December 26, 2011—January 12, 2012) 53–89.

Aprile, Dianne. *The Abbey of Gethsemani: Place of Peace and Paradox: 150 Years in the Life of America's Oldest Trappist Monastery*. Louisville, KY: Trout Lily, 1998.

Berkhof, Hendrik. *Christ and the Powers*. Translated by John Howard Yoder. Scottdale, PA: Herald, 1962.

———. *Christ and the Powers*. Translated by John Howard Yoder. Reprinted with revised author's preface and translator's epilogue. Scottdale, PA: Herald, 1977.

Berrigan, Daniel. "Act of Faith and the New Beast." *Fellowship* 32/1 (January 1966) 19–24.

———. *America Is Hard to Find*. Garden City, NY: Doubleday, 1972.

———. *The Bow in the Clouds: Man's Covenant with God*. New York: Coward-McCann, 1961.

———. *The Bride: Essays in the Church*. New York: Macmillan, 1959.

———. "Daniel Berrigan on Thomas Merton." *The Thomas Merton Life Center Newsletter* (April 1973) 6–8, 11. From address given January 28, 1973.

———. "Man's Spirit and Technology." *Fellowship* 31/5 (May 1965) 22–25.

———. *Portraits of Those I Love*. New York: Crossroad, 1982.

———. *Testimony: The Word Made Flesh*. Edited by John Dear. Maryknoll: Orbis, 2004. Originally in a lecture given at Bellarmine University, April 16, 2004.

———. "These Many Beautiful Years." In *Daniel Berrigan: Essential Writings*, edited by John Dear, 40–50. Maryknoll: Orbis, 2009.

———. *They Call Us Dead Men: Reflections on Life and Conscience*. New York: Macmillan, 1966.

———. *To Dwell In Peace: An Autobiography*. San Francisco: Harper and Row, 1987.

Berrigan, Philip. *No More Strangers*. New York: Macmillan, 1965.

Bochen, Christine M. "Censorship." In *The Thomas Merton Encyclopedia*, edited by William H. Shannon et al., 47–49. Maryknoll: Orbis, 2002.

Buell, John. *Travelling Light*. Toronto: Novalis, 2004.

Campbell, Will D. *Brother to a Dragonfly*. New York: Seabury, 1977.

Chalmers, David. *And the Crooked Places Made Straight: The Struggle for Social Change in the 1960s*. Baltimore: Johns Hopkins University Press, 1996.

Chatfield, Charles. *The American Peace Movement: Ideals and Activism*. New York: Twain, 1992.

Cornell, Thomas. "Thomas Merton on Peace." Review of *Thomas Merton on Peace* by Thomas Merton, edited by Gordon C. Zahn. *Fellowship* 40 (January 1974) 23.

Dawn, Marva J. "The Concept of 'The Principalities and Powers' in the Works of Jacques Ellul." PhD diss., University of Notre Dame, 1992.

DeBenedetti, Charles, and Charles Chatfield. *An American Ordeal: The Antiwar Movement of the Vietnam Era.* Syracuse, NY: Syracuse University Press, 1990.

Dekar, Paul R. *Creating the Beloved Community: A Journey with the Fellowship of Reconciliation.* Telford, PA: Cascadia, 2005.

———. *Thomas Merton: Twentieth Century Wisdom for Twenty-First Century Living.* Eugene, OR: Cascade, 2011.

Douglass, James W. *JFK and the Unspeakable: Why He Died and Why It Matters.* New York: Simon & Schuster, 2008.

DuMoulin, Heinrich. *A History of Zen Buddhism.* Translated by Paul Peachey. London: Faber & Faber, 1963.

Ellul, Jacques. *The Meaning of the City.* Grand Rapids: Eerdmans, 1970.

———. *The Technological Society.* New York: Knopf, 1964.

Farrell, James J. *The Spirit of the Sixties: The Making of Postwar Radicalism.* New York: Routledge, 1997.

Ferry, Wilbur Hugh. "Action at the Center: An Interview with W. H. Ferry" conducted by Gregory J. Ryan. *The Merton Annual* 4 (1991) 205–19.

Findlay, James F., Jr. *Church People in the Struggle: The National Council of Churches and the Black Freedom Movement, 1950–1970.* New York: Oxford University Press, 1993.

Flores, Mary Anne Grady. "Obituary for John Peter Grady." October 29, 2003. Cathworker Yahoo Group. Online: http://groups.yahoo.com/group/cathworker/message/236.

Forest, Jim. "A Great Lake of Beer." In *Apostle of Peace: Essays in Honor of Daniel Berrigan,* edited by John Dear, 117–22. Maryknoll: Orbis, 1996.

———. "Lessons in Peacemaking." Jim and Nancy Forest website. Online: http://jimandnancyforest.com/2012/04/lessons/.

———. *Living with Wisdom: A Life of Thomas Merton.* Rev. ed. Maryknoll: Orbis, 2008.

———. "Some Thoughts on the Resistance." *WIN* (January 15, 1969) 4–7.

———. "Thomas Merton's Struggle with Peacemaking." In *Thomas Merton: Prophet in the Belly of a Paradox,* edited by Gerald Twomey, 15–54. New York: Paulist, 1978.

Grau, Marion. *Rethinking Mission in the Postcolony: Salvation, Society, and Subversion.* New York: T. & T. Clark, 2011.

Greene, Graham. "The Author of 'The Quiet American' on Our Not-So-Quiet Use of Torture in Vietnam." *I. F. Stone's Weekly* 12/39 (November 16, 1964) 1.

———. *A Burnt-Out Case.* London: Heinemann, 1960.

Griffith, Sidney H. "Thomas Merton, Louis Massignon, and the Challenge of Isalm." *The Merton Annual* 3 (1990) 151–72.

Gude, Mary Louise. *Louis Massignon: The Crucible of Compassion.* Notre Dame: University of Notre Dame Press, 1996.

Hashimi, Muhammad Ali al-. "The Muslim and his Friends and Brothers." In *The Ideal Muslim: The True Islamic Personality–As Defined in the Qur'an and the Sunnah.* Revised 2nd edition. Translated by Nasiruddin al Khattab. N.p.: International Islamic Publishing House. Online: http://www.islamicstudies.info/family/ideal_muslim/ideal_muslim.php?id=10.

Hawkins, Merrill M, Jr. *Will Campbell: Prophet of the South.* Macon, GA: Mercer University Press, 1997.

Hedges, Chris. "Truthout Interviews Chris Hedges about Why Revolt Is All We Have Left." By Mark Kirlin. *Truthout.* No pages. Online: http://truth-out.org/opinion/

item/11032-truthout-interviews-chris-hedges-about-why-revolt-is-all-we-have-left.

Henthoff, Nat. *Peace Agitator: The Story of A. J. Muste.* New York: Macmillan, 1963.

Inchausti, Robert. *Thomas Merton's American Prophecy.* Albany, NY: SUNY, 1998.

International Thomas Merton Society. "John C. Heidbrink (1926–2006)." *International Thomas Merton Society Newsletter* 13/2 (Fall 2006) n.p. Online: http://www.mertoncenter.org/ITMS/newsletter13-2.htm.

Kunstler, James Howard. *Too Much Magic: Wishful Thinking, Technology, and the Fate of the Nation.* New York: Atlantic Monthly, 2012.

Liberation. "Editor Mugged." 9/6 (September 1964) 2.

Libreria Editrice Vaticana. 1917 Codex Iuris Canonicus. Online: http://www.jgray.org/codes/cic17lat.html.

Marcel, Gabriel. "Life and the Sacred." In *Tragic Wisdom and Beyond,* translated by Stephen Jolin and Peter McCormick, 104–19. Evanston, IL: Northwestern University Press, 1973.

Mason, Herbert. "Foreword to the English Edition." In *The Life of Al-Hallaj,* by Louis Massignon, ix–xliii. Vol. 1 of *The Passion of al-Hallaj: Mystic and Martyr of Islam.* Translated by Herbert Mason. Princeton, NJ: Princeton University Press, 1982.

———. *Memoir of a Friend: Louis Massignon.* Notre Dame: University of Notre Dame Press, 1988.

———. "An Unexpected Friendship." *Existenz* 7/1 (Spring 2012) 1–12. Online: http://www.bu.edu/paideia/existenz/volumes/Vol.7-1Mason.pdf.

Massignon, Louis. "L'Abbé Jules Monchanin" [The Abbot Jules Monchanin]. In Massignon, *Opera Minora,* 3:770–71. Unpublished translation by Hollie Markland Harder.

———. "An Entire Life with a Brother Who Set Out on the Desert: Charles de Foucauld." In Massignon, *Testimonies and Reflections: Essays of Louis Massignon,* edited by Herbert Mason, 21–38. Notre Dame, IN: University of Notre Dame Press, 1989.

———. "Foucauld au Desert Devant le Dieu d'Abraham, Agar et Ismael" [Foucauld in the Desert before the God of Abraham, Hagar, and Ishmael]. In Massignon, *Opera Minora,* 3:772–84. Unpublished translation by Virginie Reali.

———. "L'Avenir de la Science" [The Future of Science]. In Massignon, *Opera Minora,* 3:790–96. Unpublished translation by Hollie Markland Harder. First published as "L'avenir de la science." *Dieu vivant* 7 (1946) 7–16.

———. "Un Nouveau Sacral" [A New Sacral]. In Massignon, *Opera Minora,* 3:797–803. Unpublished translation by Hollie Markland Harder.

———. *Opera Minora: Textes Recueillis, Classés, et Présentés.* Edited by Y. Moubarac. 3 vols. Paris: Presses Universitaires de France, 1969.

———. *Parole donnée.* Paris: Rene Julliard, 1962.

———. "Le Respect de la Personne Humaine en Islam, et la Priorité du Droit d'Asile sur le Devoir de Juste Guerre" [Respect for the Human Person in Islam, and the Priority of the Right to Asylum over the Responsibility to Wage Justified Wars]. In Massignon, *Opera Minora,* 3:539–53. Unpublished translations by Hollie Markland Harder.

———. "The Three Prayers of Abraham." In Massignon, *Testimonies and Reflections: Essays of Louis Massignon,* edited by Herbert Mason, 3–20. Notre Dame, IN: University of Notre Dame Press, 1989.

McGowan, Edward. *Peace Warriors: The Story of the Camden 28*. Nyack, NY: Circumstantial, 2001.

McNeal, Patricia. *Harder than War: Catholic Peacemaking in Twentieth-Century America*. New Brunswick, NJ: Rutgers University Press, 1992.

Mendelsohn, Jack. "The Church and Draft Resisters." Sermon delivered at Arlington Street Church, Boston, October 22, 1967. Online: http://www.uua.org/re/tapestry/adults/resistance/workshop10/workshopplan/stories/182594.shtml.

Mennonite Church USA Archives. "Inventory of John H. Yoder (1927–1997) Collection." Online: http://www.mcusa-archives.org/personal_collections/yoderjohnhoward.html.

Merton, Thomas. "Blessed Are the Meek." In *Faith and Violence: Christian Teaching and Christian Practice*, 14–29. Notre Dame: University of Notre Dame Press, 1968.

———, ed. *Breakthrough to Peace*. Norfolk, CT: New Directions, 1962.

———. "Cargo Cults of the South Pacific." In *Love and Living*, 80–94. Orlando: Harcourt, 1979.

———. *The Climate of Monastic Prayer*. Spencer, MA: Cistercian, 1969.

———. *Cold War Letters*. Edited by Christine M. Bochen and William H. Shannon. Maryknoll: Orbis, 2006.

———. *The Collected Poems of Thomas Merton*. New York: New Directions, 1977.

———. *Conjectures of a Guilty Bystander*. New York: Doubleday, 1989.

———. *The Courage for Truth: The Letters of Thomas Merton to Writers*. Edited by Christine M. Bochen. New York: Farrar, Straus & Giroux, 1993.

———. *Dancing in the Water of Life: Seeking Peace in the Hermitage*. Vol. 5 of *The Journals of Thomas Merton, 1963–1965*, edited by Robert E Daggy. New York: HarperCollins, 1997.

———. "Gandhi and the One-Eyed Giant." In *Gandhi on Non-Violence*, edited by Thomas Merton, 3–31. New York: New Directions, 1964.

———. *Hidden Ground of Love: Letters on Religious Experience and Social Concerns*. Edited by William H. Shannon. New York: Farrar, Straus & Giroux, 1985.

———. "The Other Side of Despair: Notes on Christian Existentialism." In *Mystics and Zen Masters*, 255–80. New York: Farrar, Straus & Giroux, 1999.

———. *Passion for Peace: The Social Essays*. Edited by William H. Shannon. New York: Crossroads, 1997.

———. *Peace in the Post-Christian Era*. Edited by Patricia A. Burton. Maryknoll: Orbis, 2004.

———. "Preface to the Japanese Edition of *The Seven Storey Mountain*, August 1963." In *"Honorable Reader": Reflections on My Work*, edited by Robert E. Daggy, 63–67. New York: Crossroad, 1991.

———. *Raids on the Unspeakable*. New York: New Directions, 1966.

———. "Retreat, November, 1964: Spiritual Roots of Protest." In *The Nonviolent Alternative* (revised edition of *Thomas Merton on Peace*), edited by Gordon C. Zahn, 259–60. New York: Farrar, Straus & Giroux, 1980.

———. Review of *The Technological Society* by Jacques Ellul. *The Commonweal* 81 (December 4, 1964) 358.

———. *The Road to Joy: The Letters of Thomas Merton to New and Old Friends*. Edited by Robert E. Daggy. New York: Farrar, Straus & Giroux, 1989.

———. *Seeds of Destruction*. New York: Farrar, Straus & Giroux, 1964.

————. *Turning Toward the World: The Pivotal Years*. Vol. 4 of *The Journals of Thomas Merton, 1960–1963*, edited by Victor A. Kramer. New York: HarperCollins, 1996.

————. "The Universe as Epiphany." In *Love and Living*, 171–84. Orlando: Harcourt, 1979.

————. *The Waters of Siloe*. New York: Harcourt, Brace, 1949.

————. *The Way of Chuang Tzu*. New York: New Directions, 1965.

————, trans. *The Wisdom of the Desert: Sayings of the Desert Fathers of the Fourth Century*. New York: New Directions, 1960.

————. *Witness to Freedom: The Letters of Thomas Merton in Times of Crisis*. Edited by William H. Shannon. New York: Farrar, Straus & Giroux, 1994.

Merton, Thomas, and James Laughlin. *Selected Letters*. Edited by David D. Cooper. New York: Norton, 1997.

Miller, William Robert. *Nonviolence: A Christian Interpretation*. London: Allen and Unwin, 1964.

Mott, Michael. *The Seven Mountains of Thomas Merton*. Boston: Houghton Mifflin, 1984.

Muste, A. J. "Insecurity of Power." *Liberation* 9/8 (November 1964) 3–5.

————. "Memo on Vietnam." July 15, 1964. 12, microfilm reel 89:5, "Muste Papers."

————. "The Primacy of Peace." *Liberation* 9/9 (December 1964) 12-15.

————. *Saints for this Age*. Pendle Hill Pamphlet 124. Wallingford, PA: Pendle Hill, 1962.

————. "Unilateralism Reconsidered." *Liberation* 9/10 (January 1965) 19–23.

————. "Vietnam: The Political Reality." *Liberation* 9/7 (October 1964) 20–22.

Myers, Ched. *Binding the Strong Man: A Political Reading of Mark's Story of Jesus*. Maryknoll: Orbis, 1988.

Nation, Mark Theissen. *John Howard Yoder: Mennonite Patience, Evangelical Witness, Catholic Convictions*. Grand Rapids: Eerdmans, 2006.

Oates, Steven B. *Let the Trumpet Sound: The Life of Martin Luther King, Jr.* New York: Mentor, 1982.

O'Connell, Patrick F. "Hermitage." In *The Thomas Merton Encyclopedia*, edited by William H. Shannon et al., 197–200. Maryknoll: Orbis, 2002.

————. "Nonviolence." In *The Thomas Merton Encyclopedia*, edited by William H. Shannon et al., 330–33. Maryknoll: Orbis, 2002.

————. "Peace." In *The Thomas Merton Encyclopedia*, edited by William H. Shannon et al., 354–55. Maryknoll: Orbis, 2002.

Outler, Albert. *The Christian Tradition and the Unity We Seek*. New York: Oxford University Press, 1957.

Oyer, Gordon. "Machine Culture and the Lone Zone: Discussing Technology and Contemplation at the 1964 Peacemaker Retreat." *The Merton Annual* 25 (2011) 188–232.

Peace, Roger C., III. *A Just and Lasting Peace: The US Peace Movement from the Cold War to Desert Storm*. Chicago: Noble, 1991.

Peachey, Paul. *A Usable Past: A Story of Living and Thinking Vocationally at the Margins*. Telford, PA: Dreamseeker, 2008.

Polner, Murray, and Jim O'Grady. *Disarmed and Dangerous: The Radical Lives and Times of Daniel and Philip Berrigan*. New York: Basic Books, 1997.

Reardon, Patrick Henry. "A Many-Storied Monastic: A Critical Memoir of Thomas Merton at Gethsemani Abbey." *Touchstone* (September–October 2011) n.p. Online: http://www.touchstonemag.com/archives/article.php?id=24-05-050-f.

Robinson, Jo Ann Ooiman. *Abraham Went Out: A Biography of A. J. Muste*. Philadelphia: Temple University Press, 1981.

Shannon, Thomas A. "An Appreciation: Gordon Zahn, Prophet of Peace." *America* 198/1 (January 7–14, 2008) 4.

Shannon, William H. "Massignon, Louis." In *The Thomas Merton Encyclopedia*, edited by William H. Shannon et al., 287–88. Maryknoll: Orbis, 2002.

———. "Technology." In *The Thomas Merton Encyclopedia*, edited by William H. Shannon et al., 466–70. Maryknoll: Orbis, 2002.

Shannon, William H., Christine M. Bochen, and Patrick F. O'Connell. *The Thomas Merton Encyclopedia*. Maryknoll: Orbis, 2002.

Shearer, Tobin Miller. *Daily Demonstrators: The Civil Rights Movement in Mennonite Homes and Sanctuaries*. Baltimore: Johns Hopkins University Press, 2010.

Smith, Lisa-Marie. "Portrait of a Teacher: Anthony Walsh and the Inkameep Indian Day School, 1932–1942." Master's thesis, University of Victoria, 2004. Online: http://dspace.library.uvic.ca:8080/bitstream/handle/1828/492/smith_2004.pdf?sequence=1.

Solberg, Winton U. *A History of American Thought and Culture*. Tokyo: Kinseido, 1983.

Stringfellow, William. *Free in Obedience*. New York: Seabury, 1964.

The Thomas Merton Center at Bellarmine University. "Merton's Correspondence with: Miller, William Robert, 1927–1970." Online: http://merton.org/Research/Correspondence/y1.aspx?id=1411.

Thompson, Phillip M. *Returning to Reality: Thomas Merton's Wisdom for a Technological World*. Eugene, OR: Cascade, 2012.

van der Post, Laurens. *The Dark Eye in Africa*. New York: Morrow, 1955.

Voillaume, René. *Seeds in the Desert: The Legacy of Charles de Foucauld*. Notre Dame, IN: Fides Publishers Association, 1960.

Ward, James A. *Ferrytale: The Career of W. H. "Ping" Ferry*. Stanford, CA: Stanford University Press, 2001.

Wittner, Lawrence S. *Rebels Against War: The American Peace Movement, 1933–1983*. Philadelphia: Temple University Press, 1984.

Wylie-Kellermann, Bill. "Naming the Powers: William Stringfellow as Student and Theologian." *Student World* 247 (2003) 24–35. Online: http://www.wscfglobal.org/pdfs/247_Art2_Kellermann.pdf.

Yeasted, Rita M. *JON: John Oliver Nelson and the Movement for Power in the Church*. Bloomington, IN: iUniverse, 2011.

Yoder, John Howard. *The Christian Witness to the State*. Institute of Mennonite Studies 3. Newton, KS: Faith and Life, 1964.

———. "Karl Barth and Christian Pacifism." Study document for the Peace Section of Mennonite Central Committee. Basel: Mennonite Central Committee, 1957.

———. "Mennonites and Interdenominational Agencies." *The Mennonite* (March 20, 1962) 181–82.

———. "The Missionary Church." *Gospel Herald* (January 8, 1963) 38, 42.

———. "The Otherness of the Church." *Concern* 8 (May 1960) 19–29.

———. "The Pacifism of Karl Barth." Pamphlet in the Church Peace Mission Series 5. Scottdale, PA: Herald, 1968.

———. "The Place of the Peace Message in Missions [part 1]." *Gospel Herald* 53/50 (December 27, 1960) 1108–9.

———. "The Place of the Peace Witness in Missions [part 2]." *Gospel Herald* 54/1 (January 3, 1961) 14–5, 19–20.

———. *The Politics of Jesus.* Eerdmans: Grand Rapids, 1972.

———. "The Racial Revolution in Theological Perspective." In *For the Nations: Essays Evangelical and Public,* 97–124. Grand Rapids: Eerdmans, 1997.

———. "Reinhold Niebuhr and Christian Pacifism." *Mennonite Quarterly Review* 29 (April 1955) 101–17.

———. "Reinhold Niebuhr and Christian Pacifism." Pamphlet in the Church Peace Mission Series 6. Scottdale, PA: Herald, 1968.

———. *Täufertum und Reformation in der Schweitz: I, Die Gespräche zwischen Täufern und Reformatoren 1523–1538.* Karlsruhe: Schneider, 1962.

———. "The Unity We Have." *The Mennonite* (March 13 1962) 165–66.

———. "The Unity We Seek." *The Mennonite* (March 27, 1962) 213–14.

Zahn, Gordon C. *Solitary Witness: The Life and Death of Franz Jägerstätter.* Boston: Beacon, 1964.

Name/Subject Index

Scripture Index